ALL THAT GLITTERS

ALL THAT GLITTERS

DENISE L'ESTRANGE-CORBET
MNZM

RANDOM HOUSE
NEW ZEALAND

NOTE: Some names in this book have been changed.

A RANDOM HOUSE BOOK published by Random House New Zealand
18 Poland Road, Glenfield, Auckland, New Zealand

For more information about our titles go to www.randomhouse.co.nz

A catalogue record for this book is available from
the National Library of New Zealand

Random House International, Random House, 20 Vauxhall Bridge Road, London, SW1V 2SA, United Kingdom; **Random House Australia Pty Ltd**, Level 3, 100 Pacific Highway, North Sydney 2060, Australia; **Random House South Africa Pty Ltd**, Isle of Houghton, Corner Boundary Road and Carse O'Gowrie, Houghton 2198, South Africa; **Random House Publishers India Private Ltd**, 301 World Trade Tower, Hotel Intercontinental Grand Complex, Barakhamba Lane, New Delhi 110 001, India

First published 2008

ISBN 978 1 86979 042 4

Random House New Zealand uses non-chlorine-bleached papers from
sustainably managed plantation forests.

WORLD photos taken by Des Williams and Michael Ng
Design: IslandBridge
Cover photograph: Jessie Casson
Cover design: Anna Seabrook
Printed in Australia by Griffin Press

Dedication

This book is dedicated to my darling daughter and the light of my life, Pebbles Hooper.

Also to my husband, Francis Hooper, who has never faltered in his support of me, and has endured all my many antics, without complaint, for 20 years.

And finally, to all the people who currently suffer from depression and mental illness, and those who have gone before us, may we all find the happiness we so desperately crave.

It's a scary place to be
in my head
with my thoughts swirling in the gluggy grey matter.
Absorbed by the big sponge
and no way of squeezing out
the liquid memories.
Unable to dispose of
the bad things contained
they get pushed to the back
and sometimes creep,
ever so slowly,
to the front.
Like index cards
they're filed away for future reference
if and when they may become important enough,
to be brought out and reused.

Denise

Contents

Foreword

Who would have thought that an idea dreamed up at a Queen Street bus stop would end up all over the world?

When Denise L'Estrange-Corbet and her partner Francis Hooper first set up their WORLD brand in 1989, they did so with $200 each and no previous business experience. But what they did have was a lot of enthusiasm and sheer determination.

When Denise and Francis opened their first WORLD store, in an area less than 10 square metres, they had no idea where their ideas would take them, nor that their designs would soon be selling on the racks of some of the world's most prestigious international department stores, next to some of the world's most famous brands.

Their road to success has not been smooth all the way. Neither of them had any family in New Zealand, and necessity meant that their dream business was started just before the birth of their daughter Pebbles. But they have shown that even an idea born at a bus stop can be achieved with enough passion, commitment, and determination to succeed in the face of all odds.

Their story is one of great spirit, tenacity, and ingenuity. And along with that goes incredible generosity, as demonstrated by the fact that the profits from this book will go to the Mental Health Foundation to help promote awareness of mental health issues.

Denise was recognised for her contribution to fashion

design in 2002 when she was awarded an MNZM in the Queen's Birthday honours list. Her often funny and sometimes sad story proves that nobody can hold true creativity down, and that determination can conquer all.

WORLD is now a mainstay of the fashion industry in New Zealand after its first two decades. I wish Denise and Francis every success for the next two decades.

Helen Clark
Prime Minister
June 2008

Introduction

'If you could pick one thing you really wanted
to do in your life, what would it be?'

It was a cold, wet and windy Saturday afternoon in 1988. I was 28 years old and sitting in Rosini's, the only café open after 1pm, amid the fashion boutiques and hair salons in High Street, central Auckland.

I was a young production assistant, working for a clothing label with a shop just along the street in Vulcan Lane. I had suggested a late lunch with my friends Cris Elrick, who worked with me at the time, and Brent Lawler, a young upstart hairdresser with an incredible knack of rubbing people up the wrong way. We sat down at a table by the door, watching as the condensation dribbled down the windows, and ordered our food and coffee. We were all bored, and as we were chatting, I asked, 'If there was one wish you could have, what would it be?'

Cris was the first one off the block, and she said, 'I really want to meet a man who loves me for who I am. A man who truly, truly adores me.' It seemed like a pipedream at the time.

Brent thought for a moment before saying, 'I want to do the hair and make-up of all the famous supermodels and stars in the world, people like Linda Evangelista.' Cris and I just looked at him.

'What do you want to do, darling?' Cris asked.

'I'd love to write a book,' I said.

We sat there sipping our coffee, looking out at the rain. It all seemed ridiculously impossible.

Fast forward to today.

Cris has been married to the man of her dreams, Peter, for nearly a decade, and he was well worth the wait. They are blissfully happy together.

Brent now lives next door to Linda Evangelista in New York City, and has worked with her as well as Naomi, Claudia and a host of other superstars.

And me? Well, here's the book. I guess dreams can come true, if you really want them to.

1

Leaping into life

In 2008, I celebrated my twelfth birthday.
It was a lovely occasion, apart from the fact
that I looked — and felt — forty-eight.

I'm a leap-year baby, you see; born on 29 February, 1960. The date, I like to think, was a harbinger of my life to come. Nothing was going to be easy — not even birthdays.

My father, Donovan, was desperate for a son. 'What am I going to do with that?' he asked my mother when he discovered the squalling infant she had just delivered was another girl.

Both my parents were born in India, to wealthy British families. My mother, Elsie Ethel Williams, was the youngest of five children in a Scottish family living in Allahabad, in the northern state of Uttar Pradesh. She never met her own father, Arthur, who died aged 27 while having surgery for a brain tumour, while his wife, also named Elsie, was pregnant with my mother.

By the time the fatherless babe came into the world in 1928, the family was living with Arthur's sister, who was a senior administrator in the colonial education system. This lady, whose name was also, confusingly, Elsie (but known to all of us as Big Aunty) had deep connections to Indian politics and was wealthy in her own right, so the family had cooks, cleaners and servants.

When the children turned five, they were packed up north to board at the Wynberg-Allen School in Mussoorie, a hill station at the foot of the Himalayas.

For my grandmother, the young widow Elsie, it was a comfortable life. Her husband Arthur had, on his deathbed, asked his best friend William Trow to look after the family, and William was true to his promise, becoming my grandmother's constant companion. Nobody was ever quite sure if they married, but Grandma and William stayed together until she died in 1979.

Poor William. He was honourable and loyal, and never wavered from the deathbed oath he had taken, but life with Gran must have been hell for him. She was cold and loveless, the most undemonstrative person I have ever met.

I've often wondered why she was so awful. Certainly, the untimely death of her husband must have been traumatic for her, but the experience did not make her empathetic or soft. To put it mildly, she was a fucking bitch.

She and William adopted two children — Mickey Trow, William's nephew, and a sickly baby called Peter Smith — but when her children came home from boarding school for holidays she displayed little interest, regarding her offspring as an interruption to her life.

Big Aunty was the real maternal figure in the household. Warm and expressive, she would welcome the clattering adolescents with enthusiasm, and they adored the high-society glamour of her life. Friends were always welcome to drop around, and thus it was that Arthur, my mother's brother, brought home a young man named Donovan L'Estrange-Corbet to play tennis, one day in 1943. On seeing the very shy 15-year-old Elsie, Donovan was smitten. 'That,' he told his friend Arthur, 'is the girl I'm going to marry.' Arthur laughed out loud.

Donovan had to wait a few years, however. When he met my mother he was only 14, and their world was about to be thrown into chaos.

The indolent life of the Raj colonists was too good to last. In

1947 Britain granted independence, and in 1950 the Republic of India was officially proclaimed. For the Anglo-Indian sahibs and memsahibs, it was time to go home — although for many, England was the imperial heart they had never visited; home in name only.

As the family packed up and prepared to move to England, my mother's older brother Robin asked if she would like to remain in Allahabad and finish the secretarial course she had begun. Robin had joined the British Army as a pilot, based in India, and was just beginning a career with Air India. Their sister Phyllis also remained in India, but my grandmother sailed for England with the other children and the long-suffering William. The move meant a huge change in circumstances and status, as Gran went from a life of colonial ease to the cold reality of postwar London.

Mum had another sister, Iris, who was something of a party animal. When she left India in 1949, she left behind a baby daughter, Nancy, who was the product of a brief fling with a visiting American soldier. Even at the edge of Empire, the conservatism of postwar British society made it utterly unacceptable for a young middle-class girl to admit being the mother of an illegitimate child, so Nancy was also raised by Big Aunty.

My mother Elsie, finally free of her dreadful old bat of a mother, settled into shorthand and typing classes, enjoying her own independence as India settled into its new status as a nation. But the political changes had robbed her of her sweetheart. Donovan's father, Dennis L'Estrange-Corbet, had left his job with the resources company Andrew Yule & Co, and emigrated to New Zealand with his wife, Annie, her sister Alice, and their two sons, Cedric and Donovan. The family moved into Auckland's inner-harbour suburb of Remuera, and Donovan found work as a wool-classer; but he couldn't forget Elsie. She was a real beauty, with green eyes, dark hair and pale skin — the latter a source of much jealousy from her older sisters, both of whom had dark olive complexions.

In his regular letters, Donovan pleaded with Elsie to come to New Zealand when her secretarial course ended in 1951. She agreed, sailing to Auckland and moving into Donovan's parents' home on Ngapuhi Road, a white stucco bungalow. It couldn't have been more different from steamy India, but Elsie was happy, working as a secretary at department store Milne and Choyce.

On 18 April 1953, Elsie and Donovan married at the Winter Gardens in Auckland's Domain. Within three years a baby girl arrived, and was named Robyn after my mother's beloved brother. When Mum became pregnant for a second time, Dad was convinced he'd get a son, and announced to everyone with much joy that he would call the baby Dennis, after his own late father.

When I was born, quite clearly lacking a Y chromosome, Dad could not hide his displeasure. 'We'll call her Denise,' he said — but the name was little consolation. His disappointment was profound; he slid into a dark mood that never seemed to lift.

My mother later told me my father was quite distraught when he saw me for the first time — I was hours old and already flawed, unsatisfactory.

Dad stopped coming home after work, choosing instead to hang out with his friends and drink, sometimes for days on end. When he returned home inebriated, he was violent. Mum, a young wife in a strange country, had nowhere to turn — her mother-in-law refused to believe her son was capable of hitting a woman, and simply ignored the black eyes and bruises. She could not, would not, accept that he was capable of being an abusive husband.

Later, when my mother described my father to me, I began to recognise the same demons that have followed me through life. 'He had terrible black days,' my mother said once. 'He'd lie on the bed and he'd be miles away, just staring into space.' I've no doubt his alcoholism was an escape from his depression, but in those days a condition like his went totally unrecognised.

Alcohol lurked everywhere. My mother became close to my father's good-natured aunt, Alice, who kept a flagon of alcohol under her bed. Alice had a benign kind of alcoholism — the more she drank, the sillier and funnier she became. Dad, by contrast, became more beastly with every drink. He reserved his brutality for my mother, never hitting my sister or me. When he did come home, he would order us to come and give him a cuddle. 'No!' I'd pout, repelled by his liquor-breath.

The rejection would spark even more nastiness in Dad. 'You're putting stories in her head,' he'd snarl at Mum. It wasn't true — she never bad-mouthed him — but little children are perceptive, and I was obviously picking up the vibes. The last thing I wanted was to cuddle him.

My sister Robyn was very quiet and tolerant, whereas I was developing into a real little tomboy. If I wanted something, I got it, and I was prepared to fight. 'Alley cat,' the family called me. Something about my boisterous spirit seemed to intrigue Dad, and despite his early disdain I became his favourite. I don't believe parents should ever have favourites, but as a child I was thrilled to bask in his affection. He nicknamed me Dinya, and encouraged all my cheeky, outspoken, bossy tendencies.

I remember vividly being taken to a fair, at about the age of three. There was a running race on, and Dad said I had to enter. 'You're going to win,' he commanded. The first prize was a red, blue and yellow plastic choo-choo train. I ran, I ran with all my might, to win that train for him. As I surged for the finish-line a little boy overtook me, but I was not going to be beaten. I stuck out my foot, tripped him up and left him sprawling on the grass. I won the train. Dad was ecstatic: I was an alley cat, and nothing was going to stop me.

By this time my sister was at school, and I was at home during the day with Mum, Grandma Annie and Aunt Alice. Alice, who was a spinster, spoilt me rotten. Grandma Annie was reserved, and looked like a proper grandma, with long grey hair that was always tied up tightly in a bun.

My grandfather Dennis, who had died before I was born, was from all accounts a terrible womaniser. I think it ran in the family; infidelity was another of my father's and his brothers' unpleasant habits. Mum knew he was sleeping with other women, and she was deeply unhappy. Later she would tell me how she had to scrub the lipstick kisses from the collars of his shirts.

Finally, she had had enough. 'I'm going to leave him,' she wrote to her mother in London. Gran arranged for a friend of hers, Mrs Court the moneylender, to send over the fare, and Mum bought three tickets on a ship leaving Auckland. 'You don't have the nerve,' my father told her — but he was wrong. After several 'last' chances, Mum had finally realised Dad was not going to control his drinking and womanising.

With no job, and no money, she gathered us up and left in late 1963, taking us down to the dock to board a passenger steamer bound for England, the 'home' she had never seen.

2

Merry England

Running on the decks, playing on a rocking horse — those are my only real memories of the six-week journey from New Zealand to England. We were heading for a new life in the old country, but I was far too young to understand the grim reality of the life that awaited us.

Mum had no money, no job, and two boisterous daughters. Her relatives in England were displaced colonials, still adjusting to the strangeness of life in their reclaimed homeland, and none of them had the finances to support us. Mum would have to find work as soon as we landed — but by the time we docked at Southampton, another complication was developing.

Mum got pregnant several months after we got there. On board the ship, she had had a brief romance with one of the young stewards and they continued to see each other for a short time after we arrived in the UK. But by the time she became aware of the pregnancy, the steward was long gone. Mum did not want, and could not afford, another child. Abortion was illegal in those days — and anyway, Mum had no way of paying the extortionate fees charged by backstreet abortionists for their dangerous, unhygienic services. She decided to give the baby up for immediate adoption, and in the meantime tried to suppress the nausea and conceal her growing belly while she looked for secretarial work.

My grandmother and Aunt Iris — who was still as much of a hard-drinking party-goer as ever — met us in Southampton. I recall Mum telling me how she was struck by how dirty London seemed compared with Auckland, and as a little girl, I was utterly overwhelmed by the strangeness of it all. 'Come and sit on my lap,' Gran said when we got on the tube bound for the family's home in Tooting Bec, south London. I refused — and that was the beginning of another clash of personalities. Grandma didn't like me one little bit, and the feeling was mutual. She loathed my father for what he had put my mother through, and I looked just like him. She couldn't bear to look at me.

We lived in various rented houses in Tooting Bec before settling at number 101 Tooting Bec Road, in a two-storey brick house with a dark green painted front door. The house was owned by a friend of the family's called Kitty Brinnand, who was based in India. Kitty was fabulously sexy. She only ever wore black — black coiffed hair, jet-black eyeliner, black-rimmed glasses, a black cashmere turtle-neck sweater over her very pointy breasts, a tight, straight black-wool skirt to her knees, dark stockings, and incredibly high-heeled, pointed-toe stilettos in the softest leather. She carried a large black shiny leather handbag with a gold clasp, and wore a large black swing cashmere coat. This was topped off with pearl earrings, a row of pearls around her neck and large gold rings, bright red lips and highly manicured nails. She never wavered from this uniform and must have had a wardrobe full of black turtle-neck jumpers, black skirts, black coats and pearls.

She also had the most delicious smell and when she visited I would just inhale her gorgeous heady perfume. It wafted from room to room as she moved through the house. She only ever travelled in black cabs, and I was mesmerised by her incredible sense of style, her intense kindness to us and her odd look. She was not a classic beauty but she commanded attention. She was sophisticated, educated, wealthy — she was sex on legs. This had not escaped the attention of my Uncle Robin, and he and Kitty were conducting a very long, torrid and dangerous affair in India. Robin was married to the deeply religious Cynthia, who while sweet could never match Kitty in any department.

My aunt Iris, who I would later christen 'The Gin Queen' in honour of her predilection for spirits, had married a man named Mr Bowden after arriving in London, and had two sons with him, Tom and George. They later divorced, and the Gin Queen married Zygmund Cesenek, a lovely Polish man, who could have done so much better. When they rowed she would shout: 'What do you know, you stupid Pole, you can't even speak proper English!' The Gin Queen was truly her mother's daughter.

In reality, Zyggy's English was fine, although a little quirky. For example he'd say 'chish and fips' instead of 'fish and chips'. I thought it was endearing, and Zyggy's happy personality enlivened our lives when we later moved in with him, the Gin Queen and their three children, Andrew, Stephen and Maria, in a three-bedroom house in Tooting. I was never quite sure where Iris's two eldest sons, Tom and George, actually lived, but they were frequent visitors.

There were nine of us in that little house, including baby Mark, a gorgeous, chubby little fellow with enormous blue eyes and long, black sweeping lashes. Mum had been determined to give him up for adoption, but when he was born in 1964 her resolve had melted.

Mark was born with the umbilical cord wrapped around his neck, and when he emerged into the world, he was blue. For several terrifying moments Mum thought he was dead. The nurses in the labour ward disentangled the cord and seized the baby off the bed, slapping his little body until, at last, he opened his eyes and gasped for breath. Colour flooded into him as he went from blue to pink, dead to alive. As soon as she heard that first, outraged scream, Mum knew she could never let him go.

So now we were four: me, Mum, Robyn and Mark. For the first few months after Mark's birth we remained with Zyggy and Iris. Gran babysat while Mum went out to work. It was a tempestuous household, largely because of the Gin Queen's drinking habits.

She had a vicious temper, and when she wasn't arguing with Zyggy she'd pick a fight with whoever else happened to be in range.

One night when Mum returned from work, a huge argument blew up between her and the Gin Queen. I've no idea what the dispute was about, but it had serious consequences for our little family. The Gin Queen turfed us out into the street. 'Get out!' she screamed, as Mum flung our belongings into a suitcase, bundled us outside into the snow and darkness of a London winter night, and slammed the door.

Robyn was seven, I was nearly four and Mark was only a few months old. As we struggled down Trinity Road in the snow, Robyn and I walking next to Mum who was pushing baby Mark in his large, navy-blue Silver Cross pram, I recall asking Mum where we would go.

'Gran's place,' she said. My heart sank.

Things were terribly cramped when the four of us moved back into the house Gran and William were renting from Kitty on Tooting Bec Road. There were only three bedrooms, which meant Mum, Robyn, the baby and I were all in together. Living in close quarters with Gran was horrendous, and money was incredibly tight. William worked as a nightwatchman, leaving for work every night at 6pm and returning at 8am, and Mum was a secretary at the London Chamber of Commerce. Eventually Mum somehow managed to save 3000 pounds, and she, Gran and William were able to buy a 15,000-pound house at 57 Mandrake Road, Tooting Bec.

My grandmother, having no maternal instincts whatsoever, said she could not look after Mark while Mum went out to work. This was yet another blow — there was no such thing as childcare, and hiring a nanny was prohibitively expensive. Mum managed to find a foster-carer to mind him during the week, a local woman who minded several babies in a small house in Tooting Broadway.

Mum would drop Mark off on a Sunday night and return to collect him the following Friday, so we would spend the weekend marvelling at how much he had changed during the week. But before long Mum had to face the fact that Mark wasn't being cared for as he should have been. The foster-carer was neglectful. Her house was never clean, and she clearly had far too many children under her care. She couldn't cope.

We used to go and visit on a Wednesday, and Mark would be lying in his cot in a soaking wet terry-towelling nappy. He'd give us a huge smile, and Mum would bustle about, trying to get him changed and comfortable before she had to rush back to work. I became fiercely affectionate towards him. 'Marky Parky,' I'd coo, leaning over his cot as he beamed up at me, oblivious to the stench of his own sodden nappy. He was a lovely-natured little boy, and although he didn't seem to mind the horrid circumstances, it was obvious he wasn't getting anything like the care he needed.

The situation was dreadful for my mother. After the trauma of his birth and the emotional wrench of giving him to the foster-carer each week, she couldn't bear the sight of him in these conditions. After much negotiation, Mum eventually persuaded Gran to babysit Mark and me while she went to work. Gran was reluctant and bad-tempered about it, so everyone was astonished — including Gran herself — when she fell madly in love with little Mark. She doted on him as she had never doted on her own children, and finally discovered a nurturing side to her hard-bitten old personality. She would rock Mark gently in her arms, always making sure he was warm and comfortable and well-fed.

She still loathed me, however. Nothing I ever did was right. I had made a bad first impression on that train trip from Southampton, but I think Gran's distaste for me went deeper than mere indignation that I had dared to have a personality of my own. To her, I was my father's daughter, and Gran lost no opportunity to express her view that Dad was a useless, selfish alcoholic who had ruined my mother's life. Donovan was the devil incarnate, and I was his cloned representative.

When we were living in Kitty's house in Tooting Bec Road, Mark would spend the day gurgling away in his big Silver Cross perambulator at the bottom of the stairs. The floor was tiled, a beautiful mosaic of rust, red and cream. Every day, I would come bounding down the stairs, grab the handle of the pram and jump down, shouting: 'Hello, Marky Parky!' He would squeal with delight, and Gran would bellow at me to stop it. 'The pram will collapse,' she'd warn. But I couldn't help it; I loved seeing his smiley little face, and I loved him unconditionally.

One day, when I was about four and a half, the inevitable happened. I came skipping down the stairs, grabbed the pram handle, pushed down on it and sang 'Hello, Marky Parky!' It all seemed to happen in slow motion; as I put my weight on the handle, the two metal rings on either side slid up and the pram crumpled before me, catapulting my brother into the air, where he seemed to hover before smacking back down onto the tiled floor.

For a few seconds everything was silent, then Mark let out an almighty scream. I knew I was for it. By some miracle, the pillow from his pram had landed beneath him, cushioning his head from the blow. I've no idea how he landed with his head on the pillow, I really don't — but it undoubtedly saved his life. My grandmother went ballistic. 'You are going to get the hiding of your life when your mother gets home,' she hissed, clutching the wailing baby.

And I did.

It was the start of many beatings I would receive from my mother over the years, all due to the lies my grandmother would tell her.

'You'll never believe what that bloody child did today,' Gran would announce when Mum came home at night, before launching into some exaggerated — or blatantly untrue — account of my wickedness. Mum would be exhausted from work, and she'd lash out at me.

The beatings progressed from Mum's hand, to a slipper, to my large brown leather belt (complete with buckle) and a wooden hanger, which Mum once broke across my backside. I would wail like a banshee, until finally the crying stopped altogether. My spirit was slowly eroding, and eventually I just endured the beatings without making a sound.

I would shut my eyes and brace myself, and my mother would get more and more angry as I refused to break down. I was like a wounded animal. I didn't want anyone to know I was hurt, so I made no noise at all. I still do this today when I'm in intense pain — I completely zone out, into another place.

Mum would send me to bed, where I'd curl up and cry myself to sleep, nursing my welts. In my lonely little mind, I conjured up Dad as my saviour. I wanted him so desperately to come and rescue me; it was all too horrible, and I wanted it to stop.

One of the worst things my grandmother did to me was to shatter my vulnerability. To me, my mother was all I had in the world. Without her, we were floating, doomed to sink, and we would have been put into a children's home.

My sister Robyn and I would walk down to Tooting Bec tube station every evening as youngsters, to greet my mother when she came off the train. We would wait at the entrance barrier at 6.00pm every night, and walk home with her and chat about the day. I loved this special time with her alone, while we walked home.

As we waited, near the ticket collector's wooden and glass booth, I would be terrible and mimic the ticket collector who had a disability — every few minutes his head would jerk.

My sister would laugh at me, and tell me off and tell me to stop doing it. She said I was mean. Mum always told us to stand near his booth, and if any strangers came up to talk to us, we had to go to him. One day he caught me impersonating him and growled at me.

One evening as we left to go to the station, I told my Gran we were off.

Six o'clock came and went, 6.30 came and went, and I started to panic. Where could she be? I went up to the jerky man and asked if any of the tubes had crashed, and he said, 'No', but I was sure one had. My mother came on the Northern Line from Bank Station to Tooting Bec.

I then thought she must have had a heart attack and died, as she was never late, as she always knew we were waiting. If there was a train delay it was announced, but nothing was announced this night.

Seven o'clock came and went, and I was crying and worried about what was going to happen to us, and my vivid imagination took hold. Who would look after us? We had no money. My father was an alcoholic.

The crowds coming off the escalator were now thinning, as rush hour was over, and I said to my sister that I was going to ask Alice.

Alice had a flower stall outside the station. It was adorned from top to bottom with colour, and it lightened the dull surroundings. She would wheel her enormous barrow out each morning and away each night. Alice was there every day come rain, shine or snow.

She was in her sixties, and had a black beehive hairdo, which stayed up with enormous amounts of hair lacquer. Her hair was always covered with a pink scarf, knotted tightly under her chin. And she always wore a beige coat and black fingerless gloves, which showed her very ruddy and rather large 'man' hands.

I went up to Alice and said through the tears that my mother had failed to come home, and that she would never leave us, and that I thought she had died.

Alice said she doubted anything bad had happened, and maybe the trains were running late, but I told her, 'No, they are not, I think she is dead.' As Alice carried on serving customers buying flowers on the way home, with her cheery, 'Thanks luv,' she tried to reassure me. She said, 'Here, have a shilling,' which was a fortune in those days, and I took it, and said to my sister that we had better go home and tell Gran, as it was now very dark.

When I got to the door, I burst into tears again and told Gran that Mum had not come home and had died or been abducted.

She looked at me with those cold, steely grey eyes, and said, 'Oh yes, she rang this afternoon, she has to attend a function at work and will be late'.

I wanted to kill her at that very moment. No apology, no hug, no words of reassurance, just nothing.

I waited till Mum came home at 9.00pm and flew into her

arms and told her everything I had thought, and she cuddled me and said I should not have worried, she was fine.

She then asked my Gran why she had not told us, and she said, 'I forgot.'

I wished she had forgotten to breathe some days, it would have made my life so much easier.

I remember around this time friends of the family came to stay with us; a couple named Annie and Stan. Annie was a large, jovial woman and Stan a skinny, ginger-haired man with a cigarette always dangling from his mouth. My mother later found out Stan had molested his own son and daughter. His wife was aware of this, and both the young children were in and out of foster homes all their wretched lives. For some reason, Mum had taken pity on Stan and Annie, and allowed them to stay with us. I couldn't believe she had done this; if I even thought for a minute that a friend or acquaintance had been guilty of child rape, they would not be allowed anywhere near my house, let alone my child.

I remember once when I was visiting Mum in London as an adult, the phone rang and Mum called: 'Denise, it's Annie on the phone, come and say hello.' I shouted back: 'No thanks, but ask her how her child-molesting husband is.' Mum apologised to Annie, put the phone down and told me off in no uncertain terms, but I was an adult by then and had no intention of backing down on that one. I know I have many problems, and my behaviour can be irrational, but my God, child abuse is where I draw the line. I would willingly kill anyone who tried to harm my child — it would be worth a lifetime's jail. A mother should protect her children as best she can: to me, that is the most important thing in the world.

Annie and Stan's two children, Trevor and Linda, suffered irreparable damage from the sexual abuse they suffered at the hands of their father. Trevor lived off benefits. Linda turned to alcohol and drugs, and had children from various relationships, all of whom ended up in children's homes, just as their mother had. It is truly a very sad indictment on our society when children who are abused receive no support or help from people who are aware of what is happening and choose to turn a blind eye. All Linda's children ended up having the same sordid life as she did, moved from foster home to foster home, and put in council-run facilities. I remember as a child going with Mum and Annie to visit them at a large hostel for displaced children.

Adapting to life in 1960s England was not easy for my transplanted Anglo-Indian family. Racism was rife, and their new British friends would complain about how the end of Empire meant the country was being overrun by 'niggers' and 'Pakis'. Every bus and train seemed to have a West Indian, Sri Lankan or Pakistani conductor; the industrious new immigrants were quick to snap up any available work and property, and that infuriated some of the locals beyond belief.

Mum had a circle of Anglo-Indian friends, including Myrtle and Edwin Carter, who also lived in Tooting Bec. Whenever we visited, Myrtle would be cooking fish curry, and she and my mother would gossip in Hindustani.

All my aunts and uncles were fluent in Hindi, and would natter endlessly about matters unsuitable for childish ears. It frustrated the life out of me; from my earliest days, I've been desperate to be part of everything that's going on. I knew whatever they were saying must be fascinating.

Mum and her siblings were a feisty bunch, and there was always some family drama going on. One of the most spectacular fights occurred in the mid-1970s, when Uncle Robin came to visit us from India. Robin had enjoyed a brilliant career with Air India, rising quickly through the ranks, and even teaching Indira Gandhi's son Rajiv to fly. By now he was a director of the airline, and lived in Mumbai with his long-suffering wife, Cynthia.

Robin was a confirmed philanderer, and had continued the pattern of dangerous liaisons he had established all those years ago with the tight-skirted Kitty. Cynthia had somehow discovered Robin was sleeping with an Air India stewardess. She wrote to the airline to have the hostess fired — she had had enough — and of course the story ended up in the newspapers. It was a ripping yarn ('Director's wife takes on stewardess') and it blew up into a major scandal in the Indian press, forcing Robin to step aside temporarily from the airline's board.

Cynthia had sent the newspaper clippings to my mother, with instructions that under no circumstances were they to be shown to my grandmother. Mum, of course, did exactly what she was asked not to do, and the next time Robin visited us in London he had no idea that the family had gathered for what promised to be a spectacular confrontation. The minute he walked into the lounge, where they were all gathered, my grandmother — who was sitting on a chair like the family matriarch — waved a newspaper article in his face and asked how he could bring such shame on the family. He went ballistic; he was very charismatic, well-educated and good looking, but his temper was phenomenal.

He and I were both Pisces and shared the same temperament. We always got on well and laughed a lot, as we were so alike — he told it how he saw it, and took no prisoners. He was usually very lovely and easy-going, but when he lost his temper, he lost it, and I am the same. I have tried to curb it, but it is just the way I am. I go in with both barrels blazing, but once I have said my piece, I am over it and have cleared the air. Unfortunately my mother could never understand this. She was a Virgo and would hold on to a grudge like a large turd for days and weeks. No amount of apologies would work until she was ready to forgive you, and I could never understand that — and she could never understand me.

So now Uncle Robin wanted to know where Gran had got this article from, and when she told him his wife had sent it to my mother he turned on her, asking her how she could have been so stupid as to show it to their mother. The whole room erupted; they were all screaming and shouting at each other, in English and Hindustani. Uncle Arthur was a complete and utter gentleman and would never scream or swear at any woman, but the three sisters had mouths on them from the gutter when they were riled, and they could stand up to any man — they were completely fearless.

I was about nine or ten at the time of this confrontation, and I remember screaming at them to stop. I said, 'We can never have a get-together without you all fighting,' I shouted; 'I hate it.' And I ran out of the house in tears. Uncle Robin came after me and comforted me, walking me back to the house and saying it was just the way families were, especially ours. By the time we walked back inside everyone had calmed down a bit, partly in reaction to my being so upset.

Later Uncle Robin always brought up that episode, much to my embarrassment. When I was 21 I saved up and went for a holiday on my own to Bombay, staying with Robin and Cynthia. He was having an affair with someone else when I visited, and was very secretive toward Cynthia. He booked me on a flight to New Delhi on my own, and I travelled to Agra to see the Taj Mahal. Robin told me not to tell Cynthia that I was going — I have no idea why. She was always asking if I knew where he was, and I did not, and I did what he told me.

The night before I was to leave for Delhi he arrived home very late and I was in bed. I could hear an enormous argument develop, as Robin told her I was leaving in the morning for Delhi, and that he had arranged it. I will never forget hearing her scream at him, 'Are you fucking your niece as well now?' I was mortified. I could hear him calling her a 'fucking stupid bitch', and I hid under the covers — here it goes again! I just lay in bed not knowing what to do. Early the next morning Robin took me to the airport and gave me a tour. I told him I had heard what Cynthia said, and when I got back to Bombay from Delhi she would not talk to me! As my uncle was always at work, I spent most of the time talking, or trying to talk, to their servant, Mohammed.

There were rumours that Robin was sleeping with one of the cousins I was not close to, which shocked and appalled me, so maybe that's why Cynthia accused him of sleeping with me too — I don't know.

Life in our family was always eventful. Apart from the Gin Queen's spectacular alcoholism and fondness for public fist-fighting, there was an affair raging between my step-uncle Mickey (my mother's younger brother) and Beverly Watson, a flamboyant West Indian woman who lived in the downstairs flat in Tooting Bec Road.

When I was four and a half we moved to the house in Mandrake Road, and the Gin Queen and her family moved into Tooting Bec Road. Beverly lived in the flat with her two daughters and a monstrous son called Peter. We were never quite sure what had happened to Beverly's husband, but that didn't stop Mickey embarking on a very long affair with her. He would come over pretending to visit my aunt, and then say he had to 'pop downstairs to see Beverly'. The Gin Queen would be outraged, and shout abuse at Mickey. 'How could you have an affair with that Jamaican witch?' she would scream. I think what really riled Iris was that Mickey bought Beverly a large bottle of Mazola pure corn cooking oil every week, whereas we had to use a lump of white lard called 'Cookeen'.

Beverly Watson was mad, completely and utterly nuts. She would walk around the house singing, and told anyone who would listen that she was a witch, and that if anyone needed to curse an enemy with a magic spell, she was the person to do it. That was very convenient for the Gin Queen, who was always feuding with someone or other. Whenever she wanted to settle a score, she would overcome her moral objection to the affair between Mickey and Beverly, and ask Beverly to cast a spell on the object of her dislike. It never seemed as though Iris really needed the help of witchcraft, however — on the rare occasions when she was not passed out in an alcoholic coma on the sofa, she'd be warring with Zygmund. I distinctly recall her once chasing him down the street with a carving knife, and eventually slicing the shirt off his back.

I used to love visiting Iris's turbulent home; it was a complete free-for-all. The children were allowed to do whatever they wanted. If they didn't want to go to school, they just made up an excuse and my aunt believed them. I was so jealous; I was never allowed a day off school, even if I was near death. Whenever I visited my cousins, one of them would be lying on the couch eating and watching TV, saying they had the day off school because they had tooth/stomach/leg pains.

But one of the main reasons I liked Iris's place was that it was a relief from my unhappy life at Gran's house, as I was in her care while Mum worked and Robyn went to school. Every day, my grandmother made me sit on the third step in the cold hallway; no books, no music, no one to talk to, just my own lonely company. My mother left for work in the City early in the morning, and I had to stay on the step till my sister got home from school at 3.30. I could not go up a step or down a step.

All day I would gaze at the front door, willing my father to come through it, sweep me into his arms and take me back to New Zealand. When there was a knock, I would jump up: 'He's come to get me!' I would think. But it would always be one of Gran's friends, such as the white-haired widow, Mrs Mann. Gran would usher Mrs Mann into the sitting room and shut the door again. Often I would hear Mrs Mann say, 'Elsie, why don't you let that poor child into the lounge, it must be freezing out there; she won't be naughty.' But Gran never let me into the warmth.

When my grandmother needed to use the upstairs bathroom, she would walk past me as I sat on the step, and kick me aside, like a dog. I don't think it ever occurred to me to tell my mother what was going on. At some level, I accepted my grandmother's treatment of me. She was determined to belittle me at every opportunity, but when one of my cousins arrived, she'd make an enormous fuss. She would always look at me as she handed out sweets to my cousins, or talked fondly to them — she knew I was powerless to do anything.

On one occasion, I remember my cousin Maria visiting with her parents, Zygmund and the Gin Queen. With great ceremony, Gran took a new pair of shoes from a Marks & Spencer bag and handed them to the grinning Maria. Mum had just spent every weekend for months up a ladder painting the outside of the house in Mandrake Road. Zyg and Iris did not help once, but it was their daughter who received the gift.

When my mother found out, she was furious, and she had a row with my grandmother about why she would give Maria a new pair of shoes and not me — but there was no reasoning with the old witch. I really believed her heart was made of stone.

My fifth birthday, therefore, was an occasion for enormous joy — I could escape Gran and go to school.

3

First day at school

My mother had saved 3000 pounds and gave this to my grandmother to put towards purchasing a house that she, my step-grandfather Willy, my mother, myself, my sister and baby brother could live in.

Number 57 Mandrake Road, Tooting Bec, was a two-storey brick house in a tree-lined street, very close to the Underground, bus stops and schools. In fact, if you stood at the front gate and looked left up the street you could see my primary school, which stood on Fircroft Road, parallel to Mandrake Road. There were two large red-brick buildings, one for juniors and one for seniors. One of the buildings had a tower with a large bell, and a huge concrete plaque facing the street announced proudly that it had been built in the 1800s. Large, well-painted, glossy black railings went all the way around the perimeter, and there were two entrances with large metal gates. Above one entrance, carved into the brickwork, was the word 'Boys', and above the other the word 'Girls'.

There was a big three-sided shed in the playground, for when it rained, and a large concrete playing area that the juniors shared with the female seniors. The boys were segregated to play football around the other side of the building. On the sides of the shed were six white enamel water fountains, three on each side. These were operated by pulling on a small lever, and in winter moss would grow around the faucet. Each time I had to take a drink I would heave, or shut my eyes, as the green moss did nothing but remind me of Sally. Sally was a special needs girl, but in those days she was in the class with everyone else. She had blonde shoulder-length hair, glasses, her head was always tilted to one side, and she always had green snot running from her nose to her lips, which she would lick continually. Every time I saw the green moss on the faucet I could only ever think of Sally's green snot and it made me heave again.

The only toilets were outside, and they were freezing in winter. The toilet paper was Izal, stiff, single-sheet paper, which was like wiping your bum with crisp white baking paper. Each sheet was proudly emblazoned with the words 'London County Council', in case anyone was stupid enough to want to take a roll home.

There was never any discussion about which school I would attend. All the kids in the neighbourhood attended the nearest school, unless their parents had a specific reason to send them to another one. In England the summer holidays run from the end of July, through August and usually into the first week of September. Most children start school in September after they have turned five. I did not turn five until February 1965, too late to start in September 1964, and for some reason Mum did not want me to have to wait until the following September. I was allowed to enrol in February, just after my birthday, which meant I was five months behind everybody else. I was very nervous on my first day, as I entered the concrete playground with my mum. We walked into the main hall and met the headmistress, Miss Eatherly, who took me to my classroom. Here I met all the children I would spend the next six years with, and my teacher for the next three years, Mrs Charlton.

Mrs Charlton was in her mid-fifties, and dressed like the Queen. She had grey hair, not dissimilar in style to the Queen's, short and well-kept, and she often wore a crystal bead necklace that reflected prisms onto her turkey-like neck skin. I was always fascinated by this, and the way the colours bounced onto her skin.

The other thing about Mrs Charlton was her smell. She always wore the most glorious perfume. I have no idea what it was, but I got a whiff of a similar smell recently, and was immediately transported back to her classroom.

She was a very strict teacher, who took no prisoners — she was like Judge Judy — but she was also very thorough and very fair. I liked her immensely, except when she became angry. You could watch the blood rise all the way up her neck to her face — it was like watching mercury rise in a thermometer — and when it reached the top of her head she blew like a volcano. Luckily, I was rarely on the receiving end of her rage.

In our classroom we had a beautiful old rocking horse, complete with a real horsehair mane and tail, and if you completed your work successfully before the rest of the class you could ride the horse. It was such a treat. I spent many an afternoon on the horse, as I found the work pretty easy, and I found I could get lost in my riding.

When I first went to school there were some concerns that I would lag behind, as I was starting five months after everyone else. But before long Mrs Charlton told my mother that I had overtaken most of the other children, that I was very bright, and she shouldn't worry.

Mrs Charlton kept a stack of metallic stars in her drawer, and would stick them on our work when she marked it — blue or green was for OK work, silver for very good, and gold for excellent. Man, if you got a gold star from Mrs Charlton you felt like a star. I loved getting those stars, and would be crestfallen if my exercise book came back without a gold one.

Every afternoon she would read us wonderful stories. My favourite was 'The Adventures of Mr Twiddle', about a rather clumsy man with a bossy wife. On a Friday, she would buy packets of 'Toffos', which were toffee sweets wrapped in waxy paper. Five children were sent out of the room at a time, and Mrs Charlton would hide the sweets, then when they came back we would all shout 'Cold', 'Warm' or 'Hot' depending on how near to finding a sweet they were. It was such a great thing to do, and we all knew we had to behave and do our work, or there would be no sweet game that Friday.

The only thing Mrs Charlton and I disagreed on was the fact that I was left-handed. She did not like the fact that I wrote with my left hand, and I was regularly told not to do it, as this was not what 'young ladies' did, but I could not stop. Consequently, every time she caught me with my pencil in my left hand, I got a smack on the back of the hand with a wooden ruler. I would crumble when I got a smack from Mrs Charlton, and I never understood why Sarah Brown — a girl with carrot-coloured hair who was one of the most popular in the class — was allowed to carry on writing with her left hand while I was not.

My step-grandfather also told me more than once that when I grew up I would never be allowed in any posh restaurants, as I was 'cack-handed' and held my cutlery in the wrong hands. I tried really hard, and eventually became adept at writing with my right hand, but that was it. I still hold my knife in my left hand, brush my teeth with my left hand, eat with a spoon in my left hand, and do everything else with my left hand. I also use both hands to draw patterns with a pencil. I can still write very well with my left hand, but I'm sure the reason my writing has been likened to a doctor's is because I was forced to change hands. My brother is also left-handed, but by the time he went to school attitudes had changed and it was not seen as so barbaric.

Being left-handed made me one of a minority at school, added to which I was also one of the few children who had no father living with them, which I always found very hard. I could never understand the rule about not being allowed to write with your left hand. Today it would be seen as outrageous to smack a child for this, as it is known that the dominant side of the brain dictates which hand you write with. If you have a dominant right brain you are left-handed, and vice versa — so my poor brain was already confused, and my life had hardly started.

Despite this difference of opinion, Mrs Charlton gave me great encouragement, and at a very early age I discovered the joy of the written word. It might be difficult for people who are not into writing to understand this, but reading enables you to have the most glorious imagination. Whenever I read a book today then see the movie I am disappointed, as a movie can never live up to what you have imagined in your head.

It may have been that I found respite in the written word because my home life was so unhappy. I was fortunate in that both Mrs Charlton and my next teacher, Mrs den Hollander, encouraged me, and this continued right the way through my school years. I could think of nothing better than being given a subject and told to make up a story about it — I was in my element.

John Winston and I would always be the two best writers in the class — in fact there was very little John was not good at, and he topped the class every year for six years straight. I was also desperately in love with him, and when he professed his love for the red-headed Ms Brown I crumpled. She had freckles! But he said he loved her, and I wanted red hair after that.

Mrs Patricia den Hollander was my teacher from when I was eight until I was eleven, and she was something else. She had shoulder-length mousy, greasy hair parted in the middle, big horn-rimmed glasses, pock-marked skin, and crooked, nicotine-stained teeth. She wore old jumpers and usually a tartan kilt, with knee-high socks — the kilt finished above her knees and the socks below, and the fat would hang over the top of the socks, where they were too tight. She also wore boring shoes.

Mrs den Hollander and I did not get along. She was a mean-spirited woman, although she was always charm itself when she saw the rather good-looking music teacher from next door, Mr McNeil, who also taught me guitar. She was not long out of university, and he was also very much an ex-university boy — he usually wore a very matted green baggy jumper, drainpipe trousers and Clarks suede desert boots. Mrs den Hollander would put her lank hair behind her greasy ears and look into his eyes, and all 30 of us in the class thought they had kissed, even though she was married.

One day, after I had moved up to Mrs den Hollander's class, I bumped into Mrs Charlton in the playground and she mentioned that she needed some empty cardboard toilet roll inners, as the juniors were using them for some art they were making. I told her I would save the ones from home and give them to her. I did this, and one morning ran them over to her in the primary building, for which she was very grateful. I then rushed into class, and Mrs den Hollander asked me where I had been. I told her I had just dropped some empty toilet roll inners to Mrs Charlton as she needed them for art. Den Hollander, who specialised in art, said ominously, 'Oh really!' Soon after that she snapped, 'Everyone put your desk lids down,' turning to me and adding, 'especially you!'

'Now someone in this class is a traitor!' she went on. 'This person has given empty toilet roll inners to the juniors when they *know* we could use them in here for art.'

I could not believe what I was hearing, and my face turned puce. All the kids in front started looking around to see who this 'traitor' was, while den Hollander continued, 'I cannot believe someone in my class would do that, would give something to someone else when we could use it.'

For God's sake, we were not in wartime and talking about rationed food, but useless cardboard toilet roll inners! I desperately wanted to stand up and say, 'It was me, everybody look at me, I am the traitor — and I am going to tell Mrs Charlton what you said, you ugly bespectacled freak.'

Of course I could not summon up the courage to speak. I was so upset I was on the verge of tears. But from that moment on, the hatred I felt for this chain-smoking, kilt-wearing, greasy-haired woman came right up to the surface.

One day she brought her Dutch husband into school to talk to us about his adventures. He was very tall and gangly, but incredibly nice. He told us how he had contracted malaria from a mosquito bite when he was travelling to some far-flung corner of the earth, and that he still had to take medicine to control some of the symptoms of the disease.

I wanted to ask why he had not taken his wife on this adventure, but figured even the mosquitoes would have thought twice about wanting to suck any blood out of her. But his tale put the fear of God into me, and I kept running away from insects after that, as I hadn't a clue what a mosquito looked like. In fact there were never very many of them in Tooting Bec, but I did not know that at the time, and was too stupid to ask anybody. John Winston would have known.

John's only competitor was David Masters, who joined our class mid-year. He was a very overweight boy with glasses, hair that was always in his eyes, a huge lisp, and shorts that always twisted around his groin. He was bright, but he was no match for John.

John's father was a policeman, and his mother made him do homework every night! This was something my mother could only dream of. When the bell went at 3.30 I ran out of the school as fast as I could.

Soon after we moved into Mrs den Hollander's class she told us there were five people in the class who were exceptional at writing. She brought in five lined paperback books, which she covered in different wallpapers, and she put these books on a special shelf, which nobody but the famous five were allowed to touch. The chosen five were allowed to go and write in the books whenever the inclination took them. Den Hollander liked John, and I knew he would be one of the five, but I was very surprised when she read out my name.

Her hatred of me was legendary, so why she had picked me I could not fathom, but I went with the flow. I would get my yellow-patterned wallpaper-covered book and write stories whenever I felt like it. One day a girl from Mr McNeil's class next door told me that Mr McNeil had read them one of my stories, to show how good stories were written. I remember that the story was about a baby being abandoned in a cardboard box in a graveyard at the dead of night. It was a very morbid story for one so young, but even at that age I had very vivid thoughts.

My chest plumped with pride, until the girl added, 'And he asked us what was wrong with it, and we said it had no punctuation, and he said, "That's right, no punctuation."' My chest deflated again real quick.

How could they expect me to write something good as it came into my head, and use punctuation? I did not have the time, I was not a genius! I wrote a lot of poetry too, not rhyming but real poetry. I wrote a lot about the sea, which I love. Den Hollander thought it was great, and I always got very good marks for that. This was the only time she did not criticise my work — not once did she say anything derogatory about the writing in my wallpaper-covered book. It didn't stop her criticising everything else I did, but that was neither here nor there. I always thought it must have taken a lot for her to put me in this very exclusive club, and it was the only time John Winston and I were equals, much to my chagrin.

School had an assortment of oddities, me being one of them. Another was Roger, a half-caste boy who caused quite a few problems, and was made to sit behind me against the wall. I think this was because Mrs den Hollander knew he would scare me, which he did — I always thought he would hit or stab me when I wasn't looking.

One day Roger called to me, and I went over to him hesitantly. He handed me 50p, which was a king's ransom. 'What's this for?' I asked. 'You can have it,' he said. 'What for?' I asked. 'Because I want to give it to you.' So I took it. I have no doubt now that he had stolen it from the teacher's bag. At that time an ice cream was 3p, and for 6p you could get a '99', which was a soft serve in a cone with two Flakes! The next day, thinking we had an affinity, I went to talk to him, but he said, 'Don't talk to me today, I have no money.' I said, 'Okay,' and that was the end of our very short-lived friendship.

Mandy Smith had hair that always smelt wonderful. When the

whistle blew and we had to queue to go into the building I would always position myself behind her, standing really close so I could smell her hair. 'Get off,' she would yell, and I would say, 'Mandy, what shampoo do you use?' 'Vosene,' she would say, and I would reply, 'I'm going to get my mum to buy that for me.' But of course she never did. Vosene was a posh shampoo, it was advertised on the TV. We only bought Boots Egg and Lemon shampoo in a large plastic container — a 'no brand' shampoo — but I hankered after Vosene for years.

Lexie Jones had waist-length blonde hair, and was a friend of Sarah Brown. She was in hospital for many months with tuberculosis, and when she came out my mother and I used to go and visit her at home. We took her a fuzzy felt farm game, with little felt animals that stuck onto the green felt 'field'. When Lexie came back to school she had to have pink strawberry-flavoured powder mixed with her milk, like a milkshake; she said it was for her tuberculosis but I did not believe her and thought it was Nesquik.

One of the girls in the class, Kirsty, developed kidney failure when she was nine, and was off school for a long time. We all had to make her a card, which was sent to the hospital. I remember her face being so bloated you could hardly see her eyes, everything was pushed up around her face and neck. We all wondered why she had a 'fat face' when it was her kidneys that did not work. We thought she must have been eating a lot at home, as your face is nowhere near your kidneys. When Kirsty died we just seemed to accept it, as children do; I don't remember any of us being particularly upset, although I remember my mother was when I told her.

Susan Elliot was an only child who was in Mr McNeil's class. She and Mandy Smith of Vosene hair fame were best friends. Susan knew I was easily shocked, and it was she who told me how people 'did it'. I was horrified, but she said it was true, as she had seen her parents do it. She was always a bit too advanced for her age.

Susan's father was a fireman and they lived in a flat above the fire station. One day she invited me over after school, and a boy who also lived in the flats came over as well. We must all have been about eight. As we were playing Susan said to him, 'Show us your willy.' I nearly choked. We lived in a father-free zone and I had not even seen my brother's willy, nor anyone else's for that matter. The boy said he would not show us his willy unless we pulled our pants down, so Susan said this was a fair deal.

We were sitting in the lounge and her mother was in the kitchen, which was off the lounge. I was nervous, excited and scared all at the same time. This little pervert did not only want us to pull our pants down, but to do a show! He wanted to sit on the couch and we had to skip around it, and each time we came to face him we had to pull our pants down. Susan agreed, and I stupidly went along with this farce. We did this a few times, then the rules changed. He said he now wanted us to pull our pants down, bend over, and part our buttock cheeks near his face! I was horrified but Susan again agreed, if he would agree to pull the skin back on his willy! We had to keep our part of the bargain before he did his, so we did this, and it was embarrassing and humiliating. Susan then said we had done enough and now it was his turn.

So he undid his pants and got his tiny willy out. It was small, unattractive, and looked like a wrinkled sausage to me. She then said he had to pull the skin back. All I remember is the most awful smell as we peered closely at it, like you would at a starfish on the beach. It smelt like rotting cheese, and had bits of fluff caught between the folds. I had finally had enough, and said I wanted to go home. For years I dreaded that this gruesome story would come out, but thankfully it never did, until now!

Life in Tooting continued, and in retrospect I always seemed to be the person who attracted the disadvantaged and downright weird. The street we lived in was parallel to the 'Springfield Mental Hospital', a large brick Victorian building. The Gin Queen took a job there as a cleaner, and I remember saying to my mother, 'How would they know her from the patients?' She told me to 'shut it'.

We were always warned not to talk to people from the hospital, and I remember asking the Gin Queen what the patients were like. Her reply was, 'They're all mad,' which was pretty obvious, I suppose.

Very old men would wander up and down the streets, absolutely lost and in a world of their own. One in particular always walked the streets in his pinstriped pyjamas, burgundy corduroy slippers, and a burgundy and yellow checked woollen wrap-over dressing gown, with a burgundy-cord belt with tassels on the end.

Our grandmother had banned us from the tiny garden because of the noise we made, so we used to have to play out in the street. One day when I was out there the pyjama-clad man came up to me. 'What's your name?' he asked.

'Denise,' I said.

'Where do you live?'

'Over there,' I said. 'At number 57.'

The old man then went on his merry way.

When my mum got home I told her and she was very cross. 'What if he comes to the house to take you away!' she said. Why she said this to me I don't know. It was obviously a scare tactic, so I would not talk to other strangers, and it worked perfectly. I was beyond petrified now.

At the same time, I always felt very sorry for these people. The locals always said they were men from the war, who had seen too much and had had nervous breakdowns, which makes it even more tragic. They would wander the streets, in their own little worlds, passing the school as they did so.

During this time my sister Robyn became very reclusive and did not talk much to anyone, and she also became a victim of bullying. One day as the sleeve of her jumper moved up my mother caught a glimpse of her arm and saw a burn mark on it. She grabbed my sister's arm and pulled the sleeve up further — there were burn marks all the way up her arm. When my mother demanded to know what had happened, Robyn was at first very reluctant to tell her. But then she broke down and said that a black girl called Jessie had been putting cigarettes out on her arm — and this was in primary school!

I felt heartbroken for my sister, as I knew she had done nothing to warrant this. My mother took her straight up to the school to show the headmistress, and I decided I would confront Jessie. I was very nervous, as she was four years older than me, and what would be described today as a 'problem child'. But even though I was absolutely shaking in my second-hand shoes I went up to her and told her that if she ever did anything to my sister again, I would 'get her'. I knew I wouldn't be able to do this, as she would bash the hell out of me, but I said it anyway, and she left my sister alone. Soon after this she left the school, and we were told she had gone to 'borstal', the place all the bad people went to. My two older cousins, George and Tom, spent quite a bit of time in borstal and it only made them worse. They went in as naughty boys and came out as full-grown thugs, complete with 'Mum & Dad' tattoos on their fists!

I was always a bit scared of George — he was someone you never crossed. He was very good-looking, with piercing blue eyes, and very solidly built. He often had rolls of carpet to sell — they had always 'fallen off the back of a lorry', and as he worked as a driver for a carpet firm, it was pretty obvious where they came from! He also had car batteries to sell. We would see our neighbours trying to start their cars in the morning and wondering why they wouldn't go — we had the answer, sitting on the living-room floor. In fact, George could get you anything — watches, TVs, whatever you wanted — but my mum was onto him, and never asked him for anything.

I remember George's wedding quite vividly. He married a girl called Maureen. She was not what you would call pretty, but she had highly lacquered, back-combed, mousy hair that flicked up at the ends just above her shoulders and never moved an inch. It was the style that popstars like Lulu and Sandie Shaw were wearing, and it was terribly fashionable.

After the wedding we all went back to the Gin Queen's for the party. I remember my cousin Andrew had given me a single called 'Let's Dance', by Chris Montez, and I kept playing it over and over again on the record player. Finally George told me to turn it off, as it was driving everybody barmy, but it was the only record I had! George got a bit drunk, and after a while most people left, and he and Maureen went up to bed. We stayed on for a while, and at one stage I went into the lounge, looked around, and let out a scream. I thought George had decapitated Maureen — there, on the old oak sideboard, stood her head — well, her hair. I walked over and touched it, and there it was, all beautifully coiffed and sitting perfectly on a white polystyrene head ready for the morning.

I yelled out to my cousin Maria, 'It's Maureen's hair! Does George know she's bald?'

'She's not bald, you idiot, it's her wig!' came the reply.

I wanted to put it on, but Maria said George would kill me, so I'd better not.

I had never realised that Maureen wore a wig, and in all the time I knew her I never, ever got to see her real hair. I felt pretty disillusioned, and wondered what else was fake about her.

Along from the house in Tooting Bec Road there was a red phone box, and every time I went past it I would pop in to see if any coins had been left in the slot. I never did find any coins, but I often found needles and syringes that had been left by the local junkies, and I would sometimes pick these up. One day I struck gold and found a hand grenade! Yes, a real hand grenade. I picked it up and took it to the Gin Queen's house, and when Uncle Zyggy came in from work I showed him what I had found. He nearly had a heart attack, and told me quickly not to pull the pin out. He took the grenade from me, and I was never quite sure what he did with it, but it is probably still sitting in the garden in Tooting Bec Road waiting to blow up!

There was one area in my life that caused me no end of

embarrassment — the facts of life and periods. As most children had a father living at home, they were quite at ease with the male 'member', but I was not. In fact, apart from the very few times I saw my brother having his nappy changed, I don't think I ever saw a male appendage. As we got older Mrs den Hollander showed us the reproductive organs of a chicken, and we had to draw it in cross-section and colour it in, then it was put on the classroom wall. I was mortified. She also told us about the male and female human reproductive organs. At this point I would hum to myself, as I did not want to hear about such disgusting things. I would go bright red when she talked of 'eggs and sperm', and just wanted to shrivel up and die, it was too much for me. As for periods, well, that just about tipped me over the edge.

I don't know why, but I had a complete and utter denial phase about urinating, defecating and periods. I thought only the very lower class people suffered these. I knew I was 'very lower class', as I had free school meals, and the only kids who ever had those were either special needs or me! In my mind, there was no way the Queen, any actors, actresses, pop stars (heaven forbid!) and anyone that lived over Battersea Bridge or in America had periods or shat — it was impossible for me to imagine this. I thought only working-class people did this, and no matter how hard I tried, I could not get this tortured image out of my head. Can anyone imagine the Queen having a good crap after a curry? Or inserting a tampon? I fear not, it just did not happen — it only happened, in my head, to pond-scum like me.

When Mrs den Hollander talked of periods, I was sure all the boys in the class were momentarily made deaf and could not hear what she was saying, as they never talked about it. I knew my mother had them, but she would, as we lived in Tooting and were working class. My grandmother never had them, which just confirmed the fact that she was subhuman. And had she never had them at all, I would not have been here to endure her, so they were in fact a problem I did not want to have to endure either.

One day at school I went to the outside toilets, which were

the only ones we had — come rain or shine or snow or frost, you went outside, into a brick corridor where the toilets were housed. They had rickety, glossy black-painted doors, with cracks that you could peep through, and more often than not the bolt had come off the door, so you had to perch on the toilet, trying to hold the door shut without shitting on the floor. I was 11, and it was nearly time to start secondary school. Anyway, this day while I was in the toilet I pulled down my knickers and saw a funny-coloured smear on them. I looked closer, and thought I must be close to death. I ran inside and very quietly called my best friend, Antonia Panayi, to come out with me. I knew she would never betray a confidence, so we both huddled in the outside cubicle and I showed her what was in my knickers. 'Oh,' she said, 'I think it's your period; you'd better go and tell somebody.'

I was beyond mortified. No one in my class had their period, that I knew of, and I most certainly did not want it. It just proved to me again how very working class we were, and I had to get out of being working class. I went into the hall and saw Mrs Morgan, who was the playtime monitor, and she said she would tell Ms Wight, the PE teacher, who would deal with it, except it was the staff coffee-break. She went up the large wooden staircase to the teachers' lunch room, and returned a few minutes later to say Ms Wight would be down shortly. I was now beside myself, as for some reason I imagined she had walked into the staffroom and announced to all and sundry that Denise L'Estrange-Corbet had her period, and all the teachers, male and female, had had a jolly good laugh! I stood at the bottom of the stairs waiting for her to appear, but of course she wasn't going to before the break was over. I was convinced I was going to bleed to death, right at the bottom of the stairs, in full view of the whole school. I waited and waited, for what seemed an eternity, until finally Ms Wight appeared. She took me into a room and told me to pull my knickers down, which I did, and she peered into the crotch and said, 'Yes, that's it; pull your pants up and I'll get you a pad.'

She came back with what resembled a rather large white

hammock (a pad with a loop at either end). She said they did not have any sanitary belts (this was before the sticky liners had been invented) and went off to find two very large, nappy-type safety pins. She then proceeded to put one large pin through the front loop of the pad, and the other through the back loop, and secured these to the front and back of my vest! My mother always made me wear a vest — a white cotton one in the summer, and a cotton and woollen one in the winter. I always felt like such a twat, as Sarah Brown's mum said she didn't have to wear hers any more. But my mother said, 'I don't care what Sarah Brown's mother says, she doesn't work, and I don't have time to look after you if you get sick, so put on your vests!'

The weight of this enormous pad, which was layers and layers of swaddling jammed between my legs, made it impossible for me to walk normally, and my vest neckline was being pulled down to somewhere near my tummy. As I waddled back to class I thought all of a sudden that blood was going to gush out and I was going to flood the classroom floor, and then everyone would know my predicament. I was beyond mortification, and could think of nothing else. When I sat down on the chair, this hammock kept moving, to the left, to the right, up my crack, in fact everywhere it shouldn't. I desperately did not want anyone to know what was happening in my nether regions, and tried to act as normally as possible. Ms Wight whispered to Mrs den Hollander, and she looked over at me and I almost felt she was about to announce it to the class to further my embarrassment.

I had asked Ms Wight if I needed another pad, and she had said, 'No, you will be fine till you get home.' After school I ran all the way home in a sort of odd gait, and tried to wedge the unsightly nappy from my backside. I immediately called my mother, who was at work at the London Chamber of Commerce in the City, and started crying. I told her that I had my period (whispering in case anyone was listening) and that I didn't want it, and that I couldn't walk properly any more and that I was on the verge of bleeding to death. She told me to calm down, she was at work and could not do anything about it till she got back, but she would buy me some pads on the way home.

I remember my sister looking at me and smirking, and I yelled, 'What are you looking at?' I knew I wanted to be a boy now, as boys never had crap like this happen to them. It was awful, too awful to contemplate, and I was convinced that whenever I had it the word 'period' was emblazoned across my forehead for everyone to see.

After a few years of having to endure these awful 'nappies' I told my mother I wanted to wear tampons, as these frikken' pads were doing my head in. She agreed, and we went off to the Superdrug store to buy some. I picked the brand I wanted, Lil-lets, which were small, hard and bullet-shaped, as opposed to Tampax, which came in a cardboard tube, which I thought I would lose in my fanny.

I went into the bathroom when we got home, and gently took the cellophane off the box. I took out the instruction leaflet and peered at the cross-section of a woman's reproductive organs, and saw how you were meant to insert the tampon. Well, I have never experienced so much discomfort and pain in all my life! I tried and tried so many times to put it in but it would not go, so eventually I just managed to get the tiniest bit of the tip in and walked out of the bathroom with the rest hanging out. I thought how very uncomfortable it was, but thought that was obviously how you wore them, with the tip in and the rest hanging out, like a small penis in your pants.

My mother asked how it went, and I said it was fine but that it would not go in all the way. She said, 'Do you want me to have a look?' and I screamed, 'No thank you very much!' So then she said it had to all go in or it would not work, it would fall out! So I went back into the toilet, pulled it out in disgust, flushed it down the bog and put another hammock between my legs; life as a young woman was not going to get any easier. Friends told me that once you had sex it was easier to insert a tampon, but the chance of any boy wanting to have sex with me was even more impossible to imagine than the Queen taking a crap, so that was out of the picture.

For some reason I was one of the girls who my awful teacher Mrs den Hollander picked to look after new girls. I did this with a lot of girls, and usually once they had got their confidence they would run off with Lexie Jones and Sarah Brown, the two 'it' girls of the time. But when Winifred Lane appeared at my school one day, she and I became immediate friends. She had a curly mop of brown hair, freckles, and was funny, sweet, kind and all those things you want in a friend.

Her mother was a stay-at-home Mum, something I only dreamt of having. She never talked about where she came from or her past, but we got on famously.

I remember one day after school asking her mother if Wini could come to my house to play. I don't know what I was thinking, as my wicked grandmother absolutely forbade any of my friends to put their foot over the threshold. But I asked her mum to come with me to our house, as I felt that with her there my grandmother would not say no. WRONG! When we got to the house my grandmother answered the door, and I asked, 'Can Winifred come in to play for a bit?'

My grandmother said 'No'. I was mortified. Winnie's mother said it was fine, and not to worry about it, but I was so embarrassed. I begged my gran, who was the most stern person I have ever met, and the more I asked, the more she refused. Finally I turned to Winnie's mother, who said, 'Don't worry, you can come and play at our house another time.'

So a date was set, and after school I went to play at Winifred's house off Trinity Road. They had the ground-floor flat in a large Victorian house. Her mum made us tea, and we played until my mother came to collect me at 6 o'clock, after finishing work. Winifred's policeman father was also there, and Winifred, who was an only child, and I enjoyed ourselves tremendously.

When my mother came to pick me up I didn't want to go.

Winifred's parents chatted with my mother for a bit, then we left to make our way home through the cold winter's evening. I remember telling my mother that Winnie was my best friend, and what a great time we had had.

The next day Winnie was absent from school, but I did not think twice when den Hollander called the register. When she got to Winifred Lane she said, 'Oh yes, Winifred's not here.'

The next day Winnie was absent again, and this time I went up to den Hollander and asked if she was sick. 'No,' she said; 'she's left.'

'Left? What do you mean?'

'You know, left, not here any more, gone!'

'But she can't have left,' I stammered. 'I only played with her the other day.'

Yes, she had left. The whole family had packed up and left, and not said a word, not a single word. I kept thinking all sorts of things — that her father was a special agent and was on a secret mission, and they had to go, or that he was not a policeman at all, and the family was on the run! I just couldn't believe my best friend had gone. I went to her house and rang the bell, but there was no answer.

It was just my luck — when I meet someone I really like, they think so little of me they don't have the decency to tell me they are moving! As you can tell, I have still not got over it, and I still wonder what happened to Winnie. So if by any chance, Winnie, you happen to be reading this, can you please tell me what happened there?

Janet was a girl who lived across the road from us and down a bit, in Mandrake Road. She was the cousin of Neil, who lived next door but one to us, with his father. His rather attractive mother, who worked at The Lido, the open-air swimming pool at Tooting Common, had left them for another man, something my mother and grandmother tutted about all the time.

I always thought Janet was dead posh. She was an only child, and her parents were very proper. Sometimes, you meet people and you feel they should not be where they are. I felt this about Janet. Her parents had a very nice home, and Janet was very well behaved — never rude, never being told off continually by the neighbours for making a noise, being insolent or behaving like a street urchin.

I was reminded of Janet recently when Benny, our menswear designer, called work to say he had an appointment with the dentist in the afternoon as the cap had come off his front tooth — he was sporting half a tooth and resembled a pirate. Janet flashed into my mind, as she also had half a tooth — it had cracked diagonally and broken off, right in the front, and I was so jealous.

Janet said she had broken her tooth when she dived into a swimming pool and hit her mouth on the bottom. I wanted a chipped tooth, right in the front, and just like Janet's. I believed for some reason it would make me posh. Janet had not been living in our street for very long, and as an only child, her parents obviously thought it would be nice for her to meet the local children who lived in her street. Up till then, we had only passed in the street, and from the day I met her I tried everything I knew to crack my front tooth, painlessly.

Janet invited my sister Robyn, cousin Maria and me over to her house. They had a proper living room with armchairs and everything. Her father sat in one of the chairs and asked us what we were going to do when we grew up. Of course, I had no idea, I was just so engrossed in the house, and how neat and tidy it was. Everything was in a place, and it was the sort of house where you behaved yourself for fear of breaking something, like the mock Lladro. They also had those doily-type covers on the back of the armchairs where your head rests, so grease from your hair wouldn't get on the mock velvet — this was the time when men had a tendency to wear greasy Brylcreem in their hair. They also had carpet throughout the house, and not cracked lino.

One afternoon my cousin Maria said that Janet had invited us over again. I was so excited, and Maria said, 'I'll make you a new pair of trousers to wear!' I was going to be posh too! We were moving up in the world; we were mixing with normal, well-behaved people.

Maria cut up an old white cotton sheet, and believe me, it must have been threadbare, as there was no way she would have been allowed to cut up a good sheet, as nothing got thrown out in our house. Then she started to make me these trousers. They had no waistband, and they did not fit very well — they were basically just two legs. Maria had no pattern to follow, so she just cut out two long leg shapes, with a bit in the middle for your bum to fit into. We also did not have a sewing machine, and I don't remember how she put them together, as none of us could sew. But I didn't care, they were new, white, well sort of, trousers. So I squeezed my bottom into them, then had to hold the top up for dear life, as they had no zip or buttons, and no way of staying up on their own. I kept pulling my top down so that nobody would realise my new trousers were only half made.

We arrived at Janet's house, and again, I admired her cracked tooth, which she said she was going to have fixed! I could not imagine why. 'You're having it fixed?' I asked her incredulously. Did she not realise it made her elite, and that I wanted one? Her father, wearing a shirt, cardigan and tweed trousers with slippers, took us into the lounge and offered us a seat. I moved toward the armchair nearest the window, so I could look out through the net curtains, and hopefully the neighbours would see me sitting in Janet's house. I felt her family were all looking at me and admiring my new attire, and I blushed coquettishly. But as soon as I sat down in the pale green velour armchair, there was an almighty rip! The seat of my trousers had parted company, completely.

Janet's father asked if I was all right — I think he must have thought I had let out a huge fart. I said, 'Yes, I'm fine, why wouldn't I be?'

We declined an offer of tea, but chatted politely, mainly about school and what we wanted to be when we grew up. Maria blabbed on about what she wanted to be, as she had a very high opinion of herself, mainly because my grandmother was always saying, 'Maria is so this, Maria is so that, so clever, so pretty, so talented, blah de bloody blah.' You would have thought she was a candidate for Mensa, and my self-esteem would slowly decrease like a deflating balloon.

I could not concentrate for more than a nanosecond, as I had more important things to think about, such as the fact that my arse was no longer inside my pants! When the time came for us to leave, I did not want to stand up. Janet's father stood up, as if to tell us we really had to go, and Maria kept saying, 'Come on Denny, what's wrong with you?' I said, 'Nothing,' but I just wanted to stay seated for a bit longer. After a while, when everybody in the room was standing and looking at me, I realised I had to make a move. I slowly stood up, clutching the top of my pants, and backed out of the room, and the house.

When we got outside I told Maria that my pants had completely split, right up the bum. I remember I started complaining, and she came right back at me, telling me how ungrateful I was, that she had made me a beautiful pair of white cotton pants, and all I could do was complain about them. She started storming up the hill, as I stumbled along behind her, trying to hold on to what was left of my pants. I wanted her to walk behind me, to cover my embarrassment, but there was no way the princess was going to do that! Walking up the road seemed to take an eternity — not only did I have to clutch the top, I also had to walk backwards so that nobody could see the dreadful predicament I was in.

When we finally arrived home and I let go, the stupid pants just fell off me onto the floor. I told Maria I was never wearing them again. Janet was too posh to be our friend, and we had obviously aimed too high in thinking for a second that she was on the same level as us.

Shortly after that Janet and her parents moved, obviously to a more affluent area than Tooting Bec. They did not say good-bye, and left no forwarding address.

For as long as I can remember I wanted my ears pierced — I thought it was the height of elegance. When Mum said I could have it done for my eighth birthday, I could hardly sleep with excitement. Although she had agreed, Mum was dead against pierced ears. She kept trying to put me off having them done by telling me to look at the lobes of my grandmother's ears, which nearly touched her shoulders. I pointed out that she always wore heavy gold creole earrings, and I would never have enough money to wear those, so mine would be fine.

There was a hairdresser's next door to Tooting Bec Station called 'Ross', who did ear-piercing for three pounds, which included 9-carat-gold sleepers. We made an appointment for the Saturday morning, which was my birthday, and went along. There was a tall, thin gentleman who worked at Ross's, and he was going to do it for me. He said it would not hurt, as he would freeze my ears. He brought over a small plastic squeezy bottle, the type they used for hairspray, and proceeded to 'freeze' my earlobes. To this day I swear it was hairspray — it did cause a slight cold effect, but definitely not what I would call freezing! They did not have ear-piercing guns in those days, but used a needle on a syringe. The man sat me down in a high leather barber's type chair, put a plastic cape around me 'for the blood', and said, 'Ready?'

I said 'Yes' and shut my eyes. The pain was excruciating! I yelled at the top of my lungs. And there was blood, and I hate blood, especially my own. I thought I was going to faint. Then I thought about the look, and realised fashion is sometimes painful. He did both ears, and when I looked in the mirror my lobes were red and throbbing, but I had earrings! The man said I had to bathe them twice a day with diluted Dettol, and not remove them for six weeks. They also had to be turned daily in the ear to stop them getting crusty, and the thought of that made me cringe!

But when we walked out of there I had never felt higher. I was convinced the whole world was looking at my fabulous 9-carat-gold, yes real gold, earrings, as they looked so hot!

That afternoon Mum was also taking me ice skating for my

birthday! I had never been skating before, and I was so excited I thought I would die. I had fancy earrings and I was going skating at the Streatham ice-skating rink in the High Street. We took the 49 bus from Tooting to Streatham in the afternoon, and I remember it was a very cold day, as it was February and real winter. But I was convinced eight was my lucky birthday, as it was four years since I had had a 'real' birthday on the actual day, the 29th of February.

Mum made my sister and me wrap up warm as the ice rink was very cold. I had on a gorgeous mustard jumper that Mum had knitted, with four mustard buttons on one of the shoulders. When we got there we hired our boots and went into the changing room, which had a very wet floor from all the ice brought in by the skaters. I was chomping to get on the ice — it all looked so easy! After you put your boots on you had to walk on the blades along rubber mats till you reached the ice. People were swirling around us, there was a disc jockey playing all the latest hits really loud, and it was great! Of course, it was not even half as easy as it looked, and I spent most of the time grabbing onto the side — no doubt resembling Frank Spencer in *Some Mothers Do 'Ave 'Em*.

Mum took to it like a duck to water, as she used to roller-skate as a girl, and even my sister, who has to be the most uncoordinated person I have ever met, was at least on two legs, while I was sprawled all over the ice. My bum was soaking wet, and I had on my jeans from the 'Martin Ford' boutique, which I thought was very flash, not to mention my earrings.

For some inexplicable reason, I managed to get myself to the centre of the ring, and fell again. I got up, and slowly tried to make my way through the crowds whizzing past me, staggering like a drunk, so I could grab the trusty barrier. It was taking a while, and someone came up behind me and said, 'Excuse me dear, have you cut yourself? There's blood on you.' I said, 'No, I'm fine,' and he said, 'Are you sure — you're dripping blood all over the ice.' I then looked down at my right arm and noticed my mustard jumper was soaked in blood up to the elbow.

The man said, 'Let's get you to the side and we'll have a look.' I was in no pain, but when we reached the side and he lifted up the sleeve of my jumper the blood just gushed out like a spurting fountain from my right wrist. There was an emergency call put out, and all of a sudden all hell broke loose. The ushers skated over, swooped me up and carried me off. They asked my mum's name, and put a call out for her over the tannoy. Then they took me to the first-aid room and lifted the sleeve of my jumper again, to reveal the biggest gaping hole I have ever seen. My wrist was hanging off.

At that point I fainted, and they sat me down and put my head between my knees to get me up again. Mum came over, not having any idea what was going on, and the ushers put a large wad of serviettes over the deep gash, but it just would not stop. There was blood all over the place, and a large crowd had gathered. The usher said, 'It's like a fountain,' I think to make me laugh, but I just wanted to faint again. I swore I could see my bone.

They called an ambulance, and just sat me there taking deep breaths while we waited. They said that when I fell, I must have stood on my wrist with the blade, and sliced right through my arm. Someone took off my ice-skating boots and got my shoes and coat, then the ambulance came and I was whisked to hospital. I had never been in an ambulance before. As we scooted down Tooting Bec Road towards St James Hospital at the top of Trinity Road, we had to stop at a zebra crossing. One of the girls from my class, Linda Walsh, was crossing the road, and I desperately waved to her with my left arm, hoping she would see me and tell everyone I was in an ambulance. She didn't respond, much to my disappointment. I did not realise you could only see out of the windows, and people could not see in, which of course makes perfect sense.

I kept begging the ambulance crew to reassure me that I would not need stitches, and they said, 'No, no, you will be fine, butterflies will do.' These were little clips that held the skin together till it 'knitted' back. I was so relieved.

We arrived at the Emergency entrance to the hospital and I

was taken inside. The doctor took one look at my wrist and said, 'Stitches,' and I yelled, 'No, I want butterflies; the man said I could have butterflies.' But the doctor said the cut was too deep, and butterflies would not hold it. He also said I was very lucky not to have cut anything that would affect the use of my arm, but I didn't care, I wanted butterflies! Then the doctor asked how the accident had happened, and when he was told it was an ice-skating blade he said I would have to have a tetanus injection, and four other injections. I felt faint again. I hate needles, and I had already had to psyche myself up that day to have my ears done, and now I had to have a whole lot more.

They lay me on a bed and gave me my five injections, and then stitched me up with thick, black catgut. It was so painful. I could feel the needle and gut going through my skin, and I wanted to gag. They bandaged my arm, put me in a sling, and said I had to stay like that for a few weeks, until the stitches came out, and told me not to get them wet. We arrived home very late in the evening after all of this, and when my grandmother saw me coming through the front door in the sling, looking very sorry for myself indeed, her words of comfort were: 'What has she done now?'

I went to school on the Monday, only to be told I could not go on the 'School Pack Holiday' as I would need too much looking after. So I had to stay back, while everyone else went away for two weeks, camping somewhere. The others who stayed back were Roger (a criminal in the making) and some other children whose parents could not afford to send them. Not only that, it was two weeks with ghastly Mrs den Hollander, but I think she felt quite sorry for me, for a change. At first I don't think she believed I had really cut myself, as she asked to look at the stitches. When I unbandaged myself and showed her the stitches she said 'Yuk' and bandaged me up again.

Of course, for the weeks I was in bandages I had to use my left hand to do my schoolwork — if they had only left me alone at five I would have been fine, but now I had gone from writing with my left hand to my right, and back to my left again, so I was very confused.

So all in all, my eighth birthday was, if nothing else, one of the most memorable of my life.

4

Down in the depths

My depression was not diagnosed by a doctor
until I was in my late twenties.

Depression is one of those things that is misunderstood by some who do not suffer with it, which I guess would be the same for most illnesses — while you can sympathise, you never really know what it's like until you have it. Depression is like a cancer, and I find it so debilitating. Life can be chugging along quite nicely, and suddenly you plummet. You can go to bed fine, then wake up the next morning and this huge black cloud has enveloped you. You cannot run away from it, as it follows you everywhere. You can run all you want, but it's still there, above you, not moving, and it's so large.

When I decided to take 2007 off to concentrate on writing, I looked forward to it more than anything. The first six months were fantastic — the novelty of not having to wake up to the alarm clock was a dream come true — but then the solitude and loneliness set in. Day after day you are all alone, all your friends are at work, there is no one to talk to all day, apart from the curtains, and you start craving company, but not really, if that makes sense.

I found I became very social in the evenings, always catching up with friends and going out. In fact, if I was home for more than two nights in a row I would be going stir-crazy. Sometimes I could be having the best time, and laughing and joking all evening with friends, then I could walk straight out of a bar or restaurant and burst into tears. I would walk sobbing all the way home, and I mean sobbing — uncontrollable, body-shaking sobs, all the way home.

There is no rhyme or reason for it. Someone you care for very deeply, or someone you may never have met before, can make a comment and you will plummet, high off the shelf, down into the crevice. You fall and keep falling at a rapid pace, stopping just before you hit the bottom, and when you do hit the bottom, it's like one of those dreams where you are falling and wake up just before you hit the ground, with a huge jolt that bolts you upright.

The only difference is that sometimes you know how easy it would be to fall from the shelf and actually hit the bottom. BANG! Done, no going back. No 'I'm sorry, I didn't mean to kill myself, I want to go back'. It's too late by then. This is something I am sure every person who suffers from depression or another type of mental illness has thought about many times.

But when you are not depressed, you can handle almost anything anyone wants to throw at you, and in the fashion industry, mud is slung more often than not. When I am in the depths, I think a lot about ending it all. Not so much about the act of how to do it, but the fact that I know that whatever it is that has me clutching onto the edge of the cliff with my fingernails is all there is. I can tip at any time. The tightrope I am walking has me right in the middle and I can go either way, and it takes every ounce of my being to stop me doing it. Sometimes, the despair is so great it would almost be a relief. I have to actually talk myself out of it. It is very hard to explain, but you feel like such a tortured soul, almost as if you were put on this earth by mistake. It was not meant to happen, it was not meant to be you, and you somehow ended up in this body, and it was the wrong soul that was sent, and you so don't want to be here. You have to survive day after day, and you just want to drop off, you don't want to be here, and no matter how much friends and family tell you they love you, it just cannot penetrate that impenetrable barrier and get through to your soul to make you believe it, the torture is so great.

I attend functions and people say, 'You look great. How are you? You're the life and soul of the party.' And you smile and say that you are fine, and really you feel like vomiting, as you are lying through your teeth. No matter how bad I feel, I have never managed to say, 'Actually, I feel so dreadful, I have thought of nothing else but killing myself today.' Because that would be a real conversation-stopper — but it's the truth.

And then you pick up a magazine, and they have printed the worst possible picture, with some bitchy comment, and you spiral and start the descent again. Friends say, 'You're too sensitive,' but how can you stop it?

I never used to cry, but lately, I cry a lot. I am lying in bed reading, and it starts, and I can't stop, and I fall asleep, and I wake up in the middle of the night, open my eyes and the tears fall. I have cried rivers. And I wish it would just go away and leave me alone, but it is always there, like an invisible person sitting on your shoulder. Some days you don't notice them, and other days they prod and poke you, and you cannot budge them and you start listening to them. You can't eat, can't sleep, you are so tired but the thought of sleep is a nightmare. Other times, you just sleep and sleep and don't want to wake up and find you are still here, on earth, with all the dreadful things that happen in it.

And then I think, 'What if I got some incurable illness, would I be happy? Happy in the knowledge that I don't have to be around here much longer, or would I desperately want to stay?' I don't know.

I am sure that depression can stem from a dysfunctional childhood. I don't know if this is a proven fact, but most people I know who suffer from it have had something traumatic happen to them, not always in childhood, sometimes later in life; something they cannot erase from their memory, no matter how they try. Some people can handle it and can get over it and cope with it and others cannot, it just eats a little piece of your soul away each time it visits, until there is nothing left.

When it rains, I mean torrential rain, I put on my mac and walk without an umbrella for as long and as far as I can, until I am drenched to the skin. Till my hair is dripping, my trainers are squelching and my clothes have to be peeled off.

I love the elements of the wind and the rain and find it so therapeutic to go out and face it, instead of sitting indoors like most people. It gives me great thinking time. I realise that we are only on earth for such a short time, and the elements will always be here, and nothing can ever change that, so I just try and enjoy it, the ferocity of a good storm, with the rain lashing at you.

I often wonder how people used to cope before depression had a name. There must have been millions who have gone before us, who went undiagnosed or were just seen as 'mad' and placed in institutions because of their behaviour. Now we are told it is because the brain lacks a chemical called serotonin, some little chemical imbalance that holds the key between life and death.

There are two things I think really help depression. One is the sun and light — you need a lot of this to avoid plunging into the depths — and the other, and this sounds as corny as hell, is love. Pure, unadulterated love. Love that someone gives to you, and you can give in return. I think a lot of people in this world don't have that, and are desperate for it, and without it your self-esteem is zilch and everything pales in comparison. You can have hundreds of friends, as I do, who love and care for you, but no matter how many times they tell you, you still feel worthless and alone; it's like an impenetrable barrier has gone up, a big invisible Perspex screen, and nothing can break through it, and all the words of love and encouragement that are said to you by family and friends, you can almost watch slide down the slippery surface in front of your face, without reaching you.

Relationships are very tenuous things, and have to be worked at all the time, with workmates, friends and lovers, and when there is a glitch, it can send you right over the edge. Everything gets out of focus and perspective, and the smallest of things form into huge, cancerous growths. Ask anyone who has come out of a relationship — everything is out of kilter and there is no light at the end of the tunnel. We have all been there at some time or another, and thought we would never survive, but we do, but those of us with depression find it a lot harder to deal with.

And believe me, I have very forthright opinions on so many things, and sometimes I open my big mouth far too much and say things that maybe should have been left unsaid — as the saying goes, 'Least said, soonest mended'. But that is me, and we all come with traits we may not particularly like, but that is what makes us who we are, for better or worse. You can only hope the people who love you and who you love are understanding and forgiving when that happens.

The demons can come calling at any time, they do not make appointments, and there is no way to shake them off. They can stay for a day, a week, who knows? It brings loneliness and all your insecurities to the fore. Nothing can shake it, you cannot concentrate on anything, unless you really become focused on that and nothing else. You can watch TV and not have a clue what you have been looking at, you can forget something you have just been told, as you were not really listening, and God help anyone who wants to cross you on a day like this — you will either go on the attack or shrivel up.

Your breathing becomes so shallow you have to consciously take big, deep breaths to wake yourself, and make sure you are taking in enough oxygen. You can do mundane things, as you don't have to put any thought into that. But you don't want to eat or sleep, life feels bleak and there is nothing to look forward to. Even if you got a call to say you had won the lottery it would not cheer you up on a black day. You start wishing your life away, so it will disappear and leave — what a way to live, wishing time would go faster, in the hope that today will disappear. You can be in a room full of people and be the loneliest person on the planet, and no matter how great your friends and family are, they still cannot get through to you, the deepness is so great, it's unreachable.

It's like being at the bottom of the deepest, darkest, most desolate part of the ocean where nothing can reach you. And there you are, on the very bottom, you can't go any further; you're lying there, in the pitch black, suffocating, looking upwards for light. Light that can show you a way out, but you cannot see it, no matter how much your eyes scan upwards. And you sit and wait, and wait, wanting to be rescued, plucked out so you can gasp an enormous breath and know you are alive and safe, but nobody knows you are there, and if they don't know you are there, how can they reach you? But they can't know, as you are already there and nobody saw you reach that place. You have to get back up to the surface on your own, and it's an enormous struggle. You keep looking up, but you can't get off the bottom. It's just too hard and you don't have the energy to lift yourself up, so it's easier to lie on the bottom and float. The demons are holding you down in the blackness.

You cannot see them, but you are very aware they are there. You cannot hear or see what is happening around you unless the light starts to show through, but it's not coming. You want to scream at the demons, tell them to fuck off and leave you alone, but you can't speak under the water, as you know you could drown. And each time it happens it becomes harder and harder to get to the surface. It's an enormous battle of the wills, yours against theirs, and as you weaken they become stronger. Maybe tomorrow you can fight them, but today it's too hard. They might even win tomorrow, who can tell?

And each time you do make it to the surface, and to light and air, you inhale huge gulps of air — you made it, you're out and you know you never want to go back down again, and you will do whatever you can to stay with your head above the water. This can be days or months, and you try to be strong, as you know it is only a matter of time before they come for you again, and drag you kicking and screaming down. Down, down into the blackest depths of the earth, and you wonder how many times this can happen. How many times can you win this unbeatable battle?

Each time they come back with a new strength and a new agenda, and they are determined to get you onto their side. You know the battle is inside your head, raging like an uncontrollable fire, but you can't put it out. They want you so badly but you don't want to go yet, but it would be so much easier than fighting them, so very easy just to say 'OK, you've won.' Why do they want you so badly? Can they not just leave you alone? But once they have you in their grasp they will never let go, they want you, body and soul, and won't give up till they have squeezed out every ounce of your being, and the last breath you will ever have on earth — only then will they be satisfied. But it's never enough for them. As you leave, someone else will replace you — immediately — and the battle will start all over again. Some they win, some they lose, but they know, undoubtedly, eventually they will win.

5

Sins of the fathers

I was a sinner. I knew that much. I didn't know exactly what sins I had committed, but I knew Canon Gilliard wanted me to confess them.

Canon Gilliard was the resident priest at St Anselm's Catholic Church in Tooting — a bald, bespectacled, short-tempered man. My sister and I were regular visitors to the church, because my mother insisted we attend Sunday School each week. She was Church of England, but my father was Catholic, so Mum was raising us to be good little Catholics too.

I loathed it. While the rotund teacher, Miss Edgely, droned on about the Bible, I gazed at the beautiful paintings on the ceiling, wondering when it would be time to go home. Miss Edgely had a large mole with hairs growing out of it, and she always wore a blue single-breasted coat with large buttons, dark tan stockings, and low-heeled shoes that had become misshapen from the enormous bunions on her feet.

'What do you recall from last Sunday's lesson?' she would ask each week. I had never retained a single ounce of information. Considering all the years I was forced to attend, you'd think I should now be an expert in religion, but I don't think any of it even made it into my head. After each lesson we'd have a small Mass, and one day I was mucking around and laughing so much with one of the boys that I peed myself in the pew. The urine trickled all the way down the pew and onto the floor — surely a sin if ever there was one.

Mum dearly wanted us to have faith, and bought us St Christopher's rings, which we asked Canon Gilliard to bless. The idea of having a divinely sanctioned religious item was thrilling, and my cousin Maria and I would regularly knock on the door of the Canon's house, next to the church, and ask him to bless some new item of religious tat we had bought. He would stand on the doorstep and mumble a few words before sending us on our way. After a while he apparently tired of the practice, because he started sending his maid to the door to tell us he was out.

Canon Gilliard was more forthcoming if one crossed his palm, however. In return for a 'donation', he would say a prayer for a member of his flock at Mass. The Canon made it clear he preferred notes to coins, as my mother discovered when she and I visited on behalf of a sick friend. Canon Gilliard said he would say a prayer at the next Mass, and my mother handed him half a crown, which was 25p. He looked at the coin, then said, 'I'm sorry, I have just remembered I'm too busy to say a prayer.' Then he shut the door. My mother was furious. 'Priests shouldn't be like that,' she fumed as we walked away. 'It's not about money.'

I agreed heartily, and the experience confirmed my suspicions that the church was full of hypocrisy. One Christmas Eve, Maria had suggested Robyn and I go to midnight Mass, so we walked to the church, nearly hyperventilating with excitement at being out by ourselves so late at night. When we arrived, Canon Gilliard said: 'What are you children doing out at this time of night?'

'We've come for midnight Mass,' I told him, 'to pray to God on the eve of his birthday.'

'Well go home!' he shouted. 'You children should not be out on your own at this time of night! Where are your parents?'

'At home,' I said, 'but it's all right, Maria is here with us.' Canon Gilliard glared at me and slammed the wooden door shut.

I was so pissed off. 'I'm never going back there,' I said. 'I hope God strikes him down for being such a mean old man.'

Still, each week Mum made us go to confession. Each week, while waiting to go into this little wooden confessional box and be forgiven, I had to think up things to say.

It was always the same:

a. I hit my brother (but only after he had kicked my shins black and blue) (true)

b. I was rude to someone (true)

c. I did not do my homework (true)

d. I lied about something (true)

e. I wanted to take money out of the donation tray that was passed around at Mass, instead of putting any money in, but I did not have the nerve (very true).

And each week Canon Gilliard would solemnly order me to 'Go outside, think about what you have done, and say five Hail Marys and two Our Fathers.'

I would rush outside, mutter a couple of things, half kneel, do the sign of the cross and dash for the door, wishing for the day when I was old enough to leave the church forever.

I hated church then, and I still hate it. The altar boys would glare at me as I rattled my hand around in the donation tray, pretending to put money in. 'If I don't put any money in,' I always thought, 'I can buy a Flake on the way home. Or a Twix.'

When Mark was born, my mother decided I should be baptised with him, as I had missed out on baptism in New Zealand. I had to stand there, aged four and a half, while water was poured over my head. It was embarrassing.

I disliked the hypocrisy of Catholicism, but I adored looking at the laymen each week, trying to guess which colour ecclesiastical gown they would be wearing this week that matched the tabernacle cover. They were the most beautiful garments, rich in colours of either purple, gold, cream or red, and elaborately decorated with heavy gold trim. The purple was my favourite.

These men of God would give out communion and we would

kneel each week at the altar and everything was meant to be forgiven. A lot of the male parishioners would leave the church and cross the road to The Wheatsheaf pub, which was diagonally across the road, opposite Tooting Bec tube station, and spend all day getting plastered. The priest should have told them in no uncertain terms to seek help, not the divine sort, to stop spending their earnings on alcohol so their families went short, and stop beating up their wives. But God forgave everything apparently, and as long as you said your Hail Marys and Our Fathers you were forgiven, and could repeat this cycle week after week, year after year. It baffled me.

My feelings about the church reflected my growing awareness that the community in which we lived was, in many ways, deeply troubled. Family violence was everywhere. I'd heard the whispers of my mother and her women-friends; I knew how my schoolmates feared their fathers' tempers. And when I was about nine years old, the nasty seam of society revealed itself to be running right through the middle of our family.

Brendan was a family member, and he and Mike were brothers. Brendan was the nicer of the two, with messy dark hair and enormous lips. When I used to pout as a child, my mother would say, 'Don't do that or you will end up with lips like (either) Mick Jagger or Brendan.' Heaven forbid.

Brendan never really had a profession as such, well, none that I was ever aware of, but would do 'a bit of this and a bit of that'. He and Mike always seemed to do their own thing, since their mother had a younger brood to contend with. I never met their father, and am not sure if they ever did once their parents split.

At the time when the Gin Queen was living in Tooting Bec Road, upstairs from 'Beverly the Witch', the Carter family were also living in the street. Myrtle and Edwin Carter were also from India, and all Anglo-Indians seemed to somehow find each other and stick together like limpets. They lived in a block of grey concrete council flats, with no lifts, further up on the opposite side of Tooting Bec Road (next to the mental hospital) and right opposite Tooting Bec Common.

Gail was their eldest daughter, and she had a younger sister and an assortment of brothers. All the children were very polite and well-behaved. Whenever we went over, which was usually on a Saturday afternoon, Myrtle would be cooking fish curry, and she and my mother would talk in Hindustani so we could not understand. Myrtle was slim, with dark shoulder-length hair and the widest smile I had ever seen.

Gail was slight, with a very short black elfin-like haircut. She was the more outgoing and outspoken of the two sisters, and they seemed like a very nice family. The Carters were dark-skinned, as were all my mother's relatives, although my grandmother and my mother were both very fair. The Gin Queen was insane with jealousy over this, bizarre as it may seem.

When Brendan started seeing Gail, most of the family seemed very pleased. She was a nice, pleasant girl from a good family that was known to us, and she had a full-time job! I don't remember what it was, but she worked. After they had been seeing each other for a while Brendan announced that they were getting married. I don't remember attending the wedding; I think it was held in a registry office. After the wedding they moved into the top flat in a small two-storey house.

One afternoon the Gin Queen, Mum and I had to pop in to see them for some reason, and I clearly remember Gail opening the front door in her terry-towelling dressing gown. The Gin Queen asked for Brendan and he came down to the door with no shirt on. I remember asking my mum why they were in their night-clothes in the afternoon, and she and the Gin Queen muttered something about 'newlyweds'. We were not invited in (for obvious reasons) and left shortly after.

There were mutterings from the Gin Queen that Gail was lazy, but when they found out she was expecting, all was forgiven. She gave birth to a large, healthy baby boy, who was named John, and he was the apple of Brendan's eye. Their next child was a rather small baby girl who they called Samantha, and soon after Samantha came Susan.

When Samantha was a few months old, strange things started happening to her. First she broke a leg, which Gail said had happened when she rolled off the couch, and she was hospitalised. Then one day my cousin Maria went to visit them unexpectedly, and came home in a panic. She told her mother — and I remember this vividly, as I was with Mum in the upstairs lounge at Tooting Bec Road — that when she went into the house Samantha was in the highchair with both her hands tied behind her back and a gag in her mouth. Even as I type this now, I feel sick to my stomach.

I remember the look of shock on both the Gin Queen and my mother's faces, as they grilled Maria about what she had seen. Was she sure she had seen that? Did she ask why the child was in this condition? Maria said Gail had explained that Samantha would not stop crying, and she had just put her in the high chair.

Next, Samantha was in hospital again, this time with a broken arm and leg. Both times, Gail was alone at home, and it seemed odd that these things only happened to Samantha. John and Susan were always very well looked after, and both were very happy little children who were adored by both sets of grandparents and various aunts and uncles. I do remember my mother mentioning this incident to Myrtle, but I don't remember what, if anything, was done. Samantha always had bruises on her and was very thin compared to her brother. I remember the Gin Queen saying to Gail one day, 'Do you feed that poor child?' The Gin Queen's house was always full of food, as she had teenage boys, and when her son Steven broke his arm playing football he asked me to cook him fried eggs on toast, which I did, and he said they were very nice.

A short while after, we heard that Samantha was again in hospital, this time with burns from her neck to her feet, and everywhere in between. Mum and I went to see her, in one of the large hospitals in Tooting, either St James or St George's Hospital. St James has since closed down, but St George's is enormous now, as it looks after a good section of South West London.

I will never forget walking into Samantha's hospital room. She was in a room on her own, and we went on a Saturday afternoon. She was lying on her back, bandaged up to her neck with her legs in traction, and she turned to us and gave us the biggest smile you could imagine. Mum said, 'Hello, Darling,' and she just lay there looking at us and smiling this rather pathetic smile, unable to move. I talked to her — Mum and I were the only ones there — but at the time, and when we were leaving, my mother said she did not know how Samantha managed to smile at us, after what had happened to her. Doctors did not report incidents like this to the police in the late sixties, but thankfully, people are more aware of what goes on these days.

Brendan was in prison at the time, and was not allowed out, but I know he was distraught, and wanted to know what was going on. For all their faults, I never knew any of Brendan and Mike's family to abuse a child — it was not in their genes, it was alien and appalling to all of us, and I know that others felt as shocked as I did. Gail said she had been filling the bath, and someone had called at the front door. She had left Samantha while she went to answer the door, and Samantha had climbed into the bath. We all thought this was suspect, as there was no way this tiny little thing could have walked, let alone climbed into a large bath without help.

We then received the dreaded phone call — baby Samantha had died from her injuries. We were all shocked beyond belief. None of us realised how life-threatening her injuries were, and we did not know if there had been more internal damage that we had not heard about.

There was a card Mum had on the mantelpiece of our lounge which had a picture of baby Samantha on the front, and inside a poem Brendan had written from prison to his baby daughter. It was poetic and sad in the extreme. I don't think Samantha had even reached the age of two. I remember often reading the poem as I walked past, and thinking how terrible it all was. My only regret now is that I was not older at the time, as I would have had no hesitation in reporting what I knew.

After Brendan came out of prison he and Gail divorced, and the last I heard was that she had remarried. I doubt her new husband has any idea about what had gone on. It is very hard to accuse someone of something so terrible, but we all know babies have very soft limbs, and Samantha had at one time or another had both arms and both legs broken, and was burnt from her neck down. I'm sorry, but my alarm bells would have been ringing all over the place had I worked in the hospital — it just did not happen.

I don't know how Myrtle and Edwin coped either, as they too must have had their suspicions, but if they did, they kept schtum. Sometimes my heart is so heavy with what I know, I find it hard to breathe.

When I came to New Zealand, and after I had become a mother myself, Samantha's death absolutely haunted me. I talked to Francis about it, and said I did not care how many years had passed, Gail needed to be brought to justice for what she had done. I believed she had murdered her child. Francis agreed, and it took an enormous amount of courage for me to go to the police station in Ponsonby and report what I knew. I was hoping they would contact the police in Tooting and it could be looked into. There was a policewoman on the front desk, and she asked what I wanted. When I told her I wanted to make a report on a murder, she looked at me as though I had just reported seeing a spaceship land. I was taken into a room and gave a long account of what I knew, but nothing was done — I never heard another thing about it, which I pretty much guessed was going to happen by the way the report was taken. The police pretty much told me nothing could be done, but I feel there must have been something if someone had really wanted to take the time to investigate. I doubt the report was ever passed on to the UK police — most likely it was just shredded. I just wanted to do something for baby Samantha, as nobody seemed to be doing what I thought was right.

Today so many people come forward with horrific things

they experienced as children, and the perpetrators are eventually brought to justice, regardless of how many years have passed. And so they should be — just because time has passed, it does not make the crime any less evil.

I cannot imagine how John and Susan, now as adults, would view what had happened, if they remember it at all. It haunts me to this very day, and I cannot imagine that it does not haunt Gail. How can you sleep at night with something like that lying on your conscience?

This all came back to me one day when I was flying from Auckland to Wellington and picked up a *Metro* magazine on the plane. It had the story of Delcelia Whittaker. I scanned it, and the story of Samantha all came flooding back to me. I had to rush to the bathroom as I thought I was going to be sick. I know her killer is out, but if I had my way, he would never see the light of day again.

Brendan later married a lovely quiet girl called Veronica, who was crazy about him. I don't think he was ever the same person again. He has remained on the straight and narrow since the sixties, and still lives with Veronica in a council flat in Battersea. They have had children together, but I have no idea how many. I wonder how he feels sometimes, when we all have those times alone with our thoughts, and if he thinks about what he could have done. I am sure he feels extreme guilt, as he was not an abuser, and had he not been in prison maybe this terrible incident could have been avoided.

As someone who suffers from depression, I know how bad it can be, and Gail may well have been suffering from post-natal depression, but that does not give you the right to kill a child, or anyone else. And if she was suffering from this, then why were the other children so well looked after and Samantha not? Surely her parents would have been suspicious? At the end of the day, we are all responsible for our actions. Gail could have left Samantha with either of the grandparents, who would have taken care of her, if she felt she was not able to cope, and Samantha could have had the chance to grow up into a beautiful woman, which I know she would have been.

For a time in my life I seemed to be surrounded by abuse. We had moved out of my grandmother's house and Mum had got us a one-bedroomed flat in Tooting. We had our own lounge and kitchen, but Mum, Robyn and I all shared a bedroom, and we shared the bathroom with the tenants from both downstairs and upstairs. The house had not been divided into flats, but rooms, so you had to lock each room when you left, as anyone could go in. It was a beautiful old Victorian house, in a tree-lined street called Streathbourne Road, with Tooting Bec Common running along the bottom.

Our neighbours were the Archers — Paul, his very young wife Christine, and their daughter Mandy, who Christine's mother always called 'Miss Fish'. Paul was short, with a funny shaped mouth and leather shoes that always curled up at the toes, as if they were too big for him. Christine was lovely, with very beautiful blue eyes and the thickest, blackest sweeping eyelashes I had ever seen. She had gone to the same secondary school I went to, Garratt Green, and Paul had attended the local boys school. Christine had become pregnant after leaving school, and had married Paul. They were both just teenagers. Paul worked for the railways, but they had very little money. Paul used to beat his young wife, and I would cower when I heard this. She would run through the house pleading with him not to hit her, begging, screaming, 'No Paul don't, please don't hit me, please, please!'

I was eight when we moved to Streathbourne Road, and I used to spend a lot of time with Christine during the school holidays when Mum was at work. She was very thin, and I remember they ate baked beans and blancmange a lot! She was such a kind girl. She would take me to visit her mother and family, and always kept an eye on me.

One night Paul came up and knocked on our bedroom door when we were asleep, and asked my mum to come down and help as Christine had gone into labour. In the morning Mum told me that Christine had had a healthy baby boy in the night, and that she had been at the birth. All I could say was, 'Did you see her bum?' I was shocked, and later when I thought about where the baby comes out, I could not believe my mum had done that!

Richard was born after Christine had had a lot of miscarriages, and he was a gorgeous little boy. I adored him. He was the cutest little fellow, but before long Paul started beating him too. He would kick him across the room in his baby walker. Christine, who was about 20 at that time, would scream at Paul, pleading with him to stop. A few times, when Paul was at work, Mum went down to talk to Christine. She would have black eyes and be bruised, but would always say she had fallen, or something like that. But we could hear and see it all, as the flats were so open, and there was no such thing as sound insulation. I would see and hear her running from room to room, slamming the doors, and although Paul was a short man, she was no match for him. He would push open the door and drag her out like a dog. All I had to do was peer over the hall bannister, and I could see everything.

After we had been there for a while another Anglo Indian family moved in. He was the son of one of my grandmother's friends, and had a young wife who never said a word. They were a couple of kooks. His name was Jeffrey. He was tall and dark, with a big black moustache, and unbeknownst to us, had mental problems. One day, my mother had a friend over, Vanessa Taylor, a girl who worked in her office. Mum was cooking mince. Jeffrey came out onto the landing and started shouting, 'Stink, stink, stink.' No rhyme, no reason — he just did it. My mother is no shrinking violet, and she flew out of the kitchen. An enormous row ensued as she told him it was none of his business what she did in her kitchen, and this went on and on. Paul, who we had known for years, came up the stairs, and I was so grateful as I thought he had come to stand up for us, but instead he told my mother to stop swearing! She turned on him like a rattlesnake, and I hid in a room with my hands over my ears; it was so horrible and embarrassing, especially as we had a guest over.

Jeffrey then came downstairs from his flat and tried to strangle my mother. He put his hands around her throat, held her on the landing and tried to kill her. I don't know who called the police, but they came and Jeffrey was arrested. He had to appear in court, but he was not taken away and we still had to see him every day! He wasn't sent to prison as it was discovered he was a schizophrenic. His mother told my grandmother that they thought he had got better, and hoped that being married and having his own flat would curb him, though where the hell they got that notion from I have no idea.

So we had no friends in the house any longer. Paul banned me from seeing Richard, and Christine was ordered not to talk to us. I found this very sad as I really liked her, and I know she would have remained friends with us, but she feared Paul's temper, so I don't blame her.

Years later, in the nineties when I was visiting London, I was watching television and who should pop up being interviewed, but Paul Archer. He was still working for the the railways; there had been a crash, and he was talking about it. He looked exactly the same, and all I could think of was, 'Does he still bash his poor wife and child?' I hope not.

After a while we moved back to my grandmother's flat — from one madhouse to another. Gran still disliked me as much as ever, and although I was a few years older, I was still a fragile little girl. In the years since we had last lived with Gran I had seen enough sadness and violence in the families around me to know that our own dysfunctional clan was not unusual.

6

Mean girls

At high school, I learned one lesson very fast:
if the world was going to be this tough,
I would have to stand up for myself.

Sandra Baxter was at the secondary school I attended. She was a large black girl with an enormous afro, which she was constantly lifting her afro comb through. Now, there were afros and there were afros. Sandra's was never a dense, shiny black afro, but brown and dull. I think she put some kind of funny powder in it. Although it was big, it was not thick or particularly impressive, but nobody would dare say that to Sandra.

I learnt a lot about afros when I was at school, as there was a large contingent of black girls, and they polished and oiled their hair, and if it was black and shiny, they were very proud of it. Sandra's was not. Black girls had a thing about getting their hair wet, as it shrank, which always amused me for some reason. Apparently big hair was a status symbol.

Sandra had a large face with a big gold tooth in the front, and she sported a rather unkempt uniform. To say I was shit-scared of her was an understatement. She was older than me, and I avoided her as much as possible in the corridor as she spelt trouble.

My friends and I would meet each lunchtime either at the water fountain or on the green, but for some reason, on one particular day, two things I did not normally do happened. The first was that I actually had lunch, which I decided not to eat in the canteen, but behind the school block. The second was that I was alone. I remember I had a sausage rolled between a slice of white Mother's Pride, and I was just putting it to my lips when Sandra appeared from nowhere.

'Give me your lunch!' she demanded.

'No,' I said.

Even as the word was coming from my mouth I could not for the life of me think what had possessed me to say such a thing.

We looked at each other for a second.

'I said, give me your lunch!' she repeated, and for the second time I heard myself say, 'No.'

I stood there clutching the frigid, greasy sausage as if I had found the Holy Grail.

Sandra looked at me again, then she walked away.

I stuffed the sausage in my mouth and ran in search of my friends. When I told Jacqui what I had done, she was her usual mellow self. 'Oh dear,' she said with a giggle, which I knew to mean I was going to cop it after school.

The exit from our school resembled a large urinal. When you walked through the entrance from the street, you faced a very large coloured, tiled wall. You could walk either side of it to enter the school, but you never knew what, or who, was going to be on the other side. It was the same when you left — if someone wanted to get you after school, they would wait behind the large tiled wall, and once you had turned the corner it was too late, there was no going back.

For the rest of that day I was quietly, but absolutely, beside myself. I nearly regurgitated the sausage so many times it was hardly worth eating, but I put on the tough exterior as I had done so many times.

When the bell went, I met Jacqui and we chatted normally as we were leaving. I stared at the tiled wall as we came up to it, wishing I could see through it, that it was a one-way mirror. If I had even got a glimpse of the afro, I would have demanded a teacher put me in detention until Sandra had gone, but alas, it was a solid tiled wall.

I walked to the left of the wall, and she wasn't there. Jacqui was still talking, but I had not heard a word. I was looking all around me. She wasn't there!! She had not waited for me. I was going to live another day! I walked up the hill as fast as I could, chattering non-stop with nervousness.

After that, whenever our paths crossed Sandra would look at me, while still putting that poor comb through her hair (sometimes she just left it in her hair, and walked around with it like that during the day), but she never bothered me again.

Garratt Green might have been scary, but it was my chosen high school. When I finished primary school in 1971, my marks were high enough to get me an offer from the local grammar school, an honour none of my cousins had ever achieved. I declined the offer, however, much to my mother's disappointment, and said I wanted to go to Garratt Green, the local comprehensive. I told Mum I wanted to go there because I thought it was a better school — but the truth was, I wanted to keep an eye on Robyn, my sister, who was four years ahead of me.

I had hoped that one of the benefits of attending the local high school would be the presence of childhood friends, like our neighbours, Christine and Tish Farrell. Christine and I were old mates from primary school and our Brownies group, and I would often go to her house for afternoon tea — fresh white bread slathered in butter and jam — or dinner, which was always a vast spread involving lots of potatoes and a steaming pudding covered in Bird's custard. The house was messy, but welcoming, and I loved being part of their rambunctious family life.

The girls' parents, Bobo (Mrs Farrell) and Paddy, were staunch Irish Catholics — by comparison, my family were pseudo-Catholics at best. Bobo had tight curly red hair, freckles and glasses, and every day I would see her cycling up the hill with five pounds of potatoes in a string bag dangling from the handlebars. Paddy worked in construction. Most evenings he'd come out of Tooting Bec tube station and walk straight into the Irish pub on the corner, the Wheatsheaf, then roll home for tea. He would always say, in a thick Irish accent: 'So, how are ya?' and push his false teeth out of his mouth with his tongue. I would recoil in horror — I thought it was the most disgusting thing I'd ever seen, although I knew Paddy, in his stained string vest, was harmless.

Mrs Farrell was a tailoress, and once a year she would take us up to London when she delivered the suits she had made to the City. It was always a big adventure. We would get the train from Balham to Victoria Station in time for a screening at the cartoon cinema — usually Tom and Jerry — then we'd drop the suits at the tailor's City office, and end the day with a spread of egg and chips in a café. I loved the glamour of it all — especially visiting the tailor's office, with all its bustle and industry.

But in high school, my friendship with Christine cooled. All the students were streamed into thirteen classes, according to their academic performance. Christine's higher marks put her in the fourth-highest stream, while I was in the fifth, and she never let me forget it. Chris and I had gone through many fallings-out over the years — usually when new kids moved into the street and Christine told me they were her new best friends — but in the past we'd always patched things up.

Now, things were different. I had begun to notice that Mrs Farrell and the girls all seemed very curious about my family — Mrs F was always asking me when we had arrived in England, and when my brother was born. 'I can't remember,' I'd say. For as long as I could remember, Mum had drilled me to give this answer when anyone enquired about when we had arrived in England — she didn't want anyone to twig that Richard was not my father's son. All I was allowed to say was that we had arrived in 1964, the same year Richard was born.

One day, under cross-examination from Mrs Farrell, I blurted out the truth — we had arrived in 1963. Mrs F smirked.

It wasn't long before the scandal became public. One day at Garratt Green someone marched up to me and said: 'Christine Farrell said your brother is not your brother.' Within hours, everyone in the school knew, thanks to Christine's public awareness campaign. 'You and your brother are not the same,' she taunted me on the stairs one day, while her gaggle of friends cackled. Tish had jumped on the bandwagon, and although I don't think she was mean, she was easily led by her older sister.

I was afraid my brother would find out and be terribly hurt — he had always been led to assume he was Dad's son. I felt some drastic action was needed to permanently silence Christine and Tish. Living in such a violence-soaked community, the solution seemed fairly obvious. One of them would have to be bashed.

So one morning before school I waited at the upstairs window for one of the sisters to walk past. Tish was the unlucky one. My stomach was in knots — even though I was enacting the traditional revenge of my family, I was very nervous.

As soon as I saw Tish leaving the house I raced downstairs, out the door, across the road, and smashed my fist into her face. All my aggression came out in one right hook to the nose. Tish clutched her face and ran home, screaming. I skipped home, grabbed my schoolbag, shouted good-bye and left for school before Mum could investigate the commotion.

That evening when Mum arrived home from work she was frowning.

'The police came around today,' she said.

I tried to sound innocent. 'What for?' I said.

'You punched Tish in the face and gave her a nosebleed,' Mum said. 'Don't do it again. I don't like the police knocking on the door.'

She didn't seem as cross as I had expected — it wasn't the fact that I had hurt someone that bothered her, only that she didn't like the neighbours seeing the police at our house.

'OK,' I said meekly. It was never mentioned again. There was no need for further police action; Christine and Tish gave me a very wide berth thereafter.

It was one of the most horrible things I've ever done. I had never hit anybody in my life before apart from my siblings and Jacqui Manning, a Barbadian girl who had been my friend since we were five years old and at primary school together. And I've never hit anyone since. It went against all my non-violent instincts, but I couldn't see any other way of dealing with the problem.

My brother lived in the same street until very recently, and he told me that one day a few years ago he was walking towards Tooting Bec station when he saw Christine with her husband, who was carrying a suitcase. Christine was crying and saying goodbye. She had a couple of children by then. Her husband started to descend the steps of the tube station, and Christine walked away. 'Then,' my brother said, 'her husband came out of the Underground, looked both ways, and headed straight into The Wheatsheaf, suitcase and all.'

Anyway, I didn't need the Farrells to be my friends; I had Jacqui.

Jacqui vividly remembers the first day she met me. I asked her to do something, she said 'No,' so I hit her. When she went home she told her mother, Theresa, and her mother's words still resonate in Jacqui's ears today: 'Don't ya go playin wi' dat naarsty goirl Denise, ya' stay away from 'er, she be trouble.'

I have always called Jacqui by her surname of Manning, and she always calls me Corbet, and we have been friends for 43 years! And when I am in London I still visit her parents, Gary and Theresa, in Tooting, and Mrs M still says in her thick West Indian accent, 'Ah goirl, ya' still nart change since ya be little, Gard, ya' still cheeky,' and Manning says, 'Her, change, you must be joking!'

Jacqui and I were both celebrity-obsessed, and after school or on weekends we would hop on the 49 or 19 bus which took us from Tooting Bec to the famous Kings Road, Chelsea. We would go to all the shops, especially one called Kweens which made all the extraordinary platform boots for Elton John, Gary Glitter and just about everybody else. Another favourite was Terry de Havilland, which made incredible glitter and leather shoes that were worn only by the very rich and elite, which we were not.

We would walk the length and breadth of the Kings Road in the hope of bumping into a pop star, which we invariably did, and then we would walk up to Kensington High Street to the fabulous Biba store and hang out there on their luxurious fake leopard skin couches. Never did anyone ask us if we needed help, but if I had saved up enough I would buy a bottle of Biba's black nail polish for a staggering 25p. After that Miners brought out black polish for 19p, but to have the little square bottle with the gold lettering was magical.

We had read that Gary Glitter lived in a deco block of flats on Kensington High Street, so we decided to investigate. We popped into the foyers of all the apartment blocks on Kensington High Street and asked stupidly, 'Does Gary Glitter live here?' More times than I care to remember we were told 'No' by a very disgruntled concierge, but we would return to the same blocks and each time there would be a different concierge, so we would ask again. One day we struck lucky — the very kind man at the desk told us Gary Glitter did in fact live in that block, 'Troy Court'. He even gave us the number of his flat so we could call the intercom — he must have had delusional teenagers like us himself, and understood!

We felt like we had a secret nobody else knew about. We had met just about every pop star that had ever appeared on *Top of the Pops*, and we were thrilled one day to find that Rik Kenton, from Roxy Music, lived just up on Trinity Road, in Tooting. If his black Saab was in the drive, we knew he was home. We felt dead posh knowing a pop star lived a short walk up the road from us. We had met them all except the glittery Mr Glitter.

We had met other members of the group. Gerry Shephard was one of the band, and he lived with his mother in Streatham, which was also on the 49 bus route, lucky for me, but in the opposite direction to the Kings Road. I popped round once and he was not there, and on the off chance I popped in again, on the 12th of April 1976! There was a gaggle of girls standing outside a rather nice, middle-class brick house in a tree-lined street, just off Streatham High Road.

I went up and started talking to the girls, and was told Gerry was in fact at home. They were all screaming and calling his name, much the way people do today at Jerry Springer shows. They kept calling 'Gerry, Gerry, Gerry'. I was never sure if his name was pronounced Jerry with a 'J' or Gerry with a 'G' so I just pretended to call out, along with the others, but no words actually left my lips.

One girl said if he came out she was going to kiss him! I was flabbergasted! Kiss Gerry Shephard — are you nuts? The guy's a god, you can't do that. But some of the girls were quite loose, and if push came to shove, kissing would have been the very least they would do.

We waited and waited, and I was getting a bit bored, as I was on my own, and there was still no guarantee he was there. We were never told to keep the noise down by the neighbours, which was amazing, as it would drive me crazy — I'd have been throwing buckets of cold water over them to keep their temperatures down.

Suddenly, the black front door (which was in need of a new coat of paint) creaked open and Gerry's mother popped out — she told us that if we were all quiet, Gerry would come out. I got out my autograph book and got ready to push forward, as by now there was quite a collection of us.

After what seemed like an age, a rather dishevelled-looking Gerry appeared at the door. He had obviously just got out of bed, even though it was early afternoon. He was unshaven, and was wearing a rumpled jumper, jeans, and I don't think any shoes. At the time I had a foot fetish — I hated feet, and could not bear to look and see in case he was shoe- and sockless. Had he been I would have vomited over his toes. Luckily I'm over this now.

We formed a sort of semi-orderly queue, and filed through the gate, up the small path and a couple of steps to the front door.

Some of the girls had Kodak slim-line cameras, and others had the ones that took 126-mm film and had large, square plastic flash bulbs perched atop them, like giant ice cubes — if you got too excited and accidently put your eye near the bulb, instead of looking through the lens, it burnt your eyebrow! All the girls were snapping away furiously, taking pictures of Gerry, themselves with Gerry, their friends with Gerry, and so on.

I had no camera, though my mum had promised me one for my birthday, and I waited in line for my turn to meet this great, sexy guitarist. One of the girls asked him for a kiss, and he kissed her on the lips, and she started yelling, 'Gerry kissed me.' I was desperately hoping he would not kiss me, as I also had a hang-up about my teeth. Even though they were well cleaned, they were a strange colour, like green, and I did not want him to see them.

When the girl in front of me moved away, he was there in all his glory, standing waiting to take me in his arms, and tell me I was the girl of his dreams, but alas, he just said, 'What's your name?' so he could sign my autograph book. I wanted to say, 'Susan, yes, Susan, that's my name,' because at the time that was the name I wanted to be called, I thought it was cool. I thought Denise was a dumb name, and was annoyed my parents had given it to me.

Then as I looked up at him, while wearing my brown woollen swing coat with its enormous brown buttons, I shuddered. Gerry had the biggest, greenest bogey hanging from his nostril that I had ever seen, and nobody had told him! This was another enormous hang-up I had. I was now gagging, and trying really hard not to spew in my mouth. Bogeys had to be the one thing that could get me to retch, no problem, and here was this pop star, a pop star for Christ's sake, a demi-god, and he had a big, green, drippy bogey just like the rest of us. All my illusions were shattered.

I took my autograph book, very relieved that he didn't want to kiss me (fat chance) and walked myself back to the bus stop. When I told Jacqui I had met Gerry Shephard, she said, 'Ooh, he's the good-looking one, with the cool feather haircut —what's he like?' 'Nice,' I said. I could not even say the word 'bogey' without wanting to throw up, so I kept that part to myself. I wonder if those Kodak 126-mm cameras picked up the bogey in the photos — I hope not, for his sake.

Another time Jacqui and I were out and about in the Portobello Road (23rd January 1974, to be precise), a great haunt of ours where, I had read in the music paper the *NME* (*New Musical Express*), Eno from Roxy Music lived. Apparently, he lived in a flat in a little lane by the fruit and veg stalls. We tried every lane we knew, and we knew Chelsea, Kensington and Notting Hill like the backs of our hands, but to no avail, so we headed back to the Kings Road. There we bumped into John Rossall, one of the saxophonists with the Glitter Band. He was a thin little man, with red hair and freckles, and he was wearing a short fur bomber jacket with an elasticated waist, which zipped up the front, and an extremely tight pair of white drill jeans, which left nothing to the imagination in the 'packaging department'. The Glitter Band all seemed to do this, and I thought one day they would pop out of their pants. I could not see how Y-fronts fitted under them, and now realise they probably did not wear them!

We asked for his autograph, and he chatted and asked what we were doing, and we said we had just been to Eno's, but he was out! As if we frikkin' knew him, and were long-lost friends! We were truly a sandwich short of a picnic. He must have thought we had serious issues! Then he said, 'Don't you want Harvey's autograph?' We looked at Harvey — poor skinny, short Harvey, with the protruding mouth and bad hair — and John said, 'He's the other saxophonist in the band!' Harvey was not as outgoing as John, and on TV he tended to blend into the background, if that is possible when you are wearing a tight silver lamé suit! We said, 'Oh yeah, Harvey, of course we want your autograph.' Then they both asked again what we were doing, and the distinct impression Jacqui and I got was that it was an invitation to do something with them. This was something neither of us felt comfortable about, both being virginal. I could be wrong, but just let's say instinct is a wonderful thing, and also body language. But this was too scary for us, the thought terrified the life out of me. No other pop star had ever made any suggestions towards us, and afterwards we said thank God we had Eno as our excuse, as we said we were going to go back up the Portobello to see if he was home now! Even though we did not know exactly where he lived. We were both so incredibly naive, but very street cred.

Late one Friday night in the early seventies Jacqui called to ask if I wanted to go up the next day to see if Gary Glitter was home. I desperately wanted to go, but a 'family engagement party' had to be attended. The whole family were going to be bundled into two cars and driven to Bristol; as we did not have a car we had to rely on relatives. It was all very exciting for me, we so rarely went out in a car.

So I told Jacqui that I had to attend my cousin Andrew's engagement party in Bristol the next day, and that we would all be driving up there. I told her I would much prefer to go with her, but every time we had been, Gary Glitter was never home, and my mother would not be happy if I tried to bail out of such a big, boring occasion. Jacqui said she would find someone else to go with, and hung up.

Andrew, my cousin, had met his fiancée Jackie at some caravan holiday camp he had gone to with his friends. He had originally fancied her older sister, but the sister told him she had a boyfriend, so he asked, 'What about your sister?' Hardly love at first sight, methinks, but he started dating Jackie. The only problem was that he lived in Battersea with his mother, the Gin Queen, and Jackie's family lived in Bristol near the Wall's pork sausage factory. So she would come to London one weekend, and Andy would travel to Bristol the next.

Jackie was extremely thin, and had shoulder-length, naturally dead-straight blonde hair (no ghd hair straighteners in those days) and big blue googly eyes. She also spoke with this strong Bristol accent that none of us could understand. My cousins and I would always ask her to pronounce certain words, so we could fall about laughing, but she soon clicked on to this and stopped doing it. She had to realise, taking the piss out of people was our only form of entertainment; our lives were very dull.

At the time, Andrew was the most good-looking of all my cousins, but being a few years older than me he had very little time for me apart from trading insults. All my cousins had the sharpest tongues, and never worried about making everything into a joke. Andrew was the first of the Gin Queen and Zyggy's sons to get engaged, and me, my mum and my sister were all going up to Bristol to celebrate with my cousins. The Gin Queen never thought any of the people my cousins dated were good enough for them, but I always thought we were pretty lucky anyone wanted to date any of us, considering the family we were from.

So we all bundled into cars, squashed like sardines, kids sitting on kids' laps, no seat belts, and drove to Bristol, all bouncing around like balls. Jackie lived in a brick terraced council house. All the houses looked the same, and they went in the shape of a horseshoe, with a patch of green in the middle. Kids were supposed to use this for playing, but it was usually full of dog poo.

We arrived in Bristol in the early evening, and later the festivities began. I was very bored. The house was full of people I had never met, mostly Jackie's relatives, who were all jabbering in these weird thick Bristol accents, and I knew we would never meet again. It was like being in a foreign country. Usually I hung out with Stephen, Andrew's younger brother and my favourite cousin. He and I shared, and still do share, the same ridiculous warped, dry sense of humour, that very few people got. They would look at us as we were rolling around hysterical with laughter about something nobody else understood, which was probably just as well, as it was always bad!

As the evening progressed, the Gin Queen became more and more inebriated. The reason I had named my aunt the Gin Queen was very simple — she had a penchant for gin. Straight, mixed, who cares, gin is gin, and the more she could get the better. Whenever we had an event to attend, a birthday, wedding, etc., she would always say, 'I am going to lose weight and be as thin as your mother,' and I always waited to see if she would be, but she never was.

So this night, what always happened at any of our family events happened — the Gin Queen got smashed and started a fight. Not just a verbal assault, but a full-on physical fight. She was never one to do things by half. I can't remember what it was about, but suddenly everybody poured out onto the street, and fists and insults were flying in all directions. Somebody pushed the Gin Queen into a privet hedge, which a lot of houses had, and when she was pulled out she left a big dent in it.

I stood back, as I hated these fights. All the neighbours came out to watch, and I stood thinking, 'Not again; can't we ever go to anything without a fight breaking out?'

By now the whole family had joined in, and Jackie's brothers and other family members came out with fists flying. There were insults being thrown left, right and centre by both sides, like 'My daughter isn't marrying your son — you're all scum,' and, 'I wouldn't let my son marry your stupid daughter who can't speak proper English.'

Poor Zyggy was always mortified on these occasions. He told the Gin Queen to be quiet, which made her even worse, and she then launched an attack on him. Eventually the fights were broken up, after someone had got a bloodied nose, and we all got into the cars and set off home. It was hardly a good start to Andrew and Jackie's life together. I think Andrew stayed in Bristol and returned home later. He refused to speak to the Gin Queen for a while. By then the family were all telling him he couldn't possibly marry Jackie as she was not good enough for him, and he was saying, 'But I love her.' She came down to London a few weeks later, and said in her funny accent, 'I lurve Andy and I am going to marry him,' through great quantities of tears. I just stood back with Stephen and laughed. They were all mad, and still are.

On the Sunday morning after the party, the phone rang and it was Jacqui. 'He was IN,' she screamed; 'Gary Glitter was in.' I nearly died. I could not believe I had given up my one and only chance of meeting Gary Glitter to attend a fight outside a block of council houses in Bristol!

'What, what, what ?' I stammered.

'We rang the intercom, and a man answered, we asked if Gary was in, and he said yes, and buzzed us in. We went into his flat, and he was with his manager, and Gary was cooking a curry.'

'What type?' I asked. As my family was born in India, I wanted to know.

'I don't know what type of curry it was,' she said. 'But it was very smelly.'

'Did he ask if you wanted any?' (I also had a food fetish, which has not subsided with age.)

'NO! But I did get his autograph for you.'

'Was he wearing glitter?'

'No! But he is gorgeous, and he chatted to us, and was really sweet and kind and nice and fab and oooooh, I think I love him.'

I was so jealous I could hardly contain myself. I was never going to meet him, ever, it was all over, that much I knew. I had been in the wrong place at the wrong time.

After a while Jacqui asked how the engagement party was, and I said, 'The usual — lots of alcohol, a punch-up, which my family started, then we came home.'

Recently, in light of how Gary Glitter's life has now panned out, I asked Jacqui whether he tried anything on when she was at his flat all those years ago.

'God no, you're so disgusting,' she replied.

'I'm sorry, it was just something I had to ask,' I said.

I never did get to meet Gary Glitter, and I doubt I would want to now.

7

Time to go home

After twelve years apart, my parents decided to reconcile. Ever since we had left New Zealand in 1963, I had longed for this — I desperately missed my father, and all the difficulties of our life in England made me more deeply homesick for him and New Zealand.

Dad and Mum had kept in regular touch over the years, through letters and phone calls, and Dad never failed to send us Christmas and birthday cards. He also sent Mum money every month — albeit a minuscule amount — to help with our upkeep. Mum would take the cheque to Mr Patel at the local corner shop, and he would cash it in return for a small fee.

When Dad called, we would gather around to shout down the crackly line to Auckland. I was terribly homesick for New Zealand. Often, I would berate him for not being with us, and for not helping us more. He had been working full-time since we left, and I suspect lived a fairly easy bachelor's life. Our departure must have been a huge shock, however, and I've no doubt he was heartbroken. He had no idea Mum had the financial wherewithal to leave him.

Dad often asked Mum to bring us home, but she would reply, 'Not until you've given up drinking.' Sometimes she would say

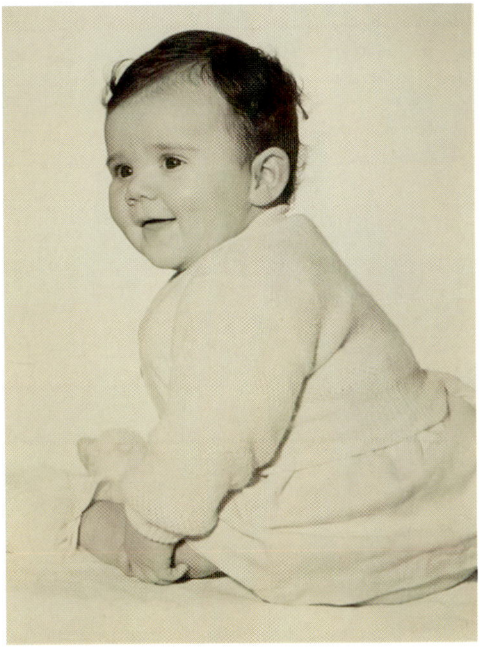

Above Me, 1960, aged six months in Auckland

Above Me, 1963, with choo-choo train that I won after tripping up another child. My dad had told me, 'You have to win the race', so I did.

Below Mum and Dad's wedding at the Wintergarden in Auckland, 18 April 1953

Below Donovan L'Estrange-Corbet in 1960

Above left School photo, 1967

Above right Francis aged three, Hong Kong, 1966

Below Last photo before we left for England (from left): me, Dad, Robyn and Ma, 1963

Cousins and friends, Christmas 1965. Back (left to right): Stephen Tychitsky and cousin Andrew; Front: Robyn, cousin Maria, Father Christmas, me, cousin Stephen and Helen Grodosfski

My brother Mark, 1968

Me, modelling for Freemans catalogue, 1965

The Williams clan, late 1960s. Back (left to right): Gin Queen Iris, my mother Elsie, anorexic Phyllis. Front: Uncle Arthur, hideous Gran and Uncle Robyn

Above Me aged 15 with first-ever haircut

Right Eastbourne, 1973

The three sisters (left to right): Gin Queen Iris, my mum Elsie and anorexic Phyllis, 1990s

Above Francis, 1989

Right The marriage, 20 May 1989

Left Pebbles aged six months in London, 1990

Below Pebbles and me in London, April 1990

Opposite top Pebbles, 1990, in her cot which collapsed after I painted it!

Opposite below All three of us in Sydney, 1991

Above Pebbles the Pirate in 1993

Left Pebbles at *Style* magazine shoot, 1996

she wanted a divorce, but Dad always refused. In all the time we had been in England, Mum had never had a serious boyfriend. She worked full-time, leaving home early and returning late, and simply had no time for herself.

During one of Dad's precious and expensive calls in 1974, he again begged Mum to return. 'I've been sober for two years,' he told her. After a long discussion, Mum said she accepted his word, and agreed to come home.

I was ecstatic. A new life in New Zealand with Dad — we could be a normal family again, after years of struggling. We could leave the dark and the cold and the violence; I envisaged us living carefree lives of laughter in sunny New Zealand.

Best of all, we would hopefully never have to see Grandma's sullen face and grey eyes again. There was a bit of short-term pain to endure; we had to move back in with Grandma temporarily before we left — but I didn't care. We were leaving.

Mum and my sister gave notice at their jobs, and I told everyone at school that I would be leaving in the new year. They were all impressed with the exotic destination we were headed for; New Zealand seemed so far away.

We celebrated Christmas 1974 as our last in London, and even the Gin Queen's grumpy face couldn't dent our happiness. She was jealous of us, I'm sure. She had taken every opportunity over the years to be mean to Mum, and would frown in disapproval if Mum ever bought herself a little treat. 'I've cleaned that burnt pan for you,' she announced one day, after having babysat my ill sister while Mum worked. It was a brand-new Teflon pan for which Mum had carefully saved up; the Gin Queen had somehow managed to scrub off all the non-stick coating. I don't know how she managed it — an electric grinder, perhaps. Mum nearly wept. The Gin Queen knew perfectly well the black coating on the pan wasn't a burn mark; she just didn't want Mum to have anything special for herself. At the same time, the Gin Queen did have a soft side, and she could be enormously generous and kind — a real contradiction. I suspect she might have been quite nice if it hadn't been for the booze.

One day around Christmas-time, Mum was walking home from Tooting Bec market when she bumped into Beverly Watson, the 'witch' from Tooting Bec Road. Beverly said she had heard we were returning to New Zealand, and Mum nodded.

Then Beverly said the strangest thing. 'You are not going to get there,' she said. 'You will not go.'

Mum was quite adamant that yes, Dad had booked the tickets for a flight departing in mid-February, so we could be in New Zealand in time to celebrate my fifteenth birthday on March 1 (yet again, I was missing out on a proper birthday).

'She's a mad old cow,' I told Mum when she relayed Beverly's remark.

I had a few weeks left at school, and spent most of the time daydreaming. One afternoon, during a French class, I was as usual taking very little notice as I sat at my desk against the radiator with my head resting on the window. I wanted desperately to go to sleep. All we ever seemed to talk about in French was 'hot chocolate and crispy baguettes', and I wanted to go to France again and have breakfast there.

We'd been on several school trips across the Channel. I loved catching the ferry, and had once put my name and address in a Cresta soft-drink bottle with a screw-top lid and thrown it into the sea as we steamed for Boulogne. A couple of months later, I received a letter from a boy called Hans van den Braak, who had found my message in a bottle washed up on the beach in Hilversum in the Netherlands, where he lived. He was a couple of years older than me, and we became pen-pals. On every subsequent trip, all the other girls would throw bottles into the sea in the hope of finding friends of their own.

Hans and I exchanged photos — he was tall, slim, blond and quite a looker. He was studying violin, and he told me in his letters how he had begun travelling to perform in violin concerts, and was quite the virtuoso. I could play 'Pease Pudding Hot' on the recorder, but I kept that to myself. We communicated for a couple of years, until the last black-and-white picture I received from him showed him standing at the side of the road near a bush, with his winkie out, urinating. I stopped writing after that.

On this particular afternoon in January 1975, I was jolted awake in the French class by my name being called over the school's Tannoy system: 'Denise L'Estrange-Corbet, please report to the headmistress's office immediately.'

I thought I must have been dreaming. What on earth could the headmistress want with me? I had never been called into her office in disgrace, even though I frequently deserved to be. I asked Jacqui if she had heard the message. She hadn't, because usually nobody paid attention to the Tannoy messages but I decided to check it out.

It was 12.30 and I was pissed off at the prospect of missing my lunch, but I made my way across the large play area, up the pebbledash steps to the office of the headmistress. Mrs Vaughan-Davies was a slender woman with false teeth, who was, not surprisingly, known among the girls as VD. As teenagers, we thought it was hilarious that our principal had the same initials as venereal disease. As I knocked on the door, I willed myself not to accidentally use her nickname when she spoke to me.

'How are you, dear?' she said kindly as she opened the door.

'Fine, thank you,' I replied cautiously.

Waiting in her office was my Uncle Arthur, Mum's brother. I was shocked to see him; Uncle Arthur was the only sane member of Mum's family, and had it all together — a City job, a nice house in Hertfordshire and a lovely family.

As usual, Uncle Arthur looked very smart, with his suit and tie, polished leather shoes and Brylcreemed hair. He seemed very uncomfortable. 'What are you doing here?' I asked. He said we had to go home, and that my mum was waiting outside in a taxi. 'Your mother will explain,' he added, leading me out to the street, where a black cab sat with its engine running. A black cab was not one of the things one expected to see in Tooting in 1975, and I climbed into the taxi feeling very important.

Mum looked very upset, but when I asked what was wrong, she said, 'Nothing, darling, nothing.'

The taxi turned for our home. 'Someone's died, haven't they?' I demanded. Mum didn't answer.

'Who is it?' I begged. Still no answer.

'Is it Robyn?'

'No.'

'Is it Mark?'

'No.'

'Is it Gran?' (Oh God, pleeease let it be her!)

'No.'

'Uncle Willie?'

'No.'

I sat there, thinking. 'I know — oh God, it's Spotty.' (Our Jack Russell terrier.)

Mum shook her head. They were the only people I could think of who I really loved and cared about (apart from Gran, obviously), so I figured it couldn't be that bad.

We pulled up outside our temporary digs at my grandmother's house in Mandrake Road, and stepped inside. The look on Gran's face told me immediately who had died. I screamed: 'Oh no, it's Dad — he's dead, isn't he?'

Nobody answered, they all just stood and stared. I ran to the corner of the hall and cried out: 'Please no, please tell me it's not Dad!'

Still, no one answered me.

I slid down the wall into a heap on the floor and curled up into the foetal position, and sobbed.

8

Overwhelmed

The news had arrived that morning, when Gran phoned Mum at work to say a telegram from New Zealand had been delivered. 'Oh that will be Don confirming our flight details,' Mum said; 'Open it up and read it to me.'

My grandmother slit open the telegram and unfolded it. A long silence followed.

'What does it say?' Mum asked.

'You'd better come home, my girl,' Gran said.

'What's wrong?' Mum insisted. 'Read it out.'

Gran read the telegram aloud: 'Don died suddenly. Arrangements made. Don't come.'

Mum dropped the phone and ran into the toilets, numb with shock. Someone called my uncle, and he came to collect her in the taxi at the London Chamber of Commerce.

That was it. All bets were off. It was impossible to get through to New Zealand on the phone, and Mum was beside herself. What did they mean: 'Don't come'?

Eventually, we managed to get through to my Grandma, Dad's mother Annie. She said Dad had been found dead on January 9 in their house on Ngapuhi Road, Remuera. The details were still very sketchy, but she told Mum not to come for the funeral, as the arrangements had been made, and it was to be held on January 11. We'd never get there in time.

Mum was distraught. After all the years apart from Dad, she had just begun to feel hope for a future with him. He was only 46.

A week later, Mum took me to New Zealand House in the Haymarket, so she could read about his death in the *New Zealand Herald*. We sat in a common area reading the papers, along with other ex-pats catching up on local news. It was my first visit to New Zealand House — and the next time I visited would be 24 years later, when I was preparing to show at 1999 London Fashion Week. So much had changed in my life, but as soon as I entered the building I felt fourteen again; a scared little girl.

There was a brief report in the paper on my father's death. It said he had died in suspicious circumstances. Mum and I were both shocked; we had had no indication from the family that they suspected foul play of any kind.

Later we talked to Dad's brother Ric on the phone. As it turned out, there was nothing suspicious about Dad's death.

Dad had been trying hard to remain sober. He had been living with his mother, Annie, in the same Remuera house where he and Mum had lived as newlyweds. Although Dad wasn't drinking, he wasn't very good at looking after Grandma — he spent most of his time out with his various girlfriends. Ric would visit every Thursday to do Grandma's washing, and one Thursday in June 1974 she wasn't home when Ric called. He went straight down to the local doctor's surgery to see if she had been taken ill — and there she was, sitting in the surgery. She had suffered a stroke.

Ric and his wife Margaret took Grandma home to live with them. Dad remained in the Remuera house, but when Ric visited he thought Dad seemed thinner than normal — raising his suspicions that Dad might have begun drinking again. Around the same time, Dad called Alcoholics Anonymous to say he felt he might be in danger of falling off the wagon.

On January 9, 1975, Gran tried calling the house to speak

to Dad, but he didn't answer. She hadn't been able to raise him for several days, and was worried enough to call Alcoholics Anonymous to ask if somebody could call at the house to see if he was all right.

When the counsellor from Alcoholics Anonymous arrived, it looked like a murder had taken place in the house. There was blood all over the kitchen floor and cupboards. Dad was lying dead on the couch. The pathologists who conducted the post mortem said Dad had bled to death, and had lain dead for approximately two days before being found. They said he showed signs of serious alcohol damage to his organs, and speculated that he had probably suffered an episode of delirium tremens (the DTs), a violent attack of hallucinations and shaking associated with withdrawal from alcohol.

Uncle Ric thought Dad had probably become delusional, as he had a history of seeing demons when he drank. It was thought he had cut himself on something while in a drunken stupor, and had staggered around the kitchen before falling on the couch in the lounge and bleeding to death. We are still not sure of the day he actually died.

As we heard Ric telling the story, I recalled Mum saying that during their marriage Dad had sometimes had visions — both menacing and benign — and had described seeing his dead father, Dennis, appear before him.

It was just too unbelievable for words. I still desperately wanted to go to New Zealand. Remaining in England was a prospect too dreadful to contemplate, and I would rather have shifted straight to hell than remain in Gran's house in Tooting. We had no home of our own, and all our belongings had either been sold or given away. There would be no fifteenth birthday celebrations for me on March 1, with our family reunited. Fate had decided it was not to be.

I hadn't seen Dad since I was three, but in my mind he had represented hope for the future. I knew I was his little girl, his Dinya, his alley cat — and even when I was in the depths of one of my down days, I could take some consolation from the knowledge that Dad, too, had suffered black moods and sadness. Dad would always be there, I had thought — and I told myself that one day we would somehow connect and re-establish our relationship.

I was heartbroken. Our new, exciting life had flown out the window — to me, the worst thing was that we could now end up trapped in our London life, with all the dysfunction and depression that surrounded us. I prayed Mum would decide to take us to New Zealand anyway, but every time I tried to raise the subject with her, she said she hadn't made up her mind.

My grandmother never once put her arms around me and tried to console me in the days after Dad's death. She just stood there, staring at me with those cold, grey eyes. There was no love lost between her and my father. They had never really known each other well, but as soon as he and Mum split up, Gran had decided he was the embodiment of everything that was wrong with men.

My head was swirling all over the place. I stopped eating for one whole month; I just couldn't face the thought of food. Once a day, I would mix a small amount of icing sugar with water to make a teaspoonful, and that would be my entire sustenance for the day. My weight plummeted — but nobody noticed. Everyone was simply too wrapped up in their own grief to pay any attention to me.

Instead of becoming sympathetic to our pain, Gran became even more difficult. She was obsessed with the expense of having us in the house, and put a padlock on the phone, so only she, William and my brother Mark could make calls. Even though Mum paid rent and bought all our food, Gran was always going on about things like the hot water, and limited us to one bath each a week. This had been her rule for many years, but now I was fourteen, with spots and greasy hair and periods, and I hated being unable to get clean. Bath night was Sunday, and although I felt relatively human on Monday, my long hair would grow more and more lank as the week progressed.

'God, she's a bitch,' I muttered to myself, vowing that when I grew up I would never be miserly or tight with money.

Gran displayed no shred of sympathy for Mum or any of us children after the loss of Dad — even when I lay on the floor, curled in the foetal position and weeping, she made no move to comfort me. There was no part of her that could do it, even in the most traumatic situation.

A few weeks after Dad died, the unhappiness became overwhelming. I tried to kill myself.

I remember that evening so clearly. My sweet godmother, Molly Cunningham, had come to visit. Over the years I had spent a great deal of time at Molly's flat in Gypsy Hill, near Crystal Palace. More often than not Molly would be drunk when I came to call, and would pass out on the couch while I tried to have a conversation with her husband, George. Poor old George was partly deaf, and I'd have to shout at him to make myself heard — although sometimes I suspected his deafness was a ruse he used when he wanted to ignore Molly's hectoring. Some days I would venture into the garden to watch the squirrels, but I had still not discovered the art of reading, which would have made the days at Molly's place much less miserable.

The night Molly arrived at Gran's house in Mandrake Road, I was in my dressing gown, sitting in the lounge. I heard Molly ask Mum if we were still going to go to New Zealand.

'No,' said Mum, 'we'll stay in London.' I asked her why.

Mum said: 'Darling, there is nothing to go for; where would we live? We have no money.'

I was devastated. We were stuck back in the same dreadful situation, living under the control of my evil witch of a grandmother. With sudden resolve, I went into the bedroom and grabbed Mum's bottle of sleeping tablets. The drug was Mogadon, a powerful sedative that can be fatal when taken in large doses.

I went into the bathroom and swallowed as many as I could. They were not sugar-coated, and the more I took, the harder they became to swallow. I just kept taking them, one after another, until I collapsed on the bathroom floor. Somehow, I dragged myself up and went into the room where Mum and Molly were sitting.

'What's wrong?' Mum exclaimed.

'I took some pills,' I slurred, before slipping into unconsciousness.

I don't know what made me walk out of that bathroom and seek help. I've reflected a lot on that episode — I dearly wanted to die, but something propelled me up off the floor and into the lounge to seek help. Perhaps it was the survival instinct; maybe it simply wasn't my time to die.

The next thing I knew, I was lying in a bed in St James's Hospital. It was the following morning. Mum told me I'd been rushed to Emergency, where the medics had pumped my stomach. I was lucky to be alive.

I felt even more terrible than before: 'I've failed. I can't even kill myself properly.'

I still wanted to die. The thought of living any longer in the situation we were in was too much to bear, and now I had to deal with the additional misery of being thought stupid and selfish by everyone around me. 'If only I'd locked the bathroom door,' I thought.

I told Mum I couldn't stand the idea of living with Gran any more. I was still bone-thin, and when I was released from hospital I found it difficult to walk. Mum made me promise not to tell anyone what I had done, and reassured me that I could stay home from school until I felt a little better.

Finally, Mum seemed to grasp the depth of my unhappiness. She explained the situation to our general practitioner, Dr Seal, and he wrote a letter to the London County Council explaining that we urgently needed to be housed and moved out of the situation we were in.

We had been on the council's waiting list for eleven years, and although there had always been three of us — Mum, Robyn and I — sharing one bedroom, we didn't qualify for urgent assistance. There was a points system that gave preference to people with illnesses, so the Gin Queen had no trouble getting a council flat; her stepbrother Peter lived with them, and his dicky heart qualified them for a modern, centrally heated four-bedroom flat in Battersea. It seemed terribly unfair.

The council wrote to Mum, saying they simply had no room for us, but they had put us on the waiting list for the Borough of Bromley, in the city's southeast. It worked. It wasn't long before we got a letter saying we had been allocated a three-bedroom flat in Penge. None of us had a clue where — or what — Penge might be, but finally we were to have a home of our own.

It wasn't as good as New Zealand, but it was a start.

9

'But you always seem so happy . . .'

Suicide has always been on my mind. That first attempt to kill myself, at the age of fourteen, was my instinctive response to the shock of my father's death — but it was also the product of the depression that had been churning inside me since my earliest childhood.

The thought of dying terrifies me. I wonder: How will I die? Will a terrible accident or an illness strike me?

None of us ever knows how or when life will end — unless we make it so.

That, I think, is the allure of suicide for depressed people. Perhaps, the thought of carrying out the act of killing oneself makes it all seem easier. In suicide, one at least has control.

So what stops depressed people killing themselves?

For me, it's very simple: I do not want to leave behind all the people who care about me.

I remember having a conversation with a friend at the London College of Fashion, where I studied in the late 1970s, one day as we queued for lunch. I can't remember how the conversation came about, but my friend, Leigh, said she thought people who committed suicide were utterly selfish. Leigh was someone whom I admired greatly, and still do, but I couldn't let her remark stand.

I told her how much I disagreed. Of course, Leigh had no idea I had already tried to kill myself.

'I think it's very courageous,' I told her. 'To actually end your own life can never be an easy decision. It's not like deciding what you are going to have for dinner; it's an enormous thing. I'm sure they go through a lot of soul-searching before they actually do it.' Leigh wouldn't have a word of it.

I still encounter people today who say suicide is a selfish act. I honestly wonder how they can say such a thing. Does it not occur to them that to contemplate ending life, one must be absolutely desperate; must feel there is absolutely nobody on earth who can help ease the pain?

A suicidal person doesn't suddenly think: 'Oh, I think I'll top myself today, and leave behind all the people who love me and make them feel really bad that they never saw the signs or got a chance to say goodbye.' That's a rational series of thoughts — and the mind of a suicidal person doesn't function in that kind of clear, linear way.

There is a complete blackness that shrouds the soul completely, and there is no other way out. A suicidal person doesn't want to burden friends and family with all these problems — however sympathetic they may be, they can't do anything to stop the feelings.

It's a wretched place to be in. The thought of having to survive another day becomes appalling, and the only thought is: 'I just want out.' Wealth and success can't protect us from this kind of despair, as evidenced by Kurt Cobain, Sid Vicious and so many other talented and well-loved people.

I know from personal experience that on the day one attempts suicide, the agony of decision is enormous. 'How will I do it? What steps will I take?' When the act starts, I know there is no turning back, but I care so little about myself, it doesn't matter any more.

At the age of fourteen, I had given in completely to my demons, the creatures who were determined to get me. They wanted me so badly; it was easier to surrender than continue the battle. I didn't know why they wanted me, or why they were squeezing out every ounce of my being, but I was happy for them to have me, body and soul. They had won. I couldn't fight any more.

I was lucky. I survived with no physical side effects; but I know of people who have been left permanently maimed, and now require 24-hour care because of a botched suicide attempt. That starts the whole process of depression anew.

'To Denise,' wrote a schoolteacher on my going-away card when we left Tooting for Penge; 'I hope your future is better than your past.' I'll never forget those words. I felt that teacher could see right through to my soul.

I have thought about suicide many times since I tried it the first time. I still have suicidal thoughts, and have to force myself to regain control. Sometimes, while driving the car, I think how easy it would be to drive off a cliff or into an oncoming truck. It would all be over; all the misery, all the pain.

Now, I know how to talk myself out of committing suicide. The brain is really an enormous sponge that absorbs everything around it, and so often I think how much I'd love to be able to take my brain out and wash away all the horrible bits. If only it were so easy.

I have talked to a very good friend who tried to kill himself in his twenties; he remembers vividly his soul leaving his body. He rose to the ceiling and looked down upon the doctors trying to revive him. He doesn't know the meaning of the memory; did he actually die? Did his soul somehow re-enter his body? Do we all see something similar at the moment of death? We are enormously lucky that he did survive; he is one of the kindest people I've ever met.

10

Penge

'It's miles from the nearest train station,' said Mum when she came home from investigating our new potential home in southeast London, 'and the flat is in a drab old brick block.' I didn't care. It could have been in Outer Mongolia; anything was preferable to staying on at Gran's. Finally, we were to have our own home.

My mother signed a rental agreement and we prepared to move to Penge — but Gran wouldn't relinquish my little brother Mark, who had just turned eleven. He had been living with Gran since he was a baby, and she flatly refused to allow him to leave with us. 'I'll throw myself under a bus if you take him,' she told Mum, 'and everyone will know you were responsible.'

I said: 'Call her bluff. Let's see if she does it.' I would happily have taken the wheel of the Number 49 and mown her down myself.

Mum gave in. 'I don't want that on my conscience,' she said. So we three girls moved to our low-rise block in Penge by ourselves, and it was glorious: wall-to-wall Axminster carpets, new furniture on hire-purchase. For the first time, I had a room to myself, and with my roller-blind, record player and brown carpet, I thought I was the bee's knees.

Penge still had a village atmosphere, with a daily vegetable market and a pub on every corner, but its main claim to fame was having produced Rolling Stone Bill Wyman. A short bus ride from our home, in Beckenham, lived a young singer named David Bowie, who played at the Three Tuns pub.

I had to say goodbye to all my friends at modern, gleaming Garratt Green School, where I had been learning French, German, chess and astronomy, and when I arrived for my first day at Rock Hills School for Girls I couldn't believe my eyes. It was a real nineteenth-century institution, complete with forbidding black iron gates, thick stone walls and a cemented yard.

The headmistress, Mrs Greenhalgh, disapproved of jewellery and had imposed a strict ban on the wearing of earrings. I had pierced ears. We did not hit it off.

I thought her school was dreadfully backward — they had no modern languages, let alone chess or astronomy, and I was informed on my first day that I would have to take religious studies and dressmaking. I became fond of saying: 'At my other school we used to . . .', which didn't endear me to either Mrs Greenhalgh or my fellow students. They thought I was a frightful snob.

The idea of Bible study appalled me. Since my father's death I had rejected all religion, and had announced that I would never go to church again apart from weddings and funerals. I just couldn't take the hypocrisy of the church, and I had entirely lost my faith in established religion.

The dressmaking class was equally unappealing. I did not want to be a machinist, and had no interest in making my own clothes. 'I'm not sewing a stitch,' I announced with my arms folded. 'I want to take art.' There was no room in the art class, I was informed — but I refused to budge.

Most of my classmates had been at Rock Hills since the age of eleven, and had already formed impenetrable cliques, so I found it very difficult to fit in. The girls all seemed to have boyfriends, and talked very openly about doing things with boys that my friends and I had never even dreamt of. One girl, Tracey Scarrott, told everyone how she 'wanked off' her boyfriend in the cinema. After someone had explained the term to me, I gagged.

'You touched a boy's penis?' I asked, and all the girls looked at me like I was some sort of alien.

'That's just disgusting,' I said. 'You'll never catch me doing that. They can touch their own friggin' penises.' Although I never would have dared say so, I thought they were a bunch of tarts.

Despite my reservations about my new school, moving to Penge made me feel I had been reborn. I no longer had to abide by any rules — so I decided it was time for a physical transformation too. At a disco with some of my old schoolfriends, I was struck by Debra Brazier's stunning new Cleopatra-style haircut, short and chic.

I had waist-length dark hair at the time. My mother had never cut it, and I wore it in plaits for school, which left it looking wavy and horrible. Off to a hair salon I went. 'Cut it all off,' I told the hairdresser. 'I want a shoulder-length bob.'

'Does your mother know?' asked the hairdresser.

'Yes,' I lied.

He sat me in the chair, lopped off both my plaits, then shaped my hair into a bob. I couldn't believe the transformation. Wrapped up in those tight braids, my hair had always seemed thin — but now I realised I had thick hair, just like the rest of the family. Mum soon got over the shock, and I decided I was now going to start looking after my hair. Having left Gran's house, we were allowed to have baths more than once a week, so I began to buy all the fancy shampoos on the market.

Mum told me eggs were very good for the hair (we'd always used Boots Egg and Lemon shampoo) so one day I put several raw eggs straight onto my scalp, rubbing them in and rinsing well. As I dried my hair, I noticed little lumps all over my head, and ran to show Mum.

'What did you rinse your hair in?' she asked.

'Hot water.'

'Oh silly,' she said, 'you should have rinsed it in cold. The eggs have scrambled in your hair.'

For weeks I was picking tiny bits of scrambled egg out of my tresses — and yes, it stank, just like disgusting farts. From then on, I stuck to shampoo.

The Gin Queen did everything she could to taint our happiness in Penge. I remember her visiting once when Mum and Robyn were away, to 'see if Denise is okay'. When she arrived she took a ouija board from her bag and suggested we try to raise some spirits. As we sat around the board she kept telling me there was an evil spirit trying to make contact. I found it all quite amusing — she was stooping so low to try and spoil our new home. The destructiveness in my family just staggers me sometimes. I never saw the Gin Queen with a ouija board before or since — and luckily, no evil forces entered our home that night.

When I was fifteen and three months, I was officially old enough to get a part-time job at the local Woolworths, on Penge High Street. I'd been working at a chemist in Tooting since the age of thirteen, but Tooting was now a one-hour bus ride away.

Woolworths was a much better option, but when I showed up for my first shift one Saturday morning at 9am, I was confronted by the sight of Anita Drought, standing outside the store puffing a cigarette. My heart sank. Anita, with her waist-length blonde hair, was one of the most popular girls at Rock Hills. I loathed her, and had always quietly sniggered at the fact that she dated a boy named Simon Brooks. Drought and Brooks — what a combination.

As we walked into the store, Anita turned to her best friend, Bev, and said: 'What is *she* doing here?' glancing at me. 'Oh, shut up Anita,' Bev said.

The store manager, Mrs Phillips, gave me a uniform and asked which counter I'd like to work on: make-up, sweets or toys. 'Make-up,' I said immediately, and Mrs Phillips took me over to the glass-fronted cosmetics counter. I'd been standing there for a few minutes when Mrs Phillips returned with Anita. 'Miss Drought, this is Denise,' she said. Anita scowled. 'Oh God,' she said.

We shuffled past each other with our backs arched, and barely spoke a word. We ignored each other at school, and at Woolworths tea-breaks all I could hear was Anita laughing with all the other girls from Rock Hills who worked at the store. I did have one friend at the shop — a lovely girl called Lorna Windle — and eventually I made other friends at school, too.

Anita's friend Bev was on the sweets counter, and Anita was always popping over to grab a few lollies. I knew she'd be sacked if she were ever caught, but I never grassed on her. Anita and I spent our days standing silently side by side, selling Ponds cream and Rimmel make-up, as well as Woolworths' home-brand and a tragic cosmetics line called Yvette.

One day, as Anita and I stood there working, I accidentally knocked one of the large pots of Ponds cold cream. Smash! It shattered all over the floor, propelling the cream everywhere. I stood there horrified. If this got back to Mrs Phillips or any of the other managers I'd be fired or forced to pay for the wasted cream. I couldn't afford either option.

Anita looked down at the floor, then up at me. 'Put it in a paper bag,' she whispered, 'and tell me when the coast is clear. I'll run out the fire exit and put it in the dumpster.'

I was dumbfounded, but all I could do was obey. I scooped up all the glass and cream, wiped the floor and thrust the paper bag into Anita's arms. When I gave the OK, she ran through the aisles, out the fire exit, and was back again in a few moments.

'Thank you,' I said, still astonished at her kindness. 'No problem,' she said with a smile. 'You'd do the same for me.'

From then on, we were inseparable, spending our days giggling together and our Saturday nights dancing at any nightclub that would let us in. Mum had no idea what I was up to. At 3am one Sunday in 1977, we emerged from one of our favourite clubs in the West End and strolled past the crowds thronging Pall Mall for the Queen's Silver Jubilee celebrations, which were to be held later that morning. I caught the first train from Victoria home to Penge, and arrived home at about 7am. I quietly opened the front door. As I crept in, Mum opened the door of her bedroom and came out in her dressing gown.

'Good morning, darling,' she said; 'you're up early. Can you take the dog for a walk?'

She hadn't seemed to notice my shiny silver disco outfit. 'Ah . . . yes,' I said, and grabbed the dog's leash. We walked around the block, me in my full party regalia. I told the dog to shut up and stop laughing.

Anita was always late for school on Monday mornings, and as she slid into class I'd quickly tell her what we'd done that morning. 'Good morning, Miss Drought,' the teacher said once when she noticed Anita had appeared, late as usual.

'What do you mean?' I said innocently. 'She's been here all the time.'

Anita and I have remained friends all our lives. She fell for a boy named Luciano Donadio while visiting Italy a few years after we left school. 'He's going to come to London and we'll get married,' she would say.

'Poor deluded girl,' my mum would say; 'it's just a holiday romance.'

Luciano did come, and although he spoke no English, they married and lived in Italy for a few years before returning to London, where they still live happily today, with their three children.

My other close schoolfriend was Sonia Knight, who I introduced to the joys of hanging out on Portobello Road. Sonia was very alternative, and we embarked together on a mild punk phase, scouring charity shops for mohair scarves. We had our heads shaved at the local barbers, and would spend our weekends shopping in Notting Hill or listening to bands at the Greyhound pub in Croydon. After the gigs, we'd hang out in the bar with the musos, who included Paul Weller of The Jam and Siouxsie Sioux of The Banshees. She was incredibly nice, but I was too in awe of her to speak.

Our constant companions were twin brothers, Mark and Dean, from a posh suburb called Biggin Hill. Despite the class gulf, we were all great friends, but I had no romantic interest in either of the boys; as far as I was concerned, we were all just friends.

One night when I was seventeen, we all went to the Global Village Club in London's West End. Sonia and I met two gorgeous boys and spent the whole evening dancing and talking. Around 1am, Mark dragged us out of the club, and I moaned all the way home about what a party pooper he was, as the club stayed open till 3am. Nobody else in the group said a word, so I continued bleating on and on. 'I can't believe you made us leave early, how could you do that?'

A few weeks later we went to the Rainbow in Finsbury Park to see The Jam, who by now had found fame, and I was still whining about Mark dragging us away from the club. Another friend of Mark's was with us that night, and she eventually interrupted me.

'Don't be so hard on him,' she snapped. 'Don't you know he's in love with you?'

Nobody had ever been in love with me before. I was so embarrassed. Mark and I had always had a brother/sister relationship — or so I thought. This changed everything. I refused to speak to him again, and cut him dead whenever he tried to make conversation.

Unfortunately, he had tickets to a band the following week, and I had promised already that I would accompany him, so I had to go along. After the gig, we sat opposite each other in the train carriage. I still hadn't said a word. I looked out the window, and he looked at the floor.

When we reached Penge East station, Mark got off the train with me. 'What are you doing?' I demanded. Mark looked pained. 'I can't let you walk all the way home on your own, it's too late,' he said.

'Get back on that train!' I said. Mark refused. I told him he could walk me home, but I wasn't going to talk to him. 'Fine,' he said. So for 20 minutes we walked in complete and utter silence. He saw me to my door, I went in, and never spoke to him again. I can't imagine how he got home, as by then the trains would have stopped running for the night.

I never apologised to Mark, which is one of my great regrets. I saw him again once, four years later, when I was working in a pub in Bromley, Kent, and saving to go on holiday to India on my own. One night Mark walked in, and after overcoming my initial instinct to scurry away and hide, I went up to him and we had a chat. He had been to university, although I never found out what he studied.

The loss was all mine. We had been great friends, and I cringe when I think of how I treated poor Mark. I was as headstrong then as I had been as a little girl, and loathed being told what to do — and I especially hated anyone spoiling my fun.

Anyway, since the age of fifteen I had been in love with a boy I'd never spoken to.

He passed me in the street, and it was like a lightning bolt had hit me. I became obsessed. I knew he played football with all the council estate hooligans, but his parents owned their own house in a very nice street in Penge and I'd often see him in Woolworths at weekends. Before long, it became clear he was intrigued by me, too — he asked another girl at school who I was, and seemed to spend a lot of time loitering around the make-up counter while I worked. I was so nervous I never even looked at him — I'm sure he thought I was terribly arrogant.

After a couple of years, Mr Gorgeous met a local girl and married her. I quite seriously contemplated going to the church on their wedding day and shrieking: 'It should have been me!' They are still married and living in the area, but I'll never forget him.

It seemed I was doomed to have no luck with boys. All my friends had boyfriends, but I was home alone most Friday nights, bored out of my skull — no wonder, really, when you consider how I behaved.

'I'm going to phone Kevin downstairs and ask him out for a drink,' I told Mum on one such endless Friday evening. Kevin Prosser was a gangly, goofy-toothed kid, a couple of years older than me, who lived in the flat below us.

'That's nice, dear,' Mum said; 'the poor ugly lad will be delighted.

He would never have been asked out by a girl.'

I sighed at the indignity of it — having to go out with the ugliest boy in the flats — and picked up the phone. 'Hello,' I said. 'It's Denise from upstairs. Do you want to go for a drink tonight?'

Kevin didn't hesitate. 'No thanks,' he said, and hung up.

11

Cutting my cloth

After finishing school at seventeen with just a handful of O-Level qualifications (the equivalent of School Certificate), I had no real idea of what I wanted to do with my life. The black moods were still coming, but most of the time I was relatively happy. When I started work as a secretary near Victoria Station, I renewed my friendship with Eileen, a girl with whom I'd gone to Brownies as a child. We spent our days and nights laughing uproariously together; we'd laugh until tears rolled down our cheeks — or I had to rush to the loo to avoid peeing myself, whichever came first. She and I still laugh like that whenever I visit London, where she lives with her husband and three strapping sons.

As a secretary I was earning very good money but was bored out of my mind. I had to do something creative, and decided I might give fashion design a go. I'd had a few attempts to sew things over the years and had spent many hours making my sister's wedding dress, so I thought fashion might be worth a try. At the very least, it would be more stimulating than taking shorthand.

I sent off my application to the London College of Fashion, which was the most prestigious place to study design, with branches in Oxford Street, Hoxton and the Barbican. On the day of my interview, I was one of hundreds of hopefuls. We all sat in a huge tiered auditorium, waiting to be called onto the stage for a grilling by a three-person panel. This included the principal, Alex Roll, a tall, slightly rotund woman who would swish about in her structured, Japanese-style clothes, which she wore with enormous jewellery, black cropped hair and red lipstick.

'Why do you think you deserve a place on this course?' the deputy principal demanded when I came onto the stage.

I was tetchy at having waited so long, and my nerves were a little raw. 'Because I would be good at it!' I snapped.

The deputy principal, a rather fierce-looking man, stared at me and scribbled something down. I walked off the stage, stormed out into Oxford Circus and burst into tears, as I knew I had blown it. My forthright attitude was always landing me in trouble, no matter how I wished I could be more like my lighthearted, laid-back friends. I could be fun, too — but my weakness was a complete inability to accept criticism. I just hated being challenged. 'That's it,' I thought to myself, 'it's back to the office for me.'

A couple of months later, a letter arrived out of the blue. I picked it up off the doormat on the way to work one morning, and saw the LCF stamp. I didn't dare open it immediately, clutching it in my hand as I continued walking towards the train station.

Eventually I psyched myself up to open it. It was an offer of a place on the Production Course, which crammed two years of qualifications into a single year's full-time study, covering design, marketing, pattern cutting, grading, hand-tailoring and modelling (creating a garment to fit a mannequin and then drawing a pattern from the garment).

I was thrilled with the offer, but I had been so certain of rejection I hadn't bothered applying for a government study grant. These grants were designed to help school-leavers finance further education, but they were only available for three years after leaving secondary school. By now I was 23 and had been out of school for just over three years.

I was faced with having to fund my studies myself, which I simply couldn't afford. After a long exchange of letters, the grants board refused to give me any money. I was furious, and decided I'd go over the heads of the petty officials in charge of allocating grants.

I wrote directly to the Prime Minister, Margaret Thatcher, telling her I was incensed at the board's reasoning and telling her I disagreed with its policies. Very rapidly, a letter arrived saying an official from Mrs Thatcher's office had been placed in charge of my case and would be delighted to help me.

I wrote to him, and hey presto, I got the grant. It was a fabulous lesson for me — 'no' does not have to mean no. As a businesswoman, I've found time and time again that it's possible to achieve anything you really want, if you keep persisting.

I wanted to get into this course very badly — and I was damned if I'd let some stupid bureaucratic rule get in my way.

I was a strong-minded young woman, but in many ways still very young — and just as accident-prone as ever. I had read somewhere that sand made a great exfoliant for the skin, so the next time I went to Brighton Beach — with my mum and her new husband Billy — I took several bags of sand home to my flat in Penge.

I filled up the bath and added a bag of sand. The water immediately turned a disgusting shade of brown, and started to stink like shit — but hey, this was all part of the beauty regime. I could hear Billy outside saying, 'Is Denise mad? Why has she got all this sand?'

By now, the smell was really bothering me, so I got out of the bath, pulled the plug and watched the filthy brown water gurgle down the plughole. I had sand in every orifice of my body.

'You were meant to buy clean sand, not take it off the beach,' a friend told me when I complained about how gritty I felt. I lugged all the remaining bags of sand out into the street and put them in the bin.

'Have you got a body in here?' asked the bin-men when they came to collect the rubbish that week.

In September I started college, and immediately realised I'd struggle to keep up with my peers. Most of the students had been making clothes all their lives, or were already working for fashion companies. The workload was horrific, and we spent our days lugging enormous bags of books and folders between LCF's three campuses.

My tailoring tutor was the most dapper of men: a delightful fellow called Eddie Thornton, who always wore checked suits and had a magician's touch with a sewing needle. He never raised his voice or bawled at any of us, even though you could tell he was exasperated with our stupidity sometimes. I'd never seen anyone work a needle like Eddie — he would sit on the table with a garment resting on his knees and transform it completely. He had worked with a tailor in Savile Row in his youth.

The year came and went in a flurry. I soon found an arch-enemy; an atrocious West Indian loudmouth called Sonia who boasted of stealing goods from Marks & Spencer, where she worked part-time. She made my life hell.

One time I returned from a week's work experience with the designer David Hicks, who was related to Earl Mountbatten, to find one of my garments from our tailoring class had been cut in half. I knew exactly who had done it. Across the room Sonia was singing loudly, which she always did when she'd misbehaved. It was some sort of nervous tic, I suppose. I didn't accuse her, however; there seemed no point. The lovely Eddie stayed after hours and helped me rescue the garment. It was a good lesson — fashion was a competitive, and often bitchy, business.

Despite Sonia, I knew fashion was the world for me. Finally I had found something that fulfilled my creative urges and was great fun. I was working as a salesperson on weekends and holidays at Browns, a top fashion boutique, so I was learning about all aspects of this fascinating industry. The journey of a garment from the initial concept to the shop-floor was so laborious and time-consuming, but wonderfully exciting.

For the following year, I applied for courses in hand-tailoring and costume design. The theatrical side of fashion intrigued me.

Whenever we had a free afternoon, I would go off to the theatres in Drury Lane or Covent Garden, buy a matinee ticket and dream. One of the plays I saw was *Mother Courage*; the theatre was nearly empty, so I had a front-row view of the amazing Judi Dench, who was yet to become a dame, performing her magic.

A lot of the costume-design students went straight into theatre jobs, but I wasn't entirely sure if that was the right path for me. I liked the exacting, perfectionist nature of the fashion skills we had been learning, but in costume design the emphasis tends to be more on the overall look of an outfit. The colour of the lining or overlocking doesn't really matter when the garment is to be seen on stage; it's far more important that a piece of clothing makes a statement about the character.

I was very pleased when Eddie accepted me into the prestigious hand-tailoring course — and even more delighted when my nemesis Sonia was rejected. Sonia had an almighty tantrum, but Eddie stood firm. 'I've chosen the four students who I think will be best,' he said.

So the four of us (Leigh Polden from Putney; a girl from Brixton named Orietta Marie; a North London lass called Amanda Gunning, and me) joined the final-year students from the four-year degree course. We were based at the Hoxton campus, an old Victorian school with high studs and clanking radiators, and had a wonderful time.

The building was cold in winter, so we'd sit there in scarves and gloves with our garments on our laps, hand-sewing and hand-canvassing our coats. We were not allowed to use stick-on fusing, and used a type of horsehair for interlining garments. Every detail had to be perfect.

It was one of the happiest times of my life. We were like an old knitting group, laughing and joking and hiding our polystyrene coffee cups from Eddie, who seemed to have x-ray vision. 'Leigh, could you please put your coffee cup away?' he'd say as he walked through the room, even though there were no cups anywhere to be seen. Leigh would sheepishly remove her cup from its hiding place and put it in the bin.

I decided we needed to keep fit, so we all brought our trainers to college each day, and after lunch we would run around the blocks of east London. None of us could have weighed more than 55 kg, and Leigh could run non-stop. Diana Turnbull and I would make it to the end of the street and have cardiac arrest. We did this for a while, then gave up. I'm still friendly with Leigh and Eddie, who has continued teaching at LCF and sends me postcards from his holidays all over the world.

Towards the end of the year, we began pestering Eddie with questions about what we were going to do for jobs. None of us could ever imagine ourselves as designers or machinists in factories. In those days, 'designers' still did not have the global following they do now. Of course, there were some celebrity fashion identities like Zandra Rhodes, Vivienne Westwood and Ossie Clark, but they were in the minority.

I was incredulous when some of the girls on the four-year course said that once they left, they never wanted to see another needle or sewing machine again. They all seemed to have such natural talent, whereas my little gang of four certainly did not. Orietta was much better than the rest of us, but Leigh, Amanda and I all got through by the skin of our teeth. I asked Eddie how many LCF graduates ended up working in the industry. 'Three per cent,' he said. That was the depressing reality. Fashion has always been a low-wage trade, but in those days it was low-prestige to boot.

12

'Send the bill to the Palace'

To avoid the drudgery of being a machinist or a factory pattern-cutter, I knew I'd have to get myself a job with one of the smaller, but more creative, fashion houses. I was now 25, and living in my own flat in Penge. I sent off dozens of CVs. Most people did not reply, but I did get a letter from a company called Crolla, which had a shop on Dover Street in the City, near the Green Park tube station.

Crolla hired me, and I spent my days in their minuscule Knightsbridge studio or in the workroom in the basement below the shop, stitching and hand-finishing their inventive garments. They used luxurious, expensive fabrics for their garments, such as Liberty-print shirts, fine knitwear and trousers made from ecclesiastical fabric — gorgeous rich purple, red, green and gold.

Thus began my true education in the realities of fashion. I knew all about seams and sequins and structure; now I was about to discover the practicalities and pitfalls of running a business.

The owners were a couple who had met at Brighton Polytechnic: Georgina Godley and Scott Crolla. Georgina had all the talent and Scott had the gift of the gab, and although they'd been dating for many years, their relationship fell apart as the business grew. Georgina had a boyfriend, Tom Dixon, who would arrive in a white motorbike helmet and goggles to take her to lunch. He looked like a modern-day Biggles, and has gone on to become a very successful furniture designer.

Scott and Georgina were still trying to work together, and would have huge rows in front of me and my colleague Felicity. Felicity seemed to be perpetually afflicted by a cold; she was always sniffing and running to the toilet. It wasn't until after she left that I learnt she was an insane cocaine addict — I was still a naive young thing.

Eventually, Georgina had a breakdown, and walked out of the business. One day she just picked up her handbag and went to stay with her mother in the country, never to return. Years later she married Sebastian Conran, brother of fashion designer Jasper and son of author Shirley and Habitat founder, the famous Sir Terence Conran.

The label was doing well and the shop was always full of society figures, actors and musicians — but keeping the business afloat was still hard work for Scott. His financial backer was a very wealthy older gallery-owner named Carole Rhodes, and she was terribly eccentric and interfering. Every Thursday, Scott would be absent from work — and eventually I discovered he was spending the day at Carole's place. He said he went there to do the housework. It seemed too crazy to be true — this successful man, who owned one of the city's hottest shops, was working as a cleaner? He forbade us to call him at Carole's place, except in an emergency — and on the few occasions I did ring, I heard the vacuum being turned off before he came to the phone.

Scott told me Carole was incredibly fussy about food. She would insist on buying two lots of every grocery item — two bunches of bananas, two bags of apples — and when she got home she would decide which of the two looked better, and throw the other one away. Completely eccentric.

At the boutique, I met some fascinating people. Whenever someone grand came in, the shop staff would buzz for me to come upstairs. Whenever the hottest film stars or the latest band came in, we'd all act very cool and pretend not to stare, but as soon as they'd left we'd dissolve into giggles.

The Duchess of York, Sarah Ferguson, came in one day and bought a pair of boxer shorts — emblazoned with a Santa Claus print — for Prince Andrew. 'Send the bill to the Palace,' she said. A cheque came back, with her signature, and Scott's mother, who looked after the accounts, was in a quandary as to whether to bank the cheque or frame it.

One morning I arrived at work to see a Rolls Royce parked outside the shop. Inside were Elton John with his then-wife, Renate, and a bodyguard with a briefcase handcuffed to his wrist.

Elton was an expert shopper. 'Six of those and six of those,' he'd say, pointing at socks or shirts as I ran around collecting his purchases. He didn't try anything on; just pointed at what he wanted.

'But what if they don't fit?' I asked.

'Then I'll give them away,' he replied.

Elton wasn't very friendly; I'd met him several times during my days as an adolescent star-stalker, and had always found him very rude to his fans. He couldn't wait to get away from the throng of teenage girls who followed him around; in retrospect, I guess girls weren't really his focus.

One of the strangest people I ever served had to be the legendary Bob Dylan. He was a scrawny little person, and came in accompanied by a tall woman. He didn't say a word to any of the staff; speaking only to his companion. I was not sure if he was all there, if you know what I mean, but I leapt to attention when he went to the rack of jackets and pointed to one.

I handed it to him, and Dylan removed his leather jacket. He tried on the coat, took it off, hung it back on its hanger, put his leather jacket back on, and then went to the next coat on the rack.

Again, he removed his leather jacket, tried on the Crolla coat, took it off, hung it up, put his leather jacket back on and went to the next Crolla coat. This went on and on and on, with him putting his leather jacket back on each time before trying on the next one. I just stood and watched the weird scenario unfolding.

The woman he was with was quite bossy, and spoke to him like he was a small child. 'Do you want that one?' she kept asking. Bob would mumble something inaudible under his breath.

He eventually decided on one, but it had to be altered, as the arms were too long and the back too wide. We pinned it up and arranged to send it to Mohammed, our specialist tailor in Fulham, and Bob and his friend came over to the counter. Bob just stood there.

'Well, get out your money,' barked the tall woman. I jumped. Bob fumbled through his pockets and eventually produced not a Louis Vuitton or Goyard wallet, which was what I was expecting, but a tiny, bright pink, plastic child's purse. It had a metal clasp which opened with a noisy click, and was identical to one I had had as a five-year-old. Bob began taking out his money, but each time he unfolded a note, he would look at the woman questioningly.

'More,' she'd say in a very condescending tone. He'd then unfold another bill and show it to her.

'More,' she'd say — this went on and on until he had taken out enough money.

It was one of the oddest sights I've ever witnessed. Bob kept looking to the woman like a small child, apparently unsure of whether he was doing the right thing. When the whole ordeal was over, she gave me the address of the hotel to which she wanted the jacket delivered and they walked out together, leaving me wondering what on earth was going on inside his head.

Andy Warhol walked in one day, with his sidekick of the time, BillyBoy, who had a jewellery line in Paris called BillyBoy Bijoux and had also designed a range of outfits for Barbie.

They were two of the campest things on earth, and very funny too; no pretentiousness. They began ferreting in the sale bin, a cardboard box we kept on the floor. Scott refused to put sale items on hangers, they were all heaped into a tatty cardboard box, with a 'sale' sign on the front, and put by the front door. The store furnishings were original Le Corbusier and Eileen Gray, amongst others, and an enormous Gilbert and George artwork covered the entire back wall of the store. Billy pulled out a sleeveless summer shift dress that Georgina had designed when she was there. It was blue floral, sewn from a floral chintz furnishing fabric by Colefax and Fowler.

As Billy grabbed the dress, Andy shouted, 'I want that!'

'Well, you're not having it,' Billy retorted, snatching it out of his reach. 'That's not fair,' Andy yelled; 'I let you have the garment I wanted from that other store!'

I just stood there, staring as these two grown men tussled and pulled at the dress. The price-tag was 50 pounds.

'It won't fit you anyway,' Andy snapped, and another argument ensued. Eventually, they agreed to share the dress.

'Can I take your picture?' Andy asked me, whipping out a Polaroid camera before they left the store.

'Yes,' I stammered. The photo buzzed out of the machine, he waved it until it dried, showed it to me, and put it in his pocket as they left. I couldn't quite believe it; one of the century's most famous artists had just taken my picture. They were a couple of gorgeous kooks — and as I've come to learn, kooks make the world go round.

Scott always had an array of gorgeous models coming in to meet him, and often he was so distracted by their charms that he failed to show up to work at all. He lived with his parents in a beautiful, large apartment in Kensington Gore, with miles of red-carpeted hallways and a uniformed concierge. Whenever I went around to deliver documents or garments to Scott, I'd be overwhelmed by the grandeur. Scott lived in what must once have been the servants' quarters, but his bathroom was full of Geo. F. Trumper toiletries and there was an enormous Gilbert and George artwork on the wall. Scott was friends with Anthony d'Offay, who represented Gilbert and George and had a gallery in Mayfair.

Scott's friends were frightfully posh. He was married for a time to the Hon. Rosie Cornwallis, a girl from an ancient Suffolk family. Six foot tall and very glamorous, Rosie had gone to school with Lady Diana Spencer. She was a real Sloane Ranger, speaking in a cut-glass accent and making elaborate birdcages in her spare time. Scott met her when she took a job in the store — although she wasn't terribly well-suited to retail. 'Fuck off,' she would snap when Scott asked her to do something. He thought that was really spunky, although I'm not sure if the rest of us could have got away with such insubordination.

Scott knew all the fashion media. One in particular was a good friend of Georgina's called Sarah-Jane Hoare, who is still a fashion writer today. When I knew her, she was short and slim with cropped blonde hair. She was also partially deaf, and known for her frightful temper. She also loathed the way Scott treated Georgina. She and Scott would have the most enormous rows in person and over the phone. She would absolutely howl at him over the phone. Scott would place the receiver on the counter and potter about the store, returning now and again to pick up the phone, shout, 'Fuck off Sarah-Jane,' then place the phone on the counter, wander off again, return later and say, 'Mind your own fucking business.' He would do the same thing again and again. She had no idea he was not listening, and I would just laugh; she never stopped for breath.

Scott never hesitated about telling editors and fashion hacks what he thought of their magazines, and I'm not talking some rag, but the *Vogues*, *Tatlers* and *Harpers* — we only dealt with the top-end magazines. He did not care who you were, whether you used him again or not, he said what he thought. I admired that, and they could not get enough of him.

One day while I was upstairs in the store, which I wasn't that often, as I worked downstairs, I saw a woman with mad, curly red hair chain her bicycle up to the black railings outside the store. She walked in wearing a fawn rain-mac, belted at the waist. I immediately knew who she was, and she came up to me, and in her very quietly spoken voice asked if Scott was around, as she had an appointment with him. Of course he wasn't, which was not unusual; he always ran late for everything, so we had to rely on him telling us where he was going to be. If he wasn't at his flat, chances were he was drinking an espresso at the café around the corner.

I explained that Scott was out, then I took her downstairs and popped her into the tiny cupboard-like, windowless office, crammed with files and stock, while I rang the café. She sat there, and I offered her a drink, which she declined, and said she was happy to wait.

I went into the workroom area, and the gorgeous pattern-cutter Rion and I looked at each other, perplexed.

'What does she want?' Rion asked.

'I have no idea,' I said.

After about ten minutes Scott flew in the door, apologising and rubbing his hands through his long hair, which he always did, then he went into the office to see the woman, closing the door.

After a while she came out, thanked me and left. I did not ask Scott what she wanted, and he did not offer any explanation.

About a month later she called in again, and I asked the junior, Wendy, to run to the coffee shop in Ablemarle Street and fetch Scott. I chatted with the woman and asked her how she was. She said, in her lovely accent, that she had been away, and had left her son Joe with money to pay the phone and electricity bills in her absence. She had returned to their council flat, she said, and I will never forget her next words: 'I have just got back and the leccie [electricity] in the flat has been cut off!'

I asked her why, and she said Joe had spent the money on other things, and they were now in darkness with no heating.

Scott came running in, and I left them to it. When she left I saw her out, she unchained her bicycle, and rode off on the dark winter's afternoon.

This time I asked Scott what she had wanted. 'Oh darling,' he said (he called everyone darling), 'she wants to borrow some money to start up in business again, but I can't help her; you know how tough it is.'

I told Rion, and we both agreed what a shame it was. She was so talented, humble and unassuming, that I wanted to hug her. Rion and I agreed that if we had had any money we would have leant it to her. I also know now how desperate you would have to be to approach someone in your industry to help you out, but desperation makes us do desperate things.

Today, I wonder if Scott ever wishes he had helped her out. Her name was Vivienne Westwood. She had split from Malcolm McLaren, their shop had closed in the Kings Road with punks having grown older, and she was a solo mum, living on a council estate in London.

When I see what she has achieved today, I am so proud she realised her dream. I am sure when she arrived back at her dark flat she would not have seen the light at the end of the tunnel, but true talent is a great thing and must never be underestimated.

Her son Joe opened a lingerie store, and released a perfume, both called Agent Provocateur, and has become very successful in his own right. Vivienne deserves it all.

13

Back to blue skies

In 1985, Scott was approached by a Japanese firm to open a boutique in Tokyo. 'Would you like to come and help me set it up?' he asked. I didn't hesitate — I was always keen for adventure, and I was thrilled at the prospect of visiting Japan with Scott. I had another motive, too: it was a chance to visit the country of my birth.

After leaving school and moving into my own flat, I had tried to push thoughts of New Zealand out of my head and try to focus on life in London. There were plenty of distractions — the assorted flotsam I was meeting through work; the exciting fashion scene in London, and my own increasing satisfaction with the work I was doing.

But despite the joy I found in fashion, I was still struggling with my demons. Dad's death had unleashed a great deal of unhappiness, and I was tormented by episodes of the darkest misery imaginable. There was no predicting when it would happen. I could go to bed fine, then wake in the morning and find the demons had come calling in the night. I would open my eyes, and the weight of the depression would be so heavy I could hardly breathe.

When I could see my way through the clouds, the prospect of returning at long last to New Zealand thrilled me. All the homesickness I had tried to suppress for so long began to resurface, and I spent all my spare time dreaming of green grass and blue skies.

Scott and I flew to Tokyo with a very well-connected public relations agent named Camilla Lowther, who was working on the boutique project. The store was amazing; it was studded with huge pillars, one of which was covered in sharkskin. I suggested we tile another, so we smashed up a stack of brightly coloured tiles and stuck them to the pillar in a mosaic. When we had finished the boutique looked stunning. There was a huge launch party, then Scott and Camilla returned to London, while I flew on to New Zealand for a fortnight's holiday.

On the flight from Tokyo to Auckland the airline had not put me down as a vegetarian, hence I had no food. The Japanese stewardess apologised profusely, and plied me with vodka and peanuts. I don't know how much I drank, but when we landed in Auckland and I stood up, I realised it was a fair bit.

I put on my Ray-Ban wayfarers and staggered through Customs, then went outside to meet my father's brother Ric and his wife Margaret. Of course the last time Ric had seen me I was three years old, and I am sure that after greeting me he must have thought to himself 'Like father, like daughter', as I was as drunk as a skunk.

When I arrived in New Zealand, I kept blinking up at the wide sky, amazed at how blue and clear it seemed. The heavens seemed larger in New Zealand, uncrowded by skyscrapers. In central London, the closest beach was Brighton, which was always covered in Coke cans, dog poo and tar. In Auckland, a ten-minute drive from the city brought me along Tamaki Drive, with little coves sparkling at every turn.

During the London winters, for months on end I would leave for work in the dark and arrive home in the dark. One thing I had learnt about my black moods during my early twenties was that sun and light seemed to help. On bleak days, I was more vulnerable to the sadness, and seemingly less able to pull myself out of it. The warmth and fresh air of New Zealand made me feel good, and I knew I wanted to spend more time in this rejuvenating southern climate.

When my holiday was over I returned to London, gave notice on my flat and booked a ticket back to New Zealand as soon as possible. My plan was to work in Auckland for six months, move on to Australia for another six months, then work my way back to the United Kingdom. Fate, however, has a way of intervening in the plans we humans make.

When I came back to Auckland, I moved in temporarily with my aunt and uncle in Browns Bay, on the North Shore, and started work for a large fashion manufacturer as head pattern-cutter. The company had several brands under its umbrella, and I found the atmosphere difficult to deal with. I wasn't used to churning out vast numbers of patterns, and felt the company gave little thought to the creative side of the business. It made the 'look of the season', which was not me.

Eventually, my bosses and I agreed this wasn't the job for me, and I went to work for a fashion brand that had a store in Vulcan Lane, a stylish little alleyway in the centre of Auckland. I also moved into my own digs; a tiny bedroom in the back of a house in the central suburb of Parnell.

Four days a week I worked as a production assistant/cutter in the label's Parnell workroom, with one day on the shop floor in Vulcan Lane. I am a useless saleswoman, even if I say so myself, but I did manage to sell my fair share of garments, which surprised me no end.

Again, I had rather unusual colleagues. I was beginning to realise that a fashion career would mean I was always working with characters. One girl I worked with was rather loose and had a passion for alcohol and coming to work wrecked. She was sweet enough, but talked in a very slooow manner. I always talk at a hundred miles an hour, and I kept wanting to thump her on the back to get her to speed up.

A very young, well-groomed boy swanned in one day and said to my work-mate: 'Hi babe, how's it going?'

She replied in her own slow time: 'Good, all good. Oh, Brent, this is Denise, she has just come from London.'

I ventured to say 'Hello', but the boy just looked me up and down, turned his nose up, said 'Ugh' and walked out. I stood in the store with my mouth open, gobsmacked.

'Who is that?' I demanded.

'Oh, that's Brent Lawler,' she drawled. 'He's a hairdresser in Shortland Street.'

I will never forget my words to her. 'I am going to remember that name,' I said. I spent the rest of the afternoon fuming.

The next time I saw Brent was at the wedding of another girl from the shop where I worked, an anorexic-looking ex-nurse called Donna. I knew barely anyone at the reception, and was standing on the fringes of the room when Brent Lawler approached me. I just glared at him.

'Oh God,' he sighed. 'I don't know anyone here, so I might as well talk to you.'

I sniffed: 'You really don't have to, you know,' and prepared to walk off.

'Oh shut up,' Brent said; 'Come and sit with me.'

Well, that was the beginning of a very long friendship. I'd never laughed so much in my life as I did that night; Brent might have been very frank, but he was also very funny.

When the bride came out, we all scattered handfuls of rice in her direction. Brent, however, took an entire bowlful of rice grains and tipped them down the front of my dress. As I stood up in shock, rice grains scattered all over the floor. Everyone turned to stare, and I rushed to the toilet to dislodge the remaining rice from my knickers. Brent thought it was hysterically funny, and when we came to leave, he asked me to go back to his flat with him. I was a bit frightened, as I had never met anyone so forthright with their opinions, and scurried away.

The next day when I was at work in Parnell, there was a phone call for me. 'I love you,' said a voice on the other end of the line.

'Who is this?' I asked.

'Brent, you idiot,' came the laughing reply. 'Who else would be in love with you?'

We never became a couple — Brent had just come out of a long relationship with a girl, and I wasn't interested in having a boyfriend at the time. Instead, we became solid friends from then on. We shared the same sense of humour, and we are both very black-and-white with our opinions, which has never gone down too well with the fashion hacks of New Zealand. Over the years, Brent has been blacklisted many times for declaring a magazine shoot to be 'crap' — an opinion he tends to hold about the vast majority of fashion spreads.

Brent never hid a thing with me, and would tell me of orgies he had at his Anzac Avenue warehouse, with a photographer friend of his (who is now very successful and living in Sydney) and an array of pretty girls and boys. I never knew whether to believe what he said; sometimes his antics seemed too outlandish to be true.

Brent later moved to Sydney and spent ten years working his butt off on magazines and commercials. In 2000, he was hired to do the hair and make-up for the visiting American country act Dixie Chicks, who promptly hired him as their full-time hairdresser, flying him around the world to make them look sensational. After a few years, the Dixie Chicks said they really wanted Brent to be based in New York, so he moved over with his long-term partner, the very quiet Adam.

I still laugh when Adam tells the story of their meeting in a gay nightclub, surrounded by gorgeous boys, all on the lookout for erotic adventures.

'Are you gay?' Brent asked Adam. It seemed a delightfully innocent question, coming from Brent — of course Adam was gay!

I always think fondly of those days in Auckland, when Brent and I spent our evenings dancing and partying with all the bright young things who worked for the fashion boutiques and labels around town.

Brent always had firm opinions about everyone we encountered, and in 1987 he took an instant dislike to a newcomer to the fashion scene — a young man named Francis Hooper.

14

Francis

He was tall, dark and had the most gorgeous smile I'd ever seen, and he was managing a shop in Vulcan Lane, next door to the boutique where I worked one day a week.

Everyone had heard a little of Francis's past. He was an Australian passport-holder who had been born in Hong Kong, and educated in Switzerland and Auckland. He had just returned to New Zealand after being caught at Heathrow, having overstayed his visa, and been instantly deported.

Francis was very outgoing and chatty and flamboyant. In those days, I was quite reserved; I still hadn't fully found my feet in New Zealand, and was shy with new people. Our first conversation came when he walked into the store where I worked one day and asked if we would like to sign a farewell card for his friend Bridget, who was leaving for the UK. The other staff all knew her and took turns signing the card.

When it came to me, I told Francis I didn't know Bridget. 'So?' he said. 'You don't have to know her. Just sign the card.'

'But that would be stupid. I don't know her,' I repeated, as if he were deaf.

Francis looked exasperated. 'Then don't sign it,' he said, and marched out of the store. 'Weirdo,' he muttered. I felt the same about him.

Born in Hong Kong to a Chinese mother and a European father, Francis had come to New Zealand at the age of eleven when his family emigrated. They had been very wealthy, but had lost everything when the oil shocks of the 1970s sent the economy plunging. After glittering Hong Kong, Auckland seemed very provincial — a big culture shock for Francis and his two sisters.

Francis won a scholarship to the prestigious Auckland Grammar School, but made a conscious effort to stand apart from the rugby-saturated blokiness, bleaching his hair and customising his school uniform to reflect his individuality. He became heavily involved in Auckland's creative scene, making friends with musicians, designers and artists. When he was sixteen the family moved on to Australia, but Francis decided to stay in New Zealand. He finished school, started a Bachelor of Arts degree at Auckland University, and got a job washing dishes in a restaurant kitchen.

He dropped out of university in his final year and moved to London, where he began working in the fashion industry. He worked in retail for designers like Krizia and Michiko Koshino, and became workroom assistant to an up-and-comer called John Galliano, who at the time was struggling to succeed. Nobody seemed to understand the young Galliano's work, and it would be many years — and three bankruptcies — before he became one of the world's most famous designers.

After a few years in London, Francis went to Paris for a holiday — but he was caught by Customs officials on his return to the UK. His visa had expired, and they put him on the next plane home to New Zealand.

Francis absolutely loved disco music, and had worked as a DJ in clubs and on the local alternative radio station, bFM, for years. When he was working in Vulcan Lane he'd crank the stereo up full blast, and the infectious disco beats would waft through the alley. It made a nice change from the music in our store, which was usually dark, depressing stuff like Nina Hagen, chosen by our manager. She was a fiery woman, and would periodically stomp out of the store and order Francis to turn the music down — and, of course, he'd turn it up louder, prompting even more fury from my manager.

It was obvious to Francis that his boss, who was the son of very wealthy parents, had no idea about how to run a business. Creditors frequently came into the shop demanding money, and Francis was once chased down the stairs into the basement by an enraged businessman who was owed money. 'I'm not the owner,' Francis protested — and the man left, promising to return and pummel Francis if the money wasn't paid pronto.

On the days I worked in the shop, Francis and I would pass each other and say hi. 'What have you sold today?' he asked one day.

'Nothing, how about you?' I said.

'A pair of socks,' he replied.

This sent me into a frenzy. I was very competitive then, and had to outsell him, come what may. So each Monday, when I worked in the shop, we'd have the same conversation, each trying to outdo the other.

I soon discovered Francis loved nightclubbing as much as I did, and we started hitting the clubs together. Nearly every day, we'd meet up for a bite to eat or a movie after work — but we were always just friends. Brent took an immediate dislike to Francis; I was never quite sure why.

'How's Geeling?' Brent would sneer, referring to Francis. Geeling Ng was a gorgeous Auckland actress of Chinese heritage who had appeared in the video clip for David Bowie's hit 'China Girl'. I made the mistake of mentioning this to Francis, who was seriously unimpressed — but eventually, they both got over their distaste and became close friends.

Francis would always ensure I got home safely, and I really enjoyed his company; he was outgoing and worldly, able to talk about any subject he chose. He was as comfortable discussing politics as he was with fashion or geography, which is one of his pet topics. Name any obscure place on the globe, and Francis would know all about it. He found it greatly amusing that I had such a total lack of geographic knowledge; it took me years to remember I lived on the North Island of New Zealand. Francis would just roll his eyes.

We found that we had been working in streets parallel to each other at the same time in London — me in Dover Street and him in Bond Street — and each Friday we would both buy groceries from Marks & Spencer in Oxford Circus. We had no doubt passed each other many times on the street.

For well over a year we were just friends. I dated other guys, and he was like my brother — I'd ask his opinion of my boyfriends, and he would be very honest and forthright in his assessments. Neither of us was very happy in our work; I was bored with my job and Francis was constantly on the lookout for angry creditors or debt-collectors chasing his errant boss.

In 1988, Francis was offered a job by Nigel Richards, who owned the label Parachute and was part-owner of Workshop, with a store on High Street, which runs at right angles to Vulcan Lane. Francis became the store's part-time manager, but in his spare time he was always creating something; whenever he had his hands free, he'd be sketching garment ideas or making button badges or jewellery, which he sold around town. Once he had some fake Rolex watches, and managed to sell one to his boss, Chris Cherry.

'That watch has given up the ghost,' Chris complained after a couple of weeks.

'Oh well,' said Francis, with his trademark insouciance, 'What did you expect for $50!'

15

Sex — and love

Francis and I were bored with the fashion scene. We both spent our spare time working on our own designs, and would enter fashion competitions together.

The industry was frustratingly small. It enraged us that the shops closed at 1pm on Saturday and were shut all day Sunday, and we both earned very little; for us, a flash meal out meant sharing a $3 rice bowl and a slice of cake at a café called DKD, just off the main city avenue, Queen Street. We were both very thin, and either walked or rode our bikes everywhere; Francis on his racing model and me on my lilac girly number, complete with a little shopping basket on the front.

One day, after we had been to a movie at the Civic Theatre in Queen Street, we were waiting for a bus back to Ponsonby. 'How would you feel about going into business with me?' Francis asked suddenly.

I was taken completely by surprise, but as Francis began to explain his idea, I caught some of his excitement. He thought we should host a glamorous nightclub evening once a month, featuring the hottest DJs of the moment and models parading the latest clothes.

It would blend our love of nightclubbing with our connections in the worlds of fashion and music, and by charging revellers a small entry fee we'd cover our costs and make a profit. It would also, he said, inject some energy into Auckland's nightlife. 'Honestly, it's like Albania here some nights,' he said.

I sat at the bus stop, looking over at one of the city's most venerable retailers, the Smith & Caughey department store. I told Francis I thought the idea sounded great, but I couldn't commit to anything just yet.

'All I have is $500,' I said slowly, 'and I can't afford to lose it.'

It had taken me so long to save my paltry amount of money, and I was reluctant to do anything expensive or hasty — I had no support network in New Zealand to fall back on if I lost my shirt.

'But all we need is $200 each to get started,' Francis said, 'and who knows how big it will grow?'

I told him I'd have to think about it. To this day, he ribs me about my reluctance; he says he was flabbergasted that I had to think about such a great offer. I've always tended to err on the side of caution, however — and although I liked the fact that he trusted me so completely, I knew friendship and business often don't mix. I didn't want to jeopardise the great friendship we had.

I asked for a bit of time to think about it, and he shrugged his shoulders and said: 'Okay.'

Francis didn't seem to understand my aversion to risk. To him, the idea was so exciting that hesitation was ridiculous.

After a few days, I realised the offer was too good to pass up. 'What the hell,' I thought, and told Francis I'd take the plunge with him. We opened a bank account and pooled our savings. The trust between us was implicit — it didn't occur to either of us that the other could have just taken the money and disappeared.

We approached the owner of a club called Berlin in Wellesley Street, right in the centre of town, and asked if we could take over the venue one Wednesday every month. We'd keep the door takings — $5 per head — and he'd keep the takings from the bar. The owner, a large Yugoslav man, agreed readily.

We approached every top-end fashion designer in Auckland

and asked them to give us an item we could customise for the show — in return, we were offering great exposure for their brands to a young, hip crowd. They all agreed, so each night after work Francis and I would go back to his flat in Ponsonby and work on customising the outfits for maximum runway impact. One garment was completely covered in safety pins, and I sewed buttons all over another. We enlisted Brent to do all the hair and make-up, and he became really excited as he planned the outlandish styles he'd do on the night.

Francis wanted an enticing name that would pique clubbers' curiosity. Then, as now, the one word guaranteed to turn heads is 'sex', so that became our moniker. We emblazoned the name in huge coloured letters on hundreds of white postcards, and had the letters SEX cut from seven-foot-high free-standing polystyrene blocks. Francis approached a hip young DJ from South Auckland called Mike Haru to work the turntables.

Then F announced we had to visit a sex shop on grungy Karangahape Road to buy pornographic playing cards, which we'd use for the invitations. I was very embarrassed about visiting a sex shop, especially with a male friend in tow, so while Francis looked through all the paraphernalia I hovered among the display cabinets, trying to look nonchalant. Francis bought several packs of cards with full-colour nude sex scenes, and had them coated with coloured plastic and branded with all the details of our event.

I was still working for the fashion company in Parnell, and stupidly gave Francis my bosses' home address to add to his mailing list. The day after he sent out the titillating invitations, my boss came into work in a fury. 'Do you know someone called Francis Hooper?' she demanded. 'Oh, I know *of* him,' I lied, 'but I don't actually know him. Why do you ask?'

She said she had received the most disgusting, upsetting piece of pornography through the mail, with an invitation attached. 'Either of my children could have opened it!' she spluttered. She said she was going to call Chris Cherry and Nigel Richards, Francis's bosses at Workshop, and ask them to come to her house that evening to discuss the outrage.

My alarm bells were ringing very loudly by this point, and I desperately wanted to call Francis and warn him, but this was in the days before mobile phones. I had to wait until I saw him that night, and when I breathlessly told him what was about to transpire, he just laughed. To him, it was a great joke that anyone could be so upset about his tongue-in-cheek invitation.

The following morning, I casually asked my boss — who seemed to have calmed down — what Chris and Nigel had said about the invitations. Her reply has always stuck in my head: 'Chris Cherry said that Francis Hooper is a very smart man and should not be underestimated.' By the next day, she had calmed down completely, and no more was said about it.

My colleague Cris Elrick, who ran the workroom in the bosses' absence, told me to be careful. 'You're skating on very thin ice,' she said.

Chris Cherry was right about Francis. I was beginning to appreciate another side of his character: his capacity for energetic, passionate work.

'I'm starving,' I moaned late one night as I was sitting in his flat sewing hundreds of button on a garment, and he was working on a piece of artwork. 'Can we go and get something to eat?'

Francis didn't even look up. 'No,' he said, 'not until we've finished the job.' I was stunned into silence.

It was a good introduction to his approach: Francis is utterly obsessive about any job he is doing. Nothing can distract him — and he is still the same today as he was then. He never places time constraints on work, just continues slogging away until the job is done. He would happily work all night if he could. What really drives Francis is the adrenaline of an exciting, absorbing task, and it's wonderful to work with someone who is so dedicated.

We pulled in favours from all our friends to get our fledgling business under way. Francis was friends with plenty of models, all of whom agreed to be involved, and our young bank manager at the Bank of New Zealand, John Francis, was a great help. We needed crowd-control barriers but hadn't enough money to hire them, so I cheekily asked John if we could borrow the bank's own barriers.

'Of course,' he said. Before each show, after the bank closed, we would collect the shiny barriers, with their red velvet ropes, from the bank in Victoria Street West, then we would return them first thing in the morning before it opened to the public, much to the amusement of the tellers. We also wanted a plush red carpet to roll out on the street outside the club, and I found a delightful carpet manufacturer who agreed to lend us a bolt of the glorious stuff each month.

When the first night finally arrived, I was assigned the role of Door Bitch and perched myself on a little stool by the door. Francis gave me a list of invited guests, and strict instructions to charge everyone else $5. A gorgeous Pacific Island boy called Rosetti, who has since passed away, was in charge of keeping the crowd at bay, and together we began processing the vast queue of revellers waiting to get in.

The night was a roaring success. On what would usually have been a quiet Wednesday night, the club was packed. Mike and Francis were DJing in the tiny booth; the models were a big hit; the bartenders were run off their feet; and when it finally ended at 3am we had trouble clearing the crowds out of the club. Nobody wanted to go home.

A journalist and photographer from *The Listener* were there, and the magazine published a spread featuring a picture of Francis's face, covered in lipstick kisses from the models. As I read the story, I was horrified to read a quote from Francis, describing the reaction of my boss to the invitation and suggesting she was 'frigid'. I knew she'd instantly realise Francis's source must have been me, as I was the only person who knew him at work on the day she had been so upset. I didn't have to wait long to hear her reaction — she rang my Courtville apartment the night the magazine came out.

'Is Francis Hooper there?' she asked.

'Yes,' I said miserably, handing over the receiver and scuttling into the kitchen, where I had been baking a celebratory meal: cheese and potato pie with the word SEX in pastry letters across the top.

As I tried to busy myself with the pie, my stomach was churning. 'I'm going to be in such deep shit,' I thought to myself; 'I'll definitely lose my job.' Eventually, I heard Francis put down the receiver, and he walked into the kitchen.

'She's overreacting,' he said, which made me feel even worse. He'd told her to go away and cool off, then call him back if she was still unhappy. No sooner had he told me this than the phone rang again. 'I'm still really unhappy,' my boss told Francis. By now I was petrified and feeling physically ill. My stomach started to churn, and my bowels were loosening. As well as having spent my $200, I was about to lose my job.

'Oh dolly-chops,' said Brent, who had come around for a slice of Sex pie; 'Don't worry. She *is* frigid.'

He always managed to put a funny spin on everything, but it didn't make me feel better. During dinner, Brent announced he wanted to become the Door Bitch and wear a jacket with a crystal-embroidered slogan saying 'Fuck me, beat me, but don't steal my hairspray'.

Before the boys left that night, I told Francis I was very anxious about my job. 'It'll be fine,' Francis said.

Well, it wasn't. From then on, my boss ignored me and her husband gave me the most filthy glares. Cris Elrick, who stayed with the company for eighteen years before eventually leaving to set up her own clothing label, Pearl, said: 'You are in so much trouble. It would be best if you kept your head down and your bum up. Don't say a word until you're spoken to.'

I took her advice — Cris has always been my greatest ally, and although we've had differences over the years (usually because I've been unable to keep my enormous mouth shut) she is still my greatest confidante, and someone I view as a sister.

Every now and again I would glance sideways, to see one of them just glaring at me, this empty glare. I couldn't tell exactly what was going on behind their eyes, but I knew it wasn't pleasant.

We continued hosting the 'Sex' nights each month, and each one was a sell-out, but I was very much on the outer at work. I remember asking for a pay rise, pointing out that I had been on $10 per hour for the past eighteen months, while all the other staff had had pay rises.

'We'll have to think about it,' my bosses said.

Christmas was looming, and we were all invited to the bosses' large Parnell house for the staff party. I needed some moral support, so I invited Francis to come along as my guest, but when we arrived at the house on the night of the party I had an attack of nerves. What on earth had possessed me to bring him? I was half expecting the door to be slammed in our faces, but instead, both my bosses welcomed us inside with smiling faces.

'Well, Mr Francis Hooper, how nice to meet you at last,' they said.

It sounded slightly menacing to me, so I bustled off to get myself a drink, abandoning Francis with the bosses in the kitchen. I was sure they'd give him a bollocking, but when I worked up the courage to return I found them all sitting around the table laughing their heads off. I was stunned; he had managed to win them around, even though they'd continued to be frosty and standoffish with me.

A few weeks later, the phone rang while I was at work in Parnell. It was Francis, and he sounded very upset.

'I've just had a call from Hong Kong,' he said. 'My grandmother has passed away.'

I knew how terrible this was for him; his grandmother, Maria, had played a huge part in his upbringing until the family left Hong Kong. He idolised her.

I rushed to town, where Francis was waiting at Workshop for another staffer to relieve him so he could go and book a ticket to Hong Kong. When I arrived, Francis was inconsolable. I'd never seen him cry before, and I just felt useless. Nothing I could say or do made his grief any lighter.

We had been best friends for over a year, and our relationship had never been anything other than platonic. Francis had been a great sounding board for my dilemmas over some of the fuckwits I dated, and although friends always asked whether there was any romance between us, I had always thought of it as a simple friendship.

But when F was away in Hong Kong I missed him terribly, more than I could ever imagine. I began to realise he was far more to me than just a friend. There was no denying my feelings; I loved him, but it was only after he left that I could stand back and see my emotions for what they were. The problem was that I had no idea whether he regarded me as just a friend, or if there might be hope for something more. His absence was a time of intense nerves; I longed for and dreaded his return.

Phone calls were prohibitively expensive, so I had to wait until he came home to speak to him again. I knew what time his plane was landing, and we'd arranged that he would come straight to my flat, but it seemed to take forever for him to arrive. The hours slowly ticked by, and I kept ringing his flatmate, Ginny Kirk-Smith, to ask if she had heard anything. Every time a car stopped outside, I would rush to the window to see if it was him.

Eventually he arrived, many hours late. He'd been strip-searched at Customs; whenever the airport officials see the word 'fashion' on an arrival card, they assume there must be a suitcase full of drugs. It's too hysterical for words when you consider how little Francis and I have ever dabbled in drugs — I had my first and only puff of marijuana soon after arriving in New Zealand, and kept waiting for something to happen, as everybody around me got off their faces. I waited and waited, but nothing happened, and I decided it was boring, and that was it for me, never touched anything illegal since.

Francis has never taken illicit substances in his life and considers them a complete waste of time. Of course, we've been offered everything under the sun — when we were running the club nights, someone offered us coke, and we both said, 'No thanks, I've already got a drink.' So naive!

As soon as Francis walked into my flat, I knew things had changed between us. It was something in the way he looked at me; somehow, I could tell there was a new dynamic in our friendship.

I told him I'd missed him dreadfully.

'I missed you too,' he said.

Francis's face became serious. 'Before my grandmother died,' he said, 'I had written her a long letter. When I got the news that she'd died, I had the letter in my bag, ready to post. She never got to read it, and that was part of the reason I was so devastated when she died.'

My heart was pounding. 'What did the letter say?' I asked.

Francis looked at me. 'It said, "I've met the woman of my dreams."'

16

Honesty

I had never felt so happy in my life. All of a sudden, my best friend had become the love of my life — and even more astonishing, he adored me too.

'I always knew you were right for each other,' said Ginny, F's flatmate. She had kept quiet about her suspicions, not wanting to frighten either of us off — but she was thrilled when we finally got together.

Francis and I moved into a large warehouse flat in Anzac Avenue, on the northern fringe of the city, and life was sweet. I was still working for the same fashion company, but F had worked for several employers, including a large international brand that was not considered trendy by any of our set, but had a huge turnover.

Along the way, F was learning a great deal about the vagaries of running a fashion business, and the damage that can be inflicted on a company by irresponsible or dishonest staff. At one of the stores where he worked (which shall remain nameless) he became very aware of one of his colleagues.

The young woman in question was very insecure with an incredible number of personal hang-ups. Even though she was always very pleasant towards me, she was dreadfully insecure, and I felt she must have had a fairly unhappy upbringing. She felt the only way to find acceptance — and employment — was through sex.

As well as bringing in her own old clothes and selling them as new garments (and pocketing the proceeds), she was giving clothes away to her friends. She had a habit of filling up her empty Evian bottle from the tap and displaying it on the shop counter as a kind of status symbol — back in the late 1980s, French bottled water was still pretty rare in Auckland, and she felt it lent her a certain yuppie cachet.

She was sexually rampant, and was sleeping with both owners of the business in which she worked, as well as many other men around town, including an art director whom she described as having 'pendulous testicles'. Luckily, he escaped her clutches and went on to get married to someone else, but I was never able to look him in the eye after hearing her description of him. I kept imagining these enormous, swinging, dangling sacs, pulling the weight of his body down. 'How on earth does he manage to stand up straight and walk around?' I used to wonder.

Francis was concerned that he might get the blame when the owners eventually noticed how much stock and money was being stolen. 'It would be her word against mine,' he said. The fact that both owners were sleeping with the girl made it worse. 'There's no way they'd believe me over her,' F fretted. 'I'd lose my job for sure.'

Even if the owners did believe Francis, there was no way they would sack the girl. While sleeping with her, both were engaged to other women, whom they later married. She could easily expose their dirty little secrets if they tried to get rid of her.

Eventually I persuaded F that he should call one of his bosses and tell him about the situation.

'Honesty's the best policy,' I said. 'If someone was stealing from you, you'd want to know about it. It's not narking; it's just covering your own back.'

So Francis arranged to meet one of his bosses one evening after work, and told him everything he knew.

'It's been going on for months,' he told the boss.

'Well, Francis,' the boss said, 'what do you want to do?'

Francis replied that he didn't know.

'Well,' said his boss, 'I guess you'd better leave then. I'll take two weeks' notice.'

Francis was devastated, and the whole experience left us both with a sour taste about the realities of the fashion industry. That particular label was well respected across the industry, but Francis had been disappointed to discover they were copying many of their garments from overseas magazines. In their workroom were huge stacks of fashion magazines, the pages marked with flags to indicate which designs were to be copied.

Honesty, it seemed, was in short supply. These so-called designers were brazenly copying other people's ideas — so perhaps it was justice, in some way, that their employee was stealing from them. Francis had tried to tell the truth, and had lost his job as a result.

He was similarly unlucky at another of his jobs. After about six months in the store, also on High Street, the general manager sacked him. 'We believe you've been selling drugs,' she said. Francis was flabbergasted.

'Are you mad?' I asked when Francis told me what had happened, so gobsmacked I actually laughed. 'Where the hell did they get that idea?'

Francis was the least likely person on earth to sell drugs; he had never taken anything stronger than a painkiller. Neither of us could understand who would accuse him of being a dealer, or where this preposterous idea had come from. We were both utterly baffled, but F quickly found another job; he was well-known in the industry as a talented and responsible employee, and nobody knew about the allegation.

A few days after the sacking, a man I'll call Simon — who also worked in the shop — came around to see us.

'I'm really sorry about what happened,' he said. Francis asked where on earth the owners could have got the idea that he was selling drugs.

'It's me,' Simon confessed. 'I've been selling drugs out the back of the shop.'

It turned out Simon had been using the back office as his own private dealing room. Francis had often noticed Simon ushering customers out the back to have fittings or pick up lay-bys, but he'd never imagined what was really going on. Simon was selling marijuana, even though he himself never smoked it at all.

Simon was the most delightful of people, an absolute sweetheart who made us laugh. He was great at propping us up, as Francis' old work-mate still worked across the road from us and would walk past the stores where we worked and shout abuse at us, or stand with a gaggle of friends and laugh. Simon was always a staunch supporter of both Francis and me.

'I should have taken the rap,' Simon said, 'but I really need this job.'

Francis was astounded that he had been so stupid. In retrospect, it was obvious something was up. He had often noticed that turnover was low, despite the fact so many customers seemed to be coming and going. 'We didn't sell much today,' he'd often remark to me.

When the owner had found out about the drug-selling, she had immediately assumed Francis was the culprit, as he was the newest recruit. Simon was the manager and beyond reproach.

Today, people would take this a lot further, but Francis didn't want to get Simon into trouble, as we considered him a good friend. The company was large, and the owner a formidable woman. It was a rare creature who crossed her, but she wasn't a bitch, just a professional businesswoman. When she learnt that drugs were being sold through her shop, she had no choice but to act on it.

That sort of thing is still happening on High Street today; drugs, sadly, are everywhere in the rag trade.

A couple of years later, I bumped into the owner of the store, and went to walk straight past her. I hadn't forgiven her for sacking Francis. She stopped me, and said: 'I want to apologise to you both.'

She'd realised F was no dealer, and deeply regretted sacking him. 'If you ever want any advice or guidance, just ask me,' she said.

I thought that was enormous, and I now have incredible admiration for this woman. Our paths crossed a few times after that, and her offer always remained open. She was big enough to admit she had been wrong, and she had the courage to apologise. In the fashion industry, that's a very rare thing.

17

A whole new world

In 1989 Francis and I decided to get married. We had very little money, but not a care under the sun — just the happiness of settling into our new life and planning our wedding. That was all about to change.

One day Francis came home from work to say he had taken a $100-per-week lease on a cupboard-sized shop space in High Street. I looked at him, incredulous.

'What are we going to do with a shop?' I asked. 'We haven't got anything to sell!'

'Don't worry,' Francis said with a benign smile. 'We'll find something.'

By now I had become used to Francis's big ideas — but this was terrifying.

It wasn't just the lack of savings that frightened me, or the lease we'd have to pay. There was another complicating factor: I was pregnant, and suffering. It wasn't just morning sickness — it was early-morning-mid-morning-lunchtime-evening-and-night sickness. I couldn't even hold down a glass of water.

We held the wedding at the RKS Gallery on Victoria Street on 20 May 1989, with a small gathering of close friends. The gallery's owner, Rodney Kirk-Smith (who was the father of Francis's friend and ex-flatmate Ginny), had offered us the venue on the strict proviso that we turned it back into an art gallery by the next morning.

On the morning of the wedding, nerves made me even more nauseous than usual, but I managed to hold myself together while Brent put my long dark hair up into an elegant chignon, accentuated with yellow lilies to match my bouquet. I wore a princess-line dress in navy, my favourite colour. The top of the frock was merino wool and the skirt was navy silk georgette, and I accessorised with navy opaque cotton tights and navy suede shoes. F didn't own a suit, so he wore a shirt and tie with a jacket and mismatching pants — and, of course, the big lace-up Doc Martens he wore everywhere.

Neither of us was religious, so we'd picked a wedding celebrant from the Yellow Pages purely because we liked her name: Rae Whale. She did a wonderfully over-the-top ceremony, complete with arching arm movements.

'I wish you lots of love and sparkles,' she announced, much to everyone's amusement.

There was no time for a blissful honeymoon; the following morning we returned to the gallery to do the dishes and vacuum, and then we had to set about getting our shop ready. It was at the back of the Century Arcade on High Street, next door to a gay nightclub, and was less than 10-square-metres in area. We needed to paint all the walls, rip up the carpet, install new lighting and have glass shelves cut.

Our savings totalled $500 and we were already having to pay rent, so we really needed to come up with a winning concept for our new store. We knew we wanted to sell interesting, quirky items from all over the world, and introduce some of our favourite labels to the local scene.

We knew the name would be important. We discussed calling it World's End in a reference to New Zealand's position right at the bottom of the globe, and as a reflection of the eclectic, international nature of the goods we'd be selling. Eventually, we decided there was no need to suggest New Zealand was some kind of backwater — it could just as easily be at the beginning of the globe as at the end — so we decided on WORLD. The capitals, we felt, gave the name plenty of impact.

To begin with, we didn't have any of our own clothes on sale; there simply wasn't room in the shop for a clothing rack. Instead, Francis made button badges, and I made peaked caps from soft fabric.

We had arranged to stock the work of interesting artists and jewellers, including many of our friends. We had Helen Holmes' handpainted drinking glasses (quite avant-garde for 1989), bronze jewellery and candelabras by Matthew von Sturmer, and enormous Fymo earrings and bracelets by the artist Tracey Collins. She had also handpainted greeting cards in oils, which we planned to sell for $5 — a pretty good deal for an original Tracey Collins.

As our funds were so limited, it was crucial to invest wisely when it came to buying imported stock. After arranging to bring in products we'd always loved, like baby Doc Marten boots and the British fashion magazine *i-D*, with its iconic cover shots of models winking at the camera, we went to a wholesale company that imported badges, jewellery and knick-knacks, and chose the items we liked best. We spent every cent of our $500 savings, and were both slightly shocked when all our purchases fitted into a small cardboard box.

I took the box home to the flat we were now renting in Mission Bay, and left it on the floor of the lounge while we rushed into town to pick up the rest of the stock from our collection of artists.

That evening we returned home after dark, and my heart nearly stopped: the front door to our flat was open. I thought we had been burgled. The idea that our stock might have been stolen, along with all our wedding presents, was more than I could bear, and I told Francis to go in and investigate while I waited outside, trembling.

After a few moments, Francis came out. 'Everything's fine,' he said. I ran across the road to the dairy and asked the owner if he'd

Century Arcade in High Street, 1989. Our first 100-square foot store!

Me, Sydney, 1991

Brent, Michele and models, 1991

Early 90s WORLD show

Third store in High Street, 1995

WORLD collection, 1995. Top to bottom: Geeling Ng, Natasha Stitchbury, Fiona Knapp, Hinemoa Elder and Kendall Simich

Top Francis, Pebbles, Anna Piaggi of *Italian Vogue* and me at Australian Fashion Week, 1997. Brent Lawler is in the background

Left At Sydney Fashion Week, 1999

Above Francis and Pebbles on the Eurostar on our way to Paris, 2001

Above left Francis and me in Paris, 2001

Above right Fashion lecturer Eddie Thornton at London College of Fashion in 2001. He still lectures there.

Right Francis in New York, 2000

At designer Zandra Rhodes' birthday party in London, 2002

Me and Jacqui Manning in Paris, 2005

Pebbles' first school ball, 2005

Our coach in Tanzania being unloaded after I peed my pants, 2004

Cris Roberts, John Reynolds, Francis and me at my party, 29 February 2008.
I was being told my bathroom was on fire!

My 12th birthday cakes, 2008

seen anything. 'The door's been wide open all day,' he said. I felt I was losing my mind — I immediately knew I'd left the door open myself when I had left the house that morning. I apologised profusely to Francis, blaming pregnancy and all the stress, and he was as gracious as ever, laughing it off. I still shudder when I think what would have become of us if all the stock had been stolen.

Even though the shop was the size of a shoebox, Francis had done it out so beautifully that it shone like a little jewel, with gorgeous displays and clever lighting.

'WORLD Opening Soon' said a sign in the window — but a few days before we opened we found nightclub posters plastered all over the glass. It wasn't hard to work out who was responsible — the insecure shop assistant (she of the Evian bottle) was still working in the area, and her boyfriend was involved with the nightclub in question.

Rage came bubbling out of me. I'd always been fiery, but now that we were running our own business, and our life savings and future were at stake, I was beginning to discover a new side of my personality: the hard-nosed businesswoman. I'd had enough of this girl's snide remarks over the past few days, and this was the final straw. I marched into the shop where she was working and asked what the hell she thought she was playing at.

'Oh well, Francis is a DJ, so I thought he would be only too happy to advertise my boyfriend's gig,' she said.

I mustered all my dignity. 'It's a shop,' I said in a low, furious voice, 'not a frikkin' space for billboard flyers. If you do it again, I'll plaster them all over your face.'

I ripped the posters down, then rang her boss to let him know. His reply took my breath away.

'I can't stop her putting posters on your shop window,' he sighed. 'She's her own person. She can do whatever she likes.'

'OK then,' I said; 'I guess you can't stop me putting posters on your shop window either then, which is exactly what I am going to do.'

I was deadly serious. I was prepared to glue WORLD posters

to every inch of his shopfront, even if it made me look like a madwoman.

He said two words to me before he put the phone down. 'Point taken.' The phone clicked, and no posters ever appeared again.

We opened the store in May, just after our wedding, and our first sale of the day was a $3 button badge. I could have kissed the ground underneath that customer's feet. She paid $3 without quibbling! I couldn't quite believe it.

Mind you, by the time I had wrapped the badge and put it in a bag, we had probably come away with a loss, but I didn't care. Those button badges quickly became chic — in fact, our first shoplifter was a young man who tried to steal one of them. Francis caught him, and we still pass him in High Street today. He's a lawyer these days, but we know who he is, and he always looks sheepish when we make eye contact.

We had always known there were plenty of eccentrics and weirdos in the fashion industry, but opening our own store exposed a level of bitchiness that shocked us. Perhaps naively, we'd hoped for some sort of collegial feeling or solidarity with other retailers and designers. That hope dissipated on our first day of trading.

'Is this it?' asked Rupert, the owner of one of the biggest labels around, looking around our store with a supercilious grin on his face. At that time, he was right at the top of New Zealand's tiny fashion market, and clearly thought he was pretty special.

I don't know how I restrained myself from punching his lights out. What possesses somebody to be so mean is baffling to me; he simply had no empathy for our situation as a young couple trying to make a start. His behaviour was transparently petty. Even if I were so insecure as to feel jealous or threatened by a competitor, I'd rather walk on by and let them get on with it than resort to childish sarcasm.

'So, Rupert,' I said, with my coldest smile, 'how big was your first store?' He looked around, grunted and walked out without a word.

I think that was a turning point in my life.

Rupert had no idea of the impact his conduct had on me, but I took his words as a direct challenge. Right then and there, I decided WORLD was going to have more stores and be a better design brand than he could ever imagine in his wildest dreams.

A few years later, he was bought out of the business, and he disappeared into obscurity.

In those early days, we were living hand to mouth. I've never been so broke in my life. Each week, our very survival was dependent on sales — if we didn't do plenty of business on Friday or Saturday, we faced having to close the shop and go back to our old jobs. We were living in our rented flat in Mission Bay, with a borrowed bed, borrowed couch, borrowed stereo, and borrowed TV. All we owned was a table and a sewing machine.

Gradually, our business and brand began to make headway, and we expanded from accessories and imported T-shirts into our own line of clothing. Each night after Francis closed the shop, he'd come home and continue working. He would cut the fabric while I sewed on our second-hand industrial machine, and it wasn't until the end of our first year that we could afford to hire our first full-time machinist.

We started making slogan T-shirts emblazoned with: '99% don't care what designers think' and 'WORLD peace now'. My favourites were the 'Fuck Fashion' T-shirts, which we retailed in our own store and through the NOM*d store in Dunedin. In those days, Dunedin was a very conservative city, and someone complained about our T-shirts to the police, who ordered NOM*d to remove them from public display. Of course, the controversy guaranteed they immediately sold out. We thought it was hilarious.

Our first pattern, number 01, was a jacket we made in denim, coloured drill, fun-fur, sequins and astroturf. We had wonderful fun; nowadays, everyone takes the business terribly seriously, but our philosophy has always been that fashion is about sending things up.

Soon stylists were coming in to borrow clothes and items for magazine shoots. The power of stylists might not be apparent to consumers, but within the industry, they hold the keys to success for new and upcoming labels. Any retailer or designer can buy advertising space in a magazine or newspaper, but the real buzz comes from being included in the fashion and beauty spreads. Money simply can't buy that kind of exposure; consumers are infinitely more likely to buy an item or recognise a brand if they've seen it modelled by some gorgeous young thing in the pages of a favourite glossy.

Fashion editors and stylists are always scouring the shops and visiting designers' workrooms to discover the next big thing. For example, the stylist for *Vogue* might be planning an autumn fashion shoot, featuring two models. He or she decides which clothes, shoes, jewellery and accessories to use, then contacts the designers and arranges to borrow the items for the shoot. It can be a logistical nightmare for both stylist and retailer — for any one shoot, a stylist might request three or four times as many items as are needed, to make sure things won't be derailed by changeable weather or tricky light conditions. The retailers need to make sure their goods are available and delivered on time, and that there's plenty of backup stock in the shop ready for when the eager readers come in to buy.

Neither Francis nor I had ever run a business before, and there were plenty of little surprises awaiting us. One day, I opened a letter from the tenants who had leased the shop before we took it over. 'We would like to come in and collect our front door,' the letter said. It seemed we had leased a shop with no front door; we'd simply assumed that the glass sliding door at the front of the shop was included as part of the deal, but in reality it belonged to the ex-tenants.

Francis panicked. He has mountains of creativity and determination, but he is not the most practical of men, and these sorts of dramas tended to startle him. I tend to become ever more calmly determined in times of crisis, and have a good knack for thinking laterally. I called the landlord, who predictably said it was not his problem.

'Listen,' I said, in my best tough-businesswoman voice, 'you have leased us a doorless shop. I am not happy. You need to fix it.'

He backed down, and in an instant we had not only a new door, but a growing sense of pride in our little adventure. It seemed we were going to make it.

18

Pebbles

Pregnancy did not agree with me. I was ill from day one, and felt thoroughly unwell for the entire nine months, as we struggled through the stressful early days of our business. Midway through the pregnancy, I became so ill I couldn't even get out of bed. Francis called my doctor, but he said there was nothing to worry about. Never one to be easily put off, Francis rang his own doctor, a brilliant general practitioner called Denise Cooper.

As soon as Denise saw me, she called an ambulance. I was seriously dehydrated, and needed to be put on a drip as soon as I got to hospital. Slowly I regained my energy, and I left hospital feeling much better.

I'd love to be able to say the birth of our baby was a magical moment, but in truth it was horrific. I had two epidurals, gas, forceps, and goodness knows what else. I thought my back was breaking in half. But the minute I saw my baby's little face, I fell in love. That moment is imprinted forever on my brain; I will never forget the beauty of the pink, scrunched little person who suddenly appeared before me.

'It's a girl!' said the doctor.

I couldn't believe it. 'Are you sure?' I slurred through the anaesthetic haze. I had been convinced I was having a boy. Despite the misery of nausea, I had felt very in tune with my body during the pregnancy, and had told everyone with confidence that we'd soon be the proud parents of a son. I had chosen two names, Jarvis and Jasper — we had decided that if we had a boy, I'd get to choose the name, and if we had a girl, Francis would have naming rights.

So once the doctors were able to persuade me that our baby was female, I said to Francis: 'You pick the name.'

'Pebbles,' he said. I loved it immediately. Everyone assumes we had some sort of odd fascination with the Flintstones cartoon character — but in fact Francis simply wanted a unique name.

'I want her to stand out and be remembered,' he said. 'I never want her to have to say her surname — there will only be one Pebbles.'

So Pebbles Maria Alice L'Estrange-Corbet Hooper she became — Pebbs for short. Maria was Francis's beloved Hong Kong grandmother, and my mother chose Alice in honour of a favourite great-aunt. It's certainly a mouthful, and Pebbles gets infuriated every time we travel overseas, as there's never enough room on official forms for all those names. But apart from a brief period when she was three years old and insisted on being called Mary, Pebbles has always loved her name.

From the very beginning, Francis and I were doting parents. Pebbles has always come first — for me, that's what being a mother is all about. I didn't see the point of having a nanny; I wanted to be a big part of my daughter's life.

I continued working from the tiny spare bedroom in the house, but we imposed a regimented schedule that gave us lots of family time together. Every day, Francis finished work at 6pm and got the bus home. We would have dinner and bathe Pebbles together, then I would give her a final feed and we'd put her to bed at 7.30. Luckily, she has always loved her sleep, and would wake only once for a midnight feed. I'd change her nappy and she'd go straight back to sleep.

We had borrowed a cot from a friend, an old-style one with

wooden slats, each of which I had painted in a different primary colour: red, yellow, green and blue. Before Pebbles was born, Francis, who has never been known as a handyman, announced he was going to assemble the cot. It looked solid and convincing enough, but one night after we had put Pebbs to bed I heard a huge crash and ran into the bedroom she was sharing with us. Her cot had completely collapsed, the four sides all parting company, and baby Pebbs had been catapulted out — but luckily, she had landed on our bed. I was so relieved she was unhurt, but so cross that the cot had collapsed.

'You are banned from ever doing stuff around the house,' I bellowed at poor Francis, cradling the baby in my arms. Many years later, I forgot about the ban and bought him a cordless drill — but the only time it ever gets charged is when I need to use it. F is a creative genius; I can't expect him to be a handyman as well.

As Pebbles grew, we had an unspoken rule that we always ate breakfast and dinner together as a family, and we would talk about what had happened to us that day. We spent a lot of time teaching Pebbs good manners, and we've been firm about our opposition to drugs. As a teenager, Pebbs has told us she has been offered drugs. I always knew this would happen; any young woman who is out and about is inevitably going to find drugs on offer. All we can do is trust her good judgement; Pebbs knows it would be a massive disappointment to us if she were to experiment with illicit substances, and all bets with regard to anything would be off.

F has always been the most patient father imaginable. He has never smacked her once. If she was being particularly naughty, I'd just have to say, 'I'll tell Daddy,' and she would immediately behave. On the few occasions F had to remonstrate with Pebbs, she'd just fall to pieces. She looks up to him so much; he never shouts at her and is always calm when he explains why he wants her to do something.

Today, as Pebbles reaches late adolescence, they still have a wonderful friendship. When we're overseas they shop like whirling dervishes together, and they share a consuming passion for music;

Francis DJs once a week on Auckland radio station George FM, and he and Pebbs often get on the Technics turntables at home. A couple of times a week, they'll go out and and have dinner together (usually sushi, another shared passion — I'm a vegetarian so it's not my thing). Although Pebbs can wrap F around her little finger, I'm hugely proud that they have such an authentic bond. He is a great sounding board for her as she begins forging her own career in fashion, as a stylist and assistant.

I wanted to record all the precious moments of Pebbles' childhood, so I bought a big old tin trunk and called it the 'First Trunk'. In it I put Pebbles' first drawing, first pair of shoes, first romper suit, first favourite toy, first ballet shoes . . . everything. I wrapped each item in acid-free tissue and labelled it, and it's all still there, ready for the day she wants to look back and remember.

She's a gifted artist, and has always drawn and sketched. She had her first exhibition at the age of eleven, and sold 37 of the 40 artworks she had created. Even as a little girl, she had a wonderful imagination. Her favourite toy was a knitted badger that had lost one of his button-eyes, and Pebbles would often ask me how we got him.

'He came into the garden one day,' I'd say, 'looking for a home, because he didn't have a family. He asked all the local wildcats and birds where he should go to find someone to love and care for him — and all the animals shouted "You have to go to Pebbles Hooper's house, she will love you." So he knocked on our door, rather sheepishly, and you took him in and gave him a home.'

Pebbs loved that story, and believed it, and Badger is in the trunk.

Our parenting philosophy has always been that Pebbles has to be happy. We have indulged her, but we've always sought to help her understand the importance of personal happiness.

'When you make decisions,' we have told her, 'you have to decide if what you're going to do will make you happy.'

There's a reason for that focus on happiness. Although we fell madly in love with our little girl from the first moment, Pebbles' birth had an unforeseen consequence on our lives — my depression became worse than ever. After her birth, the black days really kicked in fully. Even though I had a loving husband, a business and a beautiful baby, there were many days when I couldn't stop crying. I was incapacitated with misery.

What on earth could make a young mother so desperate? After a great deal of reflection, I've come to realise that parenthood forced me to confront the pain of my own childhood. As I watched Pebbles grow, I couldn't help but recall flashes of my early years — the torment of living with Gran; my loneliness; desperately missing my father and, worst of all, constantly fearing the evil forces that danced around the edges of my consciousness.

But now, as a mother, I knew I couldn't let the demons take over my life. Now, I had a gorgeous, tender little person to take care of. Pebbles looked up to me and loved me unconditionally, and I knew I had to take care of myself for her sake.

I mustered all my courage and went to see Denise Cooper, the doctor who had taken such good care of me during my pregnancy. Sitting in Denise's surgery, I poured out my heart, telling her all the details of the unhappiness I was feeling.

In those days, mental illness was never spoken about in polite society. The only experience I had of anything like this was the poor deranged old men in the mental hospitals near our home in Tooting — those shuffling old ghosts who wandered the streets in their dressing gowns.

I had no idea what Dr Cooper would say when I told her my story. Would she think I was a bad mother? Did anyone else feel the same way? Denise sat quietly and listened to everything I had to say, nodding her head.

When I finally ran out of words, Denise spoke. 'You have depression,' she said.

19

Nuts

As soon as I heard the word 'depression'
a massive wave of relief washed over me.

Finally, it had a name. The mysterious *it* that had been festering inside me for so long was suddenly visible, tangible — and maybe, understandable.

At last, I could stand back from my emotional turmoil and recognise it as something distinct from me, something that could be analysed and discussed and — miraculously — treated.

Dr Cooper prescribed antidepressant medication for me, and explained how we would probably have to try many types of treatment before we found the right combination. 'We have plenty of ways to help you deal with this,' she said, in a calm, clinical voice.

Denise's manner was enormously comforting — I had shared my innermost secret with her, and instead of recoiling in shock or telling me I was an ungrateful, selfish mother, she was responding as though this were just another ailment that we could treat. I had never thought of it in those terms.

Thus began the long, slow effort to gain control over the beast.

Denise is the most fantastic doctor I've ever had. With

unfailing patience, she has guided me through many years of diagnosis and treatment. Since that initial diagnosis I've taken every antidepressant drug on the market — I often joke that I've tried every remedy short of a frontal lobotomy.

Not all of it has worked, and at times I have been incredibly frustrated, but I've learnt that all you can do with depression is try to get some kind of control. It will never go away, but with the assistance and understanding of caring professionals you can gain some perspective and insight into the condition.

I've had to change my medications frequently, because I've found the effectiveness of most drugs dwindles after a while. Nevertheless, I believe antidepressant medications have vastly improved my life.

I've also had plenty of psychotherapy. The effectiveness of any 'talking' therapy really depends on the practitioner, in my experience, and whether or not there is a click between patient and therapist. If there is a good connection, it is possible to be greatly helped by professional, confidential counselling. Although my three closest friends are always at the other end of the phone, and have given me constant support, I often feel hesitant about burdening them with my nightmare. Everyone has their own problems, and we're all trying to muddle along as best we can.

I've spoken to many kind and learned professionals, but I've also had a few bad experiences. 'You're not clinically mad,' one psychiatrist on Auckland's North Shore told me once. Well, fuck me, I knew that!

I didn't like that psychiarist at all. She was a cold, hard bitch — her attempts to probe into my mind seemed to dredge up feelings I had been working so hard to suppress for many years. After just one fruitless session, I threw my money on the table and walked out.

I'm unconvinced about the benefits of rehashing past trauma in the attempt to understand depression. For me, poking into the past can be more destructive than helpful. It works tremendously well for some people, and I think it's wonderful when people can find comprehension and comfort in examining past events. If it works for you, stick with it.

There are some mental health professionals who believe drugs are not a valid treatment for depression, and the only path to healing is talking therapy. I think this reveals a fundamental misunderstanding of mental illness. Depression is not a self-made prison we can leave by simply making a decision to think about our lives in a different way. No amount of psychotherapy can force the body to produce serotonin, the 'feel-good' chemical that helps our brain regulate our emotions.

Through all the years of depression, counselling and treatment, I've watched Pebbles grow into a beautiful young woman. She has a wonderful sense of humour, and makes F and me laugh until tears roll down our cheeks. I'm proud to have a good relationship with her — but I'm certainly not suggesting either of us is perfect. Pebbs has inherited my fieriness, and we have had enormous arguments. When we go for it, it can be pretty bad. I was the same with my mum, and sometimes it took every ounce of my being not to hit her when we were battling — it's a terrible thing to say, but sometimes parents can exasperate their children in the most insidious ways.

My mother would infuriate me by writing down all the terrible things I said to her. She would note the offending sentence, the date and time, and would get these notes out during every argument. 'Listen to what you said to me,' she'd say; 'Can you imagine how bad that was?'

Admittedly, some of my barbs were pretty appalling. 'I hope you die soon!' was one of my choice phrases, which embarrasses me enormously now. Pebbs has never said anything like that to me, but I'm sure she has thought it many times.

The one thing I never enjoyed in my childhood was unconditional love, and I've tried always to let Pebbles know how totally surrounded by love she is. She gets kisses every morning and every night. F and I both dread the day she leaves home. 'You mustn't get married before your thirties, at least,' we tell her — but in truth, we both know she has to forge her own future. All we really care about is her happiness.

20

Different by design

So what is WORLD's style, exactly? The arts editor of *Time* magazine, Michael Fitzgerald, once called it 'witty effrontery'. Italian *Vogue* creative director Anna Piaggi loved our 'originality and sense of risk'. Melbourne's *The Age* newspaper said we were 'relentlessly original, with a sophisticated, cartoon take on trends and colour blocking'.

From the beginning, we were deliberately different. Francis and I both liked clothes that combined bold (and often clashing) use of colour, and when we began designing clothes together, we used an eclectic range of fabrics and a mix of sloganeering and complex, detailed tailoring. We'd use tablecloth plastic, wall-hangings — whatever suited a particular garment best. The same season might include a jacket festooned with intricate ruffles, garments made from fluorescent fun-fur, and a cotton hoodie with a bold, simple motif. Brent Lawler has done all the hair and make-up for our shows — two-metre-high head-dresses, faces encrusted with crystals, wild hair, and always bold, brilliant colours.

I've always loved the fact that WORLD has such a distinctive sense of self. We've been on the periphery of what's called the 'New Zealand fashion industry' because we're so unlike the other labels in the market. Thank God for that. I've often thought that if you took a number of New Zealand 'designer' clothes, cut out the labels and asked the fashion critics and style writers to identify each garment, they wouldn't have a clue about most of them. With WORLD, there's no mistake.

WORLD stands for individuality and irreverence, and our clothes are an extension of Francis' and my personalities; we are WORLD. It's loud, it's brash, it does not care what people think — if you don't like it, or don't get it, you can bugger off. We are determined to be a leader in every sense — there is nothing derivative about our work.

We don't have any single source of inspiration. Ideas might come from a colour one of us happens to notice, or a shape we remember seeing somewhere. When we come to design a garment, we sit down with our sketches and work out how we can get the exuberance of our ideas onto paper, and then into three-dimensional reality.

Selecting the right fabrics is a big part of the picture. Our recent menswear collections have included ribbon-tied fur collars, bright yellow satin sashes and three-piece suits in multi-coloured checks. For women, we've featured high-waisted playsuits with long fawn gloves, jaunty little leopard-skin hats, and sexy, figure-hugging business suits in bright red cotton drill, accentuated with wildly coloured, narrow leather belts.

We're very fortunate to have our own retail stores, which we can use to showcase the collections to their best advantage, and exhibit all the wonderful imported stuff that Francis and I like to surround ourselves with. If we had to rely on our wholesale business, we'd have a big problem — coming into our stores is a wonderful experience for the customers, and they get a true sense of what we're about.

WORLD is not a store for everyone, and we often notice people edging up the stairs to the WORLDDeluxe store in Auckland, peering in the door and then retreating. Our use of colour and unconventional fabric can be a little confronting, but once customers understand the ideas behind our choices, they're guaranteed to come back.

Another great piece of fortune is that we're able to run the business without external financial backers. Because we don't have to consult anyone else, we get to pull all the strings ourselves. I've often thought it must be terribly frustrating to design collections with one eye on the financiers.

As soon as we began designing our own ranges in 1991, we found an enormous following. That first line was coloured denim, and we were selling easily 20 pairs of jeans per day in our single shop. New Zealanders have always had an appreciation for eccentricity, and beneath the conventional surface of our society is a delightful exuberance.

People loved the humour of our designs, and had no shyness about embracing the colour and varied fabrics we used. Although black always outsells every other colour by ten to one, sometimes we just won't offer a particular garment in black. We love colour, and some items really look exceptional in bright fabric, allowing all the details to pop out.

Our customers have very strong personalities, and they know what they like. Like us, they prize individuality and appreciate the fact that we still do relatively small runs per style, so they won't end up at a function with ten other people in the same outfit.

We've often heard the view that our clothes are unwearable, or too outlandish — but the truth is most people can carry off a WORLD garment.

WORLD customers are creative people who mix in circles where a great deal of attention is paid to clothes. 'People are always coming up to me and asking where I bought my outfit,' they tell us. Our most loyal clients tend to have a determined way of dressing; they know they can expect our clothes to be different.

One who springs to mind is Bronwyn Monopoli, a glamorous 50-something with shocking red hair, who lives in Nelson. She buys all our ready-to-wear and really extreme garments. Whenever we do something really spectacular, we say in unison: 'Bronwyn will love this.'

We dress every member of one fascinating family from Marlborough, at the top of the South Island — mother, father and three daughters. They fly up and just shop for hours, trying on everything in the store.

We encourage the same spirit of adventure in our staff. Often customers will say: 'I would never have thought of looking at that, but I saw it on your staff and it looked so amazing I had to have it.' That's the WORLD person — someone who can experiment.

It's still important to do the plain black trousers. At WORLD, we never allow ourselves to forget that there will always be some customers who want classic items with our special twist, and we make sure we provide something for everybody. Although it's common for customers to take a few moments to adjust to our style, we find if they're brave enough to come into the store, they're usually able to find something that excites them.

At WORLD, we're constantly trying to keep ahead of consumers' expectations, but there are a few fundamentals we always keep in mind. Everyone wants to look good — and a woman wants nothing more than to be told she looks sexy, regardless of age or body shape. That's much more important than being told she looks cool, or fashionable, or young.

I'm fascinated by the way the emphasis on clothing and beauty has exploded in recent years; who would have predicted the explosion of a concept like the nail-bar in the streamlined, enviro-sound early noughties? They're packed to the gunwales with people having their fingers and toes chemically altered. In hair salons, blue rinses and perms have given way to hair extensions that look more real than the genuine article, and colours that would put any paint selection to shame.

Part of the reason we're still trading after two decades is our rigorous attention to standards. All our garments are quality checked at head office before they leave for the store — and I do mean every single garment. Not a lot of labels do that.

When dealing with factories, we are very strict about quality control, and supply all our own thread and zips so we can ensure the colour and quality. I've seen other labels' garments fall apart because of poor thread or fastenings used in lesser factories, but we don't ever want that to happen. Falling down on the last hurdle seems ridiculous to us — if you are going to make clothes, you have to do it to the best of your ability, and to the highest standards.

I like to compare it to a meal at the French Café, one of the finest restaurants in this part of the world, which happens to be in Auckland. They're famous for their fries — just as McDonalds is famous for its fries. Both recipes involve potato slices and lots of bubbling oil, but the similarity ends there — I don't mind paying the extra for the best possible product. There will always be a market for the generic, cheaper version of any product, but that's no excuse for allowing standards to slip.

'Does anyone buy WORLD?' Auckland magazine *Metro* once asked. The next month, the question had changed to, 'Does anyone wear WORLD?' Rationally, I know I shouldn't allow little digs like that to hurt me — after 20 years of thriving retail, the answer to both questions is obviously 'Yes', but I can't help feeling personally wounded when we are criticised. It's human nature, but I do wish the writers of such garbage would allow their names to be printed, though it's pretty easy to find out who they are.

I believe the WORLD label has always been misunderstood by the fashion media. There are plenty of critics and writers who think F and I are a couple of whackos turning out an endless line of garments encrusted in glitter or glass — too quirky, too inaccessible, gimmicky, colour-saturated, just plain over-the-top.

One accusation we've never faced, however, is lack of originality. That, I believe, is the crucial difference between WORLD and many other labels. We don't give a shit about the 'look of the season'. We keep an eye on everything that's happening overseas, of course, and know exactly what's the latest look on the runways of Milan and New York, but we've no interest in copying someone else's ideas.

I'm perpetually disappointed by the plagiarism I see in some other designers' ranges. I have seen blatant rip-offs from overseas designers on the covers of New Zealand fashion mags, and it is soul destroying. There's no thought in that — any twat can copy someone else's idea. Of course, we're all subconsciously influenced by what we see around us, but I believe it is totally unacceptable to disrespect the intellectual property of other designers.

I can't count the number of times I've hired new staff who have been shocked at having to work from sketches. 'But when I worked for Designer X, we just copied samples from overseas,' they'll say in protest. I tell them to get over it.

Some New Zealand 'designers' have even used foreign garments in their own promotional shoots, while they rush to copy the designs and pass them off as their own. That attitude disgusts me. There's an implication that the integrity of a garment is somehow less important than another piece of work — nobody would dream of copying a complete painting, or an album, or book, and claiming it is original work, but somehow in fashion it seems to be the norm.

I believe the magazine establishment is at least partly to blame. There is a generation of older writers, stylists and editors who seem to think a lower standard of originality applies to New Zealand labels — as if it is all right to plagiarise because we are geographically remote. In today's connected globe, that's not good enough. No longer can this industry assume that garments from Tokyo or Reykjavik are up for grabs — anyone with a brain can recognise plagiarism when they see it.

One fashion magazine used a cover image of a dress by a local designer which was, in my opinion, very similar to a Chloe dress. I couldn't believe it. The magazine seemed to be acknowledging the dress was 'inspired' by Chloe, and the suggestion was that this was a trend in international design.

But the unfortunate thing was that the original Chloe garment was on sale in a store in Newmarket, just a few suburbs away from the CBD — so if you can buy the original in such a small town as Auckland, why bother promoting something that looks like a copy? It beggars belief.

I have seen New Zealand shows where the designer sends out the same garment in different colours, and I think: 'And the point is . . . ?' We don't need to see every available colour — we want to see the styles, the ideas. Fashion shows shouldn't be like reading the Dulux colour chart — we can all go into the stores and check out the colours on offer.

If the lazy-brained magazine crowd can't grasp global reality, they need to stand back and let a younger generation take over — there are many magazines on offer today with bright young stylists who appreciate the need to promote individual, inventive design, and the old guard need to step down.

Similarly, I hope the young designers of today strive to be individual and trademark their own looks, rather than trying to keep pace with international 'trends'. Originality is essential if we are to sustain an export trade; New Zealand designers must have something unique to offer when they try and sell into European department stores and boutiques. Copies of foreign ideas won't cut it.

Francis and I often joke that we are both unemployable. We've worked for ourselves for so long, and we have such firm ideas about the way we like things done, that we can't imagine doing it any other way. We have a lot of skills, but could never be tied down to a nine-to-five routine, and we would be appalling employees. We're all over the place, coming up with ideas at odd times, changing the subject of conversation to a completely different one at any given moment, as the mood takes us.

Our staff are used to how we work, and accept it, but I can't imagine any other employer accepting this. For both of us, design is like an irrepressible urge: when you have that creativity in your blood, you can't switch it off, and it will come out somehow, whether it is through singing, writing, painting, cooking, or fashion.

21

WORLD in the 1990s

Within a year of opening our first tiny shop, the business was growing so fast we had to move to larger premises in High Street — and before long we moved again, to a 100-square-metre space at 25 High Street, ten times the size of the original store.

Those early years seemed to go by in a blur, but my abiding memory is how poor we were, even as the business continued to expand.

When Pebbs was just over a year old, in 1990, we bought our first house in the inner-western suburb of Grey Lynn, a working-class area full of draughty old wooden villas. The house was the very embodiment of the euphemism 'do up'; it was so old and decrepit it even had an outside toilet. I didn't like it at all at first.

'It's all we can afford,' insisted Francis, 'and it's either this, or renting for the rest of our lives.' We bought it, and with lashings of colourful paint and our eclectic collection of trinkets and accessories, we made it feel like a home.

F has a natural gift for decorating. He has always been extremely pedantic about how the stores look, and has the amazing ability to transform the appearance of a display or shop window by slightly moving a few items. By contrast, I can spend a whole day trying to arrange things in the store, and still leave it looking a jumbly mess.

Whenever possible, I try to leave the aesthetics to Francis.

As I toiled away in the workroom, F's natural gift for retail saw the shop begin to thrive. He always knew exactly what was happening, and was particularly good at catching shoplifters. One day, he caught a man stealing a pair of jeans. F followed him out of the shop and challenged him. The man sprinted down the hill towards Queen Street and ran into a café with Francis in pursuit. As the café's customers screamed and fled for the door, the thief bolted into the kitchen and grabbed a carving knife, threatening to kill anyone who came close. The police then burst into the café, and as they dragged the shoplifter out onto the street, he belted Francis, cracking one of his ribs.

Ever stoic, F returned to the shop and continued working — and that very afternoon, he looked out the door of the shop to see the shoplifter sauntering down High Street. He had presumably been charged and released pending a court appearance — all while Francis was still nursing his aching ribs. It was surreal.

All around us, the New Zealand fashion scene was becoming more and more sophisticated, with new shops opening and designers launching themselves into the market. High Street was a shopper's delight — but the customers had a few quirks of their own. For some reason, it seemed completely acceptable in New Zealand to eat food while wandering through the shops, holding a greasy burger in one hand and flicking through the clothes with the other. I can't imagine anyone trying this in London's Bond Street or Park Avenue, New York, but F was reluctant to put up a sign saying 'No food and drinks' — it seemed terribly tacky.

One day I was working in the store when a middle-aged woman came in eating an ice cream. I politely asked her to take the ice cream outside.

'I beg your pardon?' she said frostily, clearly affronted that a lowly shopgirl would dare to question her. 'I can't see a sign saying "No food".'

I explained that although there was no sign, we had a strict policy against food in the shop.

'I am a very good friend of the owner, Francis Hooper,' she sniffed. 'Did you know that?'

Trying to suppress my smirk, I asked her to leave — I knew perfectly well she was not a friend of Francis.

'I'm going to report you,' she said, storming out of the shop with her ice cream.

That afternoon, F called me, laughing his head off. The woman had called to lambast him about the rudeness of his shop assistant, whom she described as 'young and short, with very dark hair.'

'Please allow me to apologise,' F had told the woman in his most obsequious voice; 'I know exactly who you mean. We've been having a lot of problems with that assistant lately. This is the last straw. I shall fire her immediately.'

The customer was appeased, and hung up, thanking Francis for his understanding.

From then on, our standing joke was: 'Denise, you're fired!' Pebbles, who was by now a fun-loving little girl, picked up on this and thought it was a great laugh. She wrote a letter to our workroom assistant, Nicky, saying: 'If you don't do what my Mummy says, you are fried!' Of course, she meant 'fired', but her mild dyslexia meant she was not the world's greatest speller. Nicky ribbed her about it for years.

'Oh Pebbles,' Nicky would say, 'are you going to fry me?'

In 1991, we opened a shop on Wellington's Customhouse Quay, and over the following twelve years our Wellington business did so well we moved twice to larger premises. WORLD now occupies a 126-square-metre site in Victoria Street in the capital — so much bigger than the original shop.

By 1997 we had opened a second Auckland store in upmarket Ponsonby (which later moved to a site further along Ponsonby Road, which is more than twice as large as the original shop). The High Street shop had again outgrown its premises, and we moved to a 270-square-metre site at number 57, which we called WORLDDeluxe.

One evening as I was entering the Deluxe store, I noticed a man with long, scruffy hair coming out, clutching several bags. It was Steve Tyler, lead singer of the band Aerosmith (and father of the actress Liv Tyler). The giveaway was his fabulous pair of crocodile-skin boots: they were luxurious and shiny, with the spine of the crocodile's skin running up the centre of each boot. He wandered down High Street, completely unrecognised by the passing crowds.

Another star whose face became familiar in the shop was Anthony Kiedis of the Red Hot Chili Peppers, who spent some time living in New Zealand during the 1990s. He is an absolute delight, a charming man, and we would often see him in High Street, again completely anonymous. I saw him one day walking down the street with two bags from a homewares store, Deka; he had bought a kettle and toaster. It was a lovely normal touch — he was one of music's true superstars, but I'm sure the staff at Deka had no idea who he was.

One Saturday the shop staff called me to say a customer had bought five pairs of trousers and wanted them hemmed before he left town that day. The workroom was closed, so I went in and hemmed all the pants. The customer was Gene Simmons from KISS.

Comedian Lenny Henry, actress Joan Collins and musician Debbie Harry are all customers, and Alannah Currie from the Thompson Twins was a great follower of ours. We still keep in touch with Alannah, who now lives in London and does furniture design.

There was no doubt which star impressed Pebbles the most. When she was a young teenager, we got a call to let us know English actress Billie Piper, of *Doctor Who* fame, was coming in. Pebbs and her friend Jessica were hugely excited — they nearly suffered coronaries when she breezed through the door. She was so sweet to them, and they have never forgotten it.

Ever since the days of Crolla in London, I've loved meeting the celebrities who come into the shop. We never know who's going to walk in, and the nice thing about New Zealand's small size is that every visiting superstar ends up in Auckland, and every visitor to Auckland comes to High Street to shop.

Even as our business grew, both Francis and I knew the whole thing could collapse at any time. It felt as though we were keeping things together by sheer force of will. The strain really told on Francis; although I have the ability to put intangible problems like money out of my mind and focus on day-to-day tasks, F tends to worry things over in his mind.

F is also a total workaholic, so I wasn't surprised one morning when he awoke to say he had a terrible headache. It was a particularly tough time for the business; we had a $5000 bill which we were struggling to pay, and F had been agonising over how we could possibly clear the debt and continue to pay our rent and all the other expenses.

He took some painkillers and hoped the headache would go away, but the medication didn't seem to make any difference. 'The pain is just blinding,' he kept saying. For weeks and weeks, the headache refused to dissipate. Rushing around attending to Pebbles and the business, I did not pay nearly as much attention as I should have to Francis's pain — something I now regret.

'Denise!' he called from bed one morning. I was already up and about, getting ready for work. I came into the bedroom, and F was lying there looking stricken. 'I can't move my face,' he said. His speech was slurred and awkward — he seemed to have lost control over his facial muscles. I sent him straight to the doctor, and within a few minutes he rang me from the surgery.

'I'm being sent up to the hospital,' he mumbled into the phone. 'The doctor thinks I might have a brain tumour.'

I felt my stomach lurch, and immediately bundled Pebbs into the car and raced to Auckland Hospital. Francis had to fill in endless forms and we sat and waited for hours before anyone had time to see us. I was terribly agitated; the right side of F's face was completely paralysed, and we had no idea what might be wrong.

Eventually, we were called in to see a doctor. He had a Canadian accent and was the rudest prick I had ever encountered. He kept barking questions at F, who couldn't really answer because his speech was so badly affected. I asked the doctor what he thought was wrong, and he turned on me in a fury.

'Get out of the room!' he shouted.

With Pebbs in my arms, I walked out into the corridor, leant my head against the wall and burst into tears. What on earth was going to happen to us? We had no medical insurance, no family support, and certainly no money to hire a nanny or get any help with Pebbles while I worked. F was only 27 — was he going to die? For the first time in my life, I felt utterly useless.

Francis underwent a brain scan, but the doctors could find no trace of a brain tumour. They were dumbfounded, and conducted all manner of tests to try and work out what might be causing the pain and paralysis. Eventually, they asked if he wanted to stay overnight, but F said he would rather go home.

When we arrived back at the house, F went straight to bed, and stayed there for weeks. I had to run the shop myself, dropping Pebbs at a nearby daycare each morning and returning at night to collect her, then drive home to see how Francis was feeling. Each day I hoped for some improvement, but he would be in just the same position in bed in which I'd left him.

The sheets would be wringing wet. Francis was suffering terrible sweats, so I'd help him out of bed, change and wash all the sheets, help him in and out of the bath, then sit him up at the table and try to give him some dinner. Often, he'd fall asleep while eating, and I'd help him back to bed. I'd then put Pebbs to bed, work on all the stock for the shop, do the book-work, clean the house, wash all our clothes, rush out to grab any groceries we needed and eventually collapse into bed, well after midnight. I just went on to autopilot: running the business, looking after Pebbs and praying F would recover.

We had wonderful support from friends, especially two delightful women called Michelle Fried and Wendy Lever, who ran a café called Flamingos, across High Street from our original tiny shop. Michelle would call around each day and leave a cooked meal for both of us on the doorstep, and most evenings she would drop by again to see if we were all right. She was a lifesaver.

While all this was going on, F's symptoms began to morph. One day, his right ear suddenly began to change in appearance, turning into a huge cauliflower-shaped lump. It looked just like the ear of a rugby prop, all swollen and distorted.

We went rushing back to the doctor for more tests — and the mystery was solved. Francis had Ramsey Hunt Syndrome, a very rare condition that is a remnant of chicken pox. After a patient suffers chicken pox, the core of the virus remains in the base of the spine, and can develop into Ramsey Hunt at a later stage. If the patient gets very stressed, the virus travels up the spine, and can come out anywhere on the face, attacking the nerve endings, which just shrivel up and die like electrical cables that have been snipped.

The doctors warned that if the virus came out near the eye, F would go blind. It seemed to be emerging in his ear — and once the ear began changing shape, the headache left.

The absence of pain was a great relief, but F was weak and terribly frightened. His speech was still slurred and the side of his face paralysed, with his ear still deformed. There was no specialist in New Zealand who knew anything about Ramsey Hunt, which was referred to in the international literature as a '90s virus', suffered by young professionals with stressful jobs.

The doctors wanted to put F on some drugs that were then being used for AIDS patients, but he refused. 'I don't want to be a guinea pig,' he said. Instead, we saw a doctor in Mt Eden who administered injections of tiny amounts of gold, to help repair the nerve damage. The injections were excruciatingly painful, but F was very brave; he said each round of treatment made him feel slightly better.

We kept struggling on; F sleeping all day and night while I tried to hold the business together. By now, Pebbs was learning to walk and talk, but F was away with the fairies most of the time, and could barely focus his eyes on her. 'Dada sick,' she'd say, toddling around the house and climbing up on the bed to give him kisses.

Whenever F asked about work, I'd tell him everything was fine. 'We're coping,' I'd say brightly. I didn't want him to take on any more worry.

Slowly, F began to recover. His ear began to return to its normal shape, and the headaches had gone. Although he was totally drained of energy by the illness, the worst seemed to be over.

But he had lost his smile. Before the illness, F had the most gorgeous smile I'd ever seen — broad and brilliant. Now, he had lost all control of the muscles that controlled one side of his face, so smiling was impossible. It was very difficult to cope with; he became very reluctant to have his picture taken, and still today loathes being photographed.

We were a young couple in the public eye, running a hot new shop and constantly engaging with the media and public, but Francis's confidence had taken a big knock. His speech was still badly slurred, and even Pebbs couldn't understand him. He constantly sounded drunk, which is terribly cruel considering I have never seen a drop of alcohol pass his lips. F has always suffered asthma, so he has avoided booze his whole life, as well as all kinds of drugs and tobacco.

It all seemed so fucking unfair on him. Seventeen years on, F still suffers from the condition. When he is stressed, I recognise the signs immediately: he rubs the right side of his head and his eye twitches.

'Switch off, go and relax, let it go,' I tell him.

From the time of the illness, I have made it my responsibility to deal with the horrible stressful stuff of the business. Landlords, rents, leases and stroppy customers are all my domain — I don't want Francis to get sick again, and I have a much stronger constitution than him. It's probably because of my tendency to fly off the handle — my temper provides me with a release mechanism, but F has never shouted or sworn at me during our entire relationship, it's just not in his nature.

22

All's fair

Our industry can be incredibly bitchy. Since F and I first began, we've been continually surprised by the lack of goodwill from some of the other designers. I don't know whether it's inspired by jealousy, insecurity or both, but I have artist friends who say there's rampant nastiness and backbiting in their circles too — so I guess whenever artistic personalities are in close quarters, conflicts are bound to arise.

Whinging and catty comments are unpleasant, but we can deal with them. On occasion, however, the competitive spirit has extended into real nastiness.

One example related to our jeans. These had always been made by a fabulous outworker named Eunice, but as demand grew and Eunice neared retirement age, I began the hunt for someone else who could handle denim for us. It was a tough ask — over the years, increasing competition from overseas has slowly eroded our local textile manufacturing industry, and scores of small operations have been forced to close, meaning a sad loss of jobs and expertise. Francis and I have always been determined to be an entirely New Zealand-made label, but it's become ever more difficult to find sewers, cutters, embroiderers and all the other skilled people we need.

I had found the name and address of a potential new cutter in Westmere, a southwestern suburb where lots of contractors and outworkers have their workrooms. Due to my utter lack of geographical sense, I unwittingly drove down the street parallel to the one I was seeking. I parked outside what I thought was the right place and walked up to the garage, where I could see a woman with rolls of fabric, ready to cut.

This lovely lady, Shirley, was a fabric cutter, but not the one I was looking for. However, once we had worked out the mix-up and started chatting, she said she might know someone who could help. She gave me the address of a friend in Grey Lynn who ran a small denim-sewing business.

What a stroke of luck. Off to Grey Lynn I went, and introduced myself to Shirley's friend Mr Little, a contractor who made jeans for several labels. That didn't bother me — New Zealand's scene is far too small to expect contractors to work exclusively for one label. Mr Little was happy to take our business, and everything worked brilliantly — until Max Browning, a denim manufacturer, discovered that Mr Little was working for us. Mr Little told me Max was upset that he was doing business with us.

'Next time Max complains,' I told Mr Little, 'you tell him I said to fuck off and mind his own business.'

I couldn't see the problem — we had never demanded preferential treatment or tried to damage Max's business. We had simply stumbled across the same contractor, and a contractor is free to work for whoever they please.

About a year after Mr Little began working for us, he called me and said, 'I can't do your jeans any more.'

He said Max Browning had walked into the factory, picked up the WORLD jeans and chucked them on the floor. Mr Little told me Max had said if he saw any more WORLD items in the factory, he would 'throw them in the street'.

I was appalled. I couldn't understand why Max was doing this — we had totally different target markets. Our jeans were aimed at a very young market, while Max's were more conventional and boring.

Mr Little said he had to obey, because Max was his biggest customer.

'I'm really sorry,' he said. 'I just can't take the risk.'

So I went to Mr Little's factory and collected my unmade bundle of jeans. I was furious — it seemed to me that Max was simply trying to damage our business. I've always hated a bully, ever since my schoolyard days of standing up to the mean girls in Tooting. Max's behaviour was exactly the same: pure, naked intimidation.

How was Mr Little supposed to survive with only one client? What would happen if Max decided to use another manufacturer at some point in the future? Surely, Mr Little risked losing his business.

'I'm going to call the bullying bastard and tell him what I think,' I told Francis when I got home. Francis, who is always the calm one, said he'd call Max himself. F asked Max why he was insisting on exclusivity.

'Because that's what I want,' Max said.

'But what have we done to you?' Francis asked. Max said he would not discuss it any further, and put down the phone.

I racked my brains over what I could do. I might have felt a smidgen of respect for Max if he had been able to come up with a reason — but the only reason was that we were becoming too successful for his liking. He was an established businessman, and he knew we ran our business on a shoestring. He wanted to stamp us out.

After pacing up and down for a few hours, I decided to write to the Commerce Commission, the government agency that regulates competition and fair trading. In a long and detailed letter, I asked the Commission to look into this example of the abuse of monopoly power. But, of course, when the Commission began investigating, Mr Little refused to confirm what had been said.

'I don't want to get involved,' he said.

I then received a letter from Max's lawyer, saying Mr Browning denied all my claims and that if I continued making allegations, he would sue me.

I made sure Max knew he did not frighten me one bit, and wrote him a letter calling him a bully — the one thing bullies hate is someone standing up to them.

The last we heard of Mr Little was not too long afterwards. Inevitably, Max switched to another manufacturer — leaving Mr Little with no work and forcing his factory to close.

To this day, when I see him, he looks the other way. He can't face me — and I have absolutely no respect for him or his brand.

While all this was going on, we were surprised one day to receive a letter from Levi's, maker of the eponymous jeans, announcing they would sue us if we didn't move the position of the tiny cloth tab featuring our brand name from the back pocket of our jeans.

It seemed Levi's considers the tab position an essential part of its brand, and will stop at nothing to enforce its intellectual property rights, no matter how different the garment itself might be.

We were startled by the letter, as it hadn't even occurred to us that the label might infringe someone else's rights. Our white tab read 'WORLD', not 'Levi's', and we certainly didn't have any intention of copying a Levi's design. We were happy to move the tab — no biggy. It did seem odd, however, that an international corporation with a reputation for making very straightforward jeans would notice — or bother pursuing — an apparent similarity in our luridly coloured items. I'm convinced someone must have dobbed us in to Levi's in an attempt to make life difficult for us.

23

To market

The journey of a garment from the initial concept to the shop floor is far more complex than most people outside the fashion industry realise.

First, we come up with an idea. This is a continual process; whenever either of us thinks of a potential garment or accessory, we sketch it and put it into a file for the upcoming season.

When the next range is due, we go through the ideas, biffing out the ones we no longer like and adding new suggestions to the mix. There must be a coherent idea running through the whole range, so it all sits well on the rack and can be mixed and matched.

At the same time, we're constantly sourcing fabric and having it ordered, shipped and held for us until we need to cut it. All our fabrics are imported, as New Zealand has a very limited fabric-manufacturing sector. When each fabric arrives, we conduct wash and wearability tests to ensure it's right for the style we've envisaged.

Then we come up with a name for the range, to be included on prints and linings of all men's and women's garments.

We give a sketch to the pattern cutter, who makes the first cardboard pattern from scratch, and then cut the first sample garment from the fabric we intend to make it in. If we're making a special order for someone, we first make a toile, which is a calico mock-up of the garment. We use black marker to note any adjustments directly on the calico, and then transfer these to the pattern.

Zips are ordered in the right size, weight and colour for the sample garments, and then we select the fusing or interlining. This is crucial; if a fusing is too heavy, the garment will look like cardboard, and if it is too light it will not hang correctly.

The buttons are then selected, engraved with our WORLD logo and dyed to match the fabric. We order thread in the correct colour, and then the sample machinist makes the garment. As she works, she records exactly how long it takes to make each piece (these figures are crucial for our costing and pricing) and works with the pattern cutter to ensure it all fits together well. Many of our garments are very complicated, with several different fabrics, so the machinist and pattern-cutter work together to see if there are any modifications that need to be made.

We then do a rough costing on the fabric, trims and timings to see whether the garment is cost-effective. If not, we go back to the drawing board.

All the labels are ordered and printed, and each garment is given a style number and name. For each fabric, we order labels giving the washing instructions and fabric content. A model tries on each garment to assess the sizing, fit and comfort, and then each sample is presented to the design team. We examine the fit and style, and change anything we think will improve the design.

Once a sample is considered perfect, it is signed off by two people — an extra precaution to ensure the right sample is sent to the production team. The pattern-cutters grade each sample into the various sizes, and when all the samples are done (100 for women and 70 for men in most collections) we then cost everything.

All this data is collated into the 'Bible', a huge bound book we produce each season, with a full line drawing of each garment and all the components, methods, timings and costs — plus wholesale and retail prices.

We then shoot a lookbook, using the same photographer and make-up team every year. We hire one male and one female model, shoot several images of each outfit, and then choose the best shot of each garment, to be bound into a full-colour book.

We make four of each sample: one to stay in the workroom, one to be sent to Sydney, one to take overseas for selling and one for shoots. That makes a total of 400 women's and 280 men's sample garments.

Next we make appointments for all our wholesale clients to view the range. Each is given a full colour lookbook, line drawings and all the style names and details. We put their orders into the Bible, which never, ever leaves the workroon.

We host all our store managers on one day to view the range, flying the Wellington and Sydney Managers into Auckland to join us. We present the range to the managers, who order for their individual stores, just like wholesalers. Each manager knows his or her clients and customers best, so we give them complete autonomy on what quantities of each garment they will order. That night, we all go out for dinner and a get-together, which is always tremendous fun.

Then the mad production process gets rolling. All the fabric and fusings are sent to the cutters, with the patterns in each size. The cut shapes arrive back at head office to be bundled with the correct trims and linings, then sent out again to the machinists, with detailed instructions for the creation of each garment.

Some days, we have hundreds of garments arriving back from factories all over New Zealand, as all our garments are made onshore. If there are any problems with a factory, our Production Manager will visit the site to investigate and try to sort things out.

Every single garment is then quality checked in-house. Any flawed items are returned to the factory to be redone. If a garment requires buttonholing, this is done, and then the buttons are put on. There is no room for error — each style has its own button and buttonhole template.

When the garments arrive back, they are sent out again to be pressed, and then sorted on racks for each wholesale client and store, according to size.

Once a complete look is ready to go, the garments are each given a computer code, label and price. We despatch the garments on a carefully projected timetable so all the stores receive a complete look on the same day, and then we send out the lookbooks to stylists, stores and wholesalers so they can see what's ahead for the whole season, and how each item can be worn. If any style sells out immediately, we can decide whether to re-cut it (which in turn depends upon fabric availability).

All the while, the design teams have been sketching the next season's look, and the new samples are starting to come through so the whole process can begin again. It never stops, and when everything is rolling smoothly, the system is a joy to behold.

24

Winning ways

Before the days of New Zealand Fashion Week, the biggest deal in the New Zealand industry was the annual Benson & Hedges Fashion Awards. Everyone in the industry watched the telecast, even those who pretended to be too highbrow for such a populist event.

We first entered the Benson & Hedges Fashion Awards in 1988, as it was an amazing vehicle for launching yourself into the fashion industry. A lot of the leading names at the time were continual entrants, as it was seen as a very prestigious event.

In 1991 we again entered, and spent hours cutting and making our outfit before sending it off with the entry form, and waiting to see whether or not it was considered good enough to be selected. For just $70 you could have your outfit paraded live in front of thousands of television viewers; love it or hate it, the show was always watched, and well talked about the next day.

A fashion designer we knew at the time would always invite us over to watch the awards at her house, saying, 'We can have such a laugh at all the crap designs.' I never went, as I thought this was an awful thing to say — people worked so hard to enter, and regardless of whether or not you liked what they produced, it was just a matter of opinion. She would prattle on about how awful it was and how useless everyone was (compared to her) — I later found out that she also entered the awards but was never selected, which was probably the reason she was so foul about it.

We would wait patiently for the letter to arrive to tell us whether we had been successful or not, and when we learnt we had been nominated we were over the moon.

In 1994 we again entered, and this time we decided we would splash out and both travel to Wellington to see the awards. Since we now had a store in Wellington, we could tie in a visit to that as well. I was absolutely convinced that we were going to win this year. We got all dressed up and headed off excitedly to the Michael Fowler Centre for the evening. We sat in the very glamorous-looking audience, agog at all the famous faces we saw — it seemed like anyone who was anyone in fashion was there. Finally our section came on, and the runners-up were announced — we were not part of the winning team. I had convinced myself our outfit was good enough to win — how could it not, when the entry was called 'Jesus was a Samoan Woman'.

In 1988 Maysie Bestall-Cohen had called me and said she thought the outfit I had designed needed a hat. I stupidly went and had one made by a very talented but completely loopy milliner who must have been 90 if she was a day. As Maysie had suggested the outfit needed a hat, I was sure we were going to be in the finals, if not winners.

When the hat was finished we collected it one Saturday morning and dropped it round to Maysie's house in Herne Bay. I was sure when she opened the door she gave me that look, the look that said: 'You are a winner!'

When I look back, my naivety makes me cringe. That fucking hat cost me $250, which was a fortune to us at the time, and money we didn't really have. I was taking home precisely $296 per 40-hour week working in the fashion industry. But the thought of winning seemed too good a chance to pass up.

Looking back now, being older and wiser, I should have said,

'That is what I have designed, and that is how it stays.'

After we learnt we were not winners in 1994, I was so disappointed. Our tickets included entry to the after-show party, so we went along. I got myself a drink and stood watching. The party seemed to consist of a load of very old people in the fashion industry who we did not know, all getting wildly drunk and groping each other. It was horrible.

There were no such things as 'fashion designers' in those days, they were not revered like they are today. Of course, there were people around who made clothes —like Patrick Steel, Adrienne Winkelmann and Trelise Cooper, who had a very dowdy brand called Limited Editions — but there was no youth culture. All the people at these get-togethers seemed to me a bunch of old drunks. When we left that evening we said very little to each other, we were feeling so low.

The following year Francis said we should enter again. It was 1995 and the business had been growing steadily. We had moved three times in the past six years, each time to bigger premises, plus we had the store in Wellington. So we paid the $70 entrance fee again, filled out the form, and carried on with what we were doing.

A little later Maysie again called, not to tell us we needed another hat, but this time to tell us we had completed all the formalities, but had failed to deliver the outfit in time. We were in trouble! With everything that was going on, we had forgotten to make one! Of course we didn't tell her this — we just said we needed a bit more time. She told us we had to have the outfit to her within 48 hours or our entrance fee would be null and void.

I told Francis that we were going to have to let this one go. There was no way I was going to be able to get a pattern cut and make it up in fabric we had not even got, all within just 48 hours. But ever the optimist, F said we had paid our $70 and could not afford to lose it — he told me to go to Whitcoulls and buy some cardboard. So off I trotted and bought pieces of white cardboard, pieces of black card and a roll of raffia. When I got back to the workroom, F said, 'Make an origami piece on the mannequin.' I was a bit perplexed, as the body form is rounded and cardboard does not mould very easily around it, but I started playing around, using brown pattern cardboard at first. After a while an idea came to me, and I could see this creation appearing before my eyes. F and I both looked at it, and we drew a line here, cut a bit there, and when we were satisfied with what we had done, I set about cutting it out in the proper card. The top was in white card, the bottom in black card, and the shawl in raffia. We did not have time to think about shoes or accessories, as we had to get the garment finished and in.

Even though it looked easy, it was in fact very difficult, as there was no flexibility with lines. In fabric, if you cut it out a bit uneven, you can straighten it up in the sewing, and once it is overlocked you would not notice. But with cardboard, there was no sewing, every join had to match perfectly and no tape could be seen. I finished it late in the evening and left it on the mannequin, and when I walked in the next morning it took my breath away. I called Brent Lawler, who was working across the road in a hair salon, and asked him to pop up as I wanted his opinion. He walked into the office and said, 'Fucking amazing — what is it?' and I knew it was something special.

We flat-packed it and took it to Maysie's office in Queen Street, which was littered with racks and garments from all over the country. We handed it to her, and she looked at us and asked us what it was! We explained, and told her the sticky velcro pieces matched up, and if she worked on that principle, she could work it out. She smiled at us, and we asked her not to bend it.

We had entered the garment into the avant-garde section, and now we waited to see if it would be selected. When we received a letter saying we had been nominated we were very happy. We decided to travel down for the show with Pebbles, who was four at the time, and stay in a nice hotel. While we were getting ready for the evening we said, 'Let's pretend we have won,' and we stood on the bed laughing and pretending we were giving our acceptance speeches.

At one point Francis popped out to get himself a takeaway sushi, and when he came back he said he had bumped into the crew who were working on the show for Maysie. I asked if they had said anything, and he said 'No.'

I was gutted. If you were one of the winners, you were rung and asked if you were going to attend the show. If you said no, you were advised to do so. We had given Maysie all our numbers and told her she could ring us anytime, day or night, if she needed to. Poor Francis had been lugging around his Motorola brick phone in case the call came. But it didn't.

I was now feeling very despondent about the whole thing. Pebbles said, 'I want to go to Georgie Pie for dinner,' so we went off to Georgie Pie all dressed up for the evening, so she could play on the jungle gym. I told Francis that this was the last time I was entering — it was just becoming embarrassing. After Georgie Pie we dropped Pebbs off at our friend Margaret's house for the night, and set off to the show.

We had been given very good seats near the front, and as each section came on we guessed who we thought would win. The avant-garde section came on and we were thrilled to find we had made the final three. Francis said the winner would be a black dress, with a sterling silver necklace.

Then the winner was announced — 'Denise and Francis from WORLD'. We both remained in our seats, we were so gobsmacked. A woman behind us tapped us on the shoulders and told us to go up and get our award. We scrambled up and were given the award by Leanne Malcolm, and a cheque for $5000, which was a king's ransom to us. We could not believe it.

I later asked Maysie why we had not received a call, saying how embarrassing it would have been had we not turned up. She just said, 'You have to buy your tickets through us, so we knew you would be here.' But while we were sitting in Georgie Pie I had told F I did not want to go. He had again said we had paid for the tickets and we had to go — we could not afford to waste that sort of money.

After the awards show Tony Hart, from the swimwear brand Moontide, who was one of the judges, came up to us and said when he first saw our outfit the hairs on the back of his neck had risen, and when he saw it again the same thing happened. He said this had never happened to him, and he had fought hard for our entry to be named the supreme winner, but Maysie could not get her head around the idea of a piece of cardboard winning! The brand Insidious Fix won the supreme award, and later disbanded after one of the owners was found guilty of cultivating marijuana for supply.

We did not care — we had won our section. When we got back to Auckland we had the outfit placed in the window of the store, with the award. It was most definitely one of the highlights of our careers so far.

Being recognised by our peers was wonderful, and we were thrilled shortly afterwards when the garment was purchased by the Auckland War Memorial Museum for its permanent collection. We were so proud — especially considering the pressure under which it had been created. Later, when we were asked to design a garment for Barbie, to celebrate the Mattel doll's 45th birthday, we recreated the origami dress in miniature. That design encapsulated our philosophy — we might use unconventional fabric and take a different approach to the traditional parameters of design, but our tailoring and finishing is always considered and careful.

By 2001 our men's range was doing so well we decided to open a dedicated WORLDMan store on High Street, and in 2006 we opened a dedicated WORLDBeauty store in Vulcan Lane. We stock hard-to-find imported perfumes, candles and beauty products, and the concept has proved such a hit that we opened another two beauty stores in 2007, in Ponsonby and Wellington.

Our first Sydney store opened in 2003, in the swish inner-city Strand Arcade, and in 2005 we moved into much larger premises on Glenmore Road in Paddington, just around the corner from Oxford Street and opposite Ksubi.

In 2004, we had a big thrill — a retrospective of our work at the

Auckland Museum. We were first approached in 2002 by Louis LeVaillant, the Curator of Applied Arts, who said it was the first time the museum had undertaken anything like this. The curator of our show was to be Dr Peter Shand, a renowned art historian and one of our first customers. Over the years Peter had become a dear friend, and he was familiar with all our collections.

We sat down with Peter and went through all the stand-out pieces we had designed, which turned into an enormous job. It took months to trawl through all our designs and decide upon the pieces, then sort through our archives to see if we still had them. Francis and I had always believed that having things in storage was not necessarily a good thing, as so much money is tied up in them. So most of our garments had either been sold to the Auckland Museum, Te Papa or the National Gallery of Victoria in Melbourne, or purchased by customers.

If we didn't have a particular piece we wanted for the retrospective, we had to recreate it exactly. This was not a problem in terms of the pattern, as we have kept every pattern since number 1, which was our denim jacket. The issue was getting hold of the right fabrics, and we put our team, led by Lou Davies, onto the task. It occupied Lou for months and months — fortunately, we still had all the records of the trims and accessories, and where we'd got them from, so she was able to purchase or recommission what was needed.

At that time, a lot of our business was not on paper, but in mine or Francis's head. Peter was relentless in ensuring he delved as deeply as he could to find out everything he needed. The nights were long and late, as Peter sat and interviewed us as we had never been interviewed before for the museum catalogue to accompany the exhibition. All the while, Lou sat at her desk and trawled through all the archives to find the things we needed. Having been with us for so long, she remembered a lot of things we had forgotten, which was a godsend.

I had several meetings with the museum organisers about who was to open the show. They wanted Pieter Stewart from New

Zealand Fashion Week, but I suggested the Prime Minister. The museum people just laughed at me, but I emailed the PM myself and said: 'Wanna open our show?'

Helen Clark said yes immediately — and in the speech she gave at the opening she said it was so unusual to get an email out of the blue that she decided to do it, because of my pure cheek! I was chuffed to bits.

For the opening night I asked that the front pillars of the museum be lit in a different colour, and they looked magnificent. The evening was clear and balmy, and the museum was packed. The exhibition, featuring 151 of our outfits, ran for four months and was a tremendous success, with thousands of people coming though the doors. We were told the students and staff of every fashion school in the country arrived at some point to be taken through. The exhibition was entitled 'We Fought Fashion and Lost: A WORLD Retrospective 1989–2005'.

For us, being recognised by 'the establishment' in this way was a tremendous honour. WORLD has always gone its own way, and we have never done things for the sake of being acclaimed. Two years previously I had received an award from the Queen, and now we had a major show at a mainstream museum. Suddenly, it felt like we were accepted.

25

Showtime

For a designer, there's nothing more exciting than seeing creations being strutted down the catwalk. The lights, the music, the models — there's a glamour about live fashion that's utterly thrilling.

Runway shows are always hugely expensive and traumatic to stage, costing tens of thousands of dollars and many grey hairs and restless nights. There are always dramas with venues, models, garments, accessories and the trillion other little details that can go wrong at any time, whether you are staging a stand-alone show or participating in a fashion week somewhere around the world. For me, one of the greatest trials is dealing with the fashion media, a tantrum-prone breed of individuals of wildly divergent talents, some of whom seem to think they have morphed into Anna Wintour.

WORLD's first proper show was the Corban's Fashion Collection in 1995. By this time, we had lost the regular showcase of the Benson & Hedges Fashion Awards (which had been rebranded under the Smokefree banner, then folded). We approached Pieter Stewart, a well-known fashion identity who was running the Corban's show, and asked if we could be involved. Pieter, an elegant and friendly woman, came to visit us at our workroom in

High Street, and although I've no idea whether or not she liked our work, she was very welcoming.

The collection ran over three nights, with shows for the general public on the first two evenings and a final show just for invited guests and media. One of the nights was filmed for a television broadcast, but all three shows had to be identical. We decided to do a tightly focused show, with just six outfits, each of which was intended to make a big impact. We didn't tell Pieter any of our plans — and to her credit, she never demanded any information. She was happy to trust us to do something impressive.

In 1995 the world was abuzz with news that the French were threatening to resume nuclear testing in the Pacific. In nuclear-sensitive New Zealand, this was a hugely controversial issue, and everyone we knew was outraged that France was preparing to use our peaceful backyard for experimenting with atoms.

We decided to make a statement, and pulled in several model friends, including Kendall Simich, Fiona Knapp, Geeling Ng and Hinemoa Elder, who was the wife of TVNZ broadcaster Paul Holmes, and two other models, Janine and Natasha.

We asked Brent to do the hair and make-up, and he was assisted by a burly Samoan drag artist named Harold Samu, also known as Bertha. Harold performed in a drag duo known as 'Buckwheat and Bertha', and although Brent was a bit apprehensive about working with someone he had never met before, we knew they'd have a great creative spark together. Harold is hugely intelligent, with a PhD in something or other, and has the sharpest wit of anyone I've ever met. He and I are constantly engaged in verbal one-upmanship. He spins on his own axis, but he's a real professional, and we knew he would be able to work productively with Brent.

At 10 o'clock on the morning of the first show, Brent and the girls arrived, and started working. In rolled Harold, all two metres of him, and before long we were all rolling about laughing. Brent is also very quick-witted, with an acid tongue, and the models gave as good as they got. With other designers fussing around preparing their shows, there was a rather tense environment around us, and we were asked many times to keep the noise down. The show started at 7pm, and we used every one of those nine hours to bring to life the elaborate concept Francis and Brent had come up with.

Backstage at the Auckland Town Hall we had our own room, as we were the only designers to engage our own models and hair-and-makeup team. We always wanted to do our own thing, and although some of the other designers were a little miffed that we were getting 'special treatment', Pieter was very happy to lock us in a room of our own. I dislike people gawping at us; none of us work well like that.

F and I were excited and apprehensive. We'd never done a show for television before, and we were determined to keep our ideas a secret until they actually burst onto the runway at showtime.

The garments were all vastly different. For Kendall, we made a skirt and shirt of a flock fabric emblazoned with the face of Elvis Presley; Geeling was in trousers and a shirt made from a photographer's backdrop showing fields of brightly coloured tulips, and Fiona was in the shortest skirt we have ever made, with a shirt depicting Jesus. I cut the Elvis and Jesus outfits by hand, painstakingly matching up the two large faces, so when the model's shirt was buttoned up it formed a composite face.

To the sound of sixties icon Donovan singing 'Hurdy-Gurdy Man', Natasha strode out wearing a full-circle, knee-length skirt with a blouse completely covered in bright blue sequins, layered over an orange organza top, also sequinned. Next came Janine, in a trouser-suit covered in white sequins, which didn't show up too well on TV (a fast lesson for us in the basics of designing for the camera).

For the finale, we pulled out our political trump card. We had made Hine a floor-length sleeveless dress, using a photographer's backdrop depicting a Pacific Ocean scene of blue water, palm trees and sand. I had engaged a florist to make a flax crown, and we put Hine in jandals, the distinctively New Zealand footwear known in Australia as 'thongs' and everywhere else as 'flip-flops'. In her hands was a huge New Zealand flag, overprinted with 'NUCLEAR

Empire Strikes Back show at the Auckland Town Hall, 2002

In the workroom and backstage at the Northern Club at New Zealand Fashion Week, 2003. The show was called 'I don't like sport but I can high-jump'.

This page and next New Zealand Fashion Week, 2003

Above WORLD Winter, 2003

WORLD collections across the years

This page and next Air New Zealand Fashion Week, 2004 at Ara Lodge, a Freemason lodge in Airedale Street, Auckland

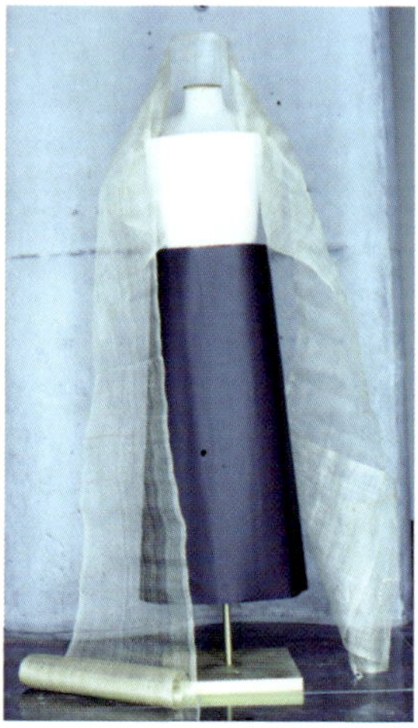

At the launch of the Retrospective of World at the Auckland Museum in 2005

FREE FASHION' in bright yellow letters.

When Hine emerged into the lights the crowd erupted in cheers, giving us a standing ovation. It might sound big-headed, but I really knew from that moment that we had a knack for putting on seriously good shows. It was an enormous buzz. Nevertheless, by the end of the third night, we were all knackered.

A few days later Brent called and invited us to dinner at a restaurant in Ponsonby. 'I want you to meet my new boyfriend,' he kept saying.

'Who is it?' I kept asking. I knew he hadn't been seeing anyone lately.

'You'll find out at dinner,' he said mysteriously.

We arrived at the restaurant and were drinking and chatting when I saw a huge figure stride through the door. 'Oh my God,' I said, 'there's Harold!' and called him over.

When he sat down at the table and looked meaningfully at Brent, the penny dropped — this was the new boyfriend. I was astounded. Their relationship did not last long, but their friendship is solid to this day. Harold went to work for Brent in Sydney and looked after all his shoots and engagements for years. He has also visited him in New York, and I was glad to have introduced this utterly odd couple.

The following year the collection, now sponsored by the hair company Wella, was held at the ASB Stadium in Kohimarama, a beachside suburb south of the harbour. We again used six looks, but this time it was all boys. The models were all the most gorgeous-looking young men, including a well-known artist, Reuben Paterson. For the finale we wanted a real blockbuster, so we decided to use drag queens.

Now this was in 1996, and drag queens had never been on national television. We asked Harold and his performance partner Edward (of Buckwheat and Bertha fame) to model for us. Harold was 'Madame Butterfly', with an amazing black polystyrene wig made by Brent, and Edward was 'Miss World', with long, natural-looking blonde tresses.

'You're taking a big risk,' Pieter warned us. She was concerned New Zealand television might not be ready for a prime-time onslaught of drag queens, and worried about the controversy the show would generate. We didn't care either way. If the bigwigs at TVNZ refused to show our strapping lads, we couldn't do anything about it. All we cared about was creating a fantastic show for the live audience in the stadium.

Harold's full-length dress was in yellow and orange swirls, with splits up the side, and huge butterflies swarmed all over him, including his boots. Edward was in a full-length silver glitter dress with a sash reading 'Miss World'. When they came out the cheers were deafening, and the boys were clearly in their element. The drag queen world is very competitive, and our two ladies faced off at the end of the catwalk, neither wanting to be the one to leave the stage first.

As Harold circled like a shark, Edward was smiling and waving his hands in the air. In full view of the cameras, Harold mouthed to him: 'Cow'. Anyone watching at home could easily have understood what had been said — it was a brilliant moment.

After the show another manufacturer, Bruce Wells, came up to me and said jokingly: 'What was the point of me showing? I might as well have gone home. My collection came after yours and nobody was interested. They just wanted WORLD.'

We laughed about it. The after-show party on the third night was great, and for the first time Francis and I were beginning to get to know lots of people in the industry. Until then, we'd been left pretty much to our own devices — others in the industry were never quite sure how to take us. The communal feeling of these shows was a great revelation for us; it was fun to be engaged in a common endeavour with our colleagues.

Unbeknownst to us, the audience that night included representatives of Mercedes Australian Fashion Week, which was then just beginning to gain steam. They liked what they saw. In early 1997 we received a letter from the office of Simon Lock, the creator of MAFW, inviting us to show our range in Sydney that year. We thought the letter was a joke from one of our friends, and biffed it in the bin.

A few months later the MAFW organisers rang us, wanting to know if we'd received their letter. I stammered and stumbled, trying frantically to think what I'd done with it. 'We've chosen four New Zealand brands to participate in our New Generation show,' the organisers told us. The others were Zambesi, Moontide and a brand I can't remember. Moontide, the swimwear label, was owned by Tony Hart, one of the judges who had awarded us the 1995 Benson & Hedges award.

This was the first time any New Zealand designers had been asked to show internationally, and we were very honoured to be invited — but we were way behind the eight ball. Since I'd thrown out the original letter we'd given no thought to preparing a show, so we hadn't a minute to waste in preparing the requisite fifteen outfits for our show.

As ever, we wanted them to be spectacular, and now that we were representing the country on the world stage we felt an extra incentive to do something thrilling. We made suits for men from Sanderson furnishing fabrics, and gave our male and female models little raffia bonnets, perched precariously on their heads and tied with bright satin ribbon. We also did leather trousers and jackets, and I spent every spare hour sewing feathers onto four women's dresses we'd made. For weeks on end, I was up till 3am working on the garments, but all the drama was worth it — the Sydney critics loved our show, and suddenly we were an internationally visible brand, with a whole new continent of potential customers interested in our wares.

After the show, as we were backstage packing up, we were told somebody wished to speak to us. I turned around to see Anna Piaggi, the creative director of Italian *Vogue*. She proceeded to tell us our show was the best she had seen all week and that most shows put her to sleep! We were flabbergasted. We were part of a group show — we had not had our own show — and she was blown away. She wrote about us in Italian *Vogue*, and has since visited us twice in Auckland.

We kept going with the New Zealand shows, each time trying to come up with something even more exciting than the previous year. With each show, expectations rose, and we tried never to disappoint. In 1997, the theme was aliens, and we hired the avant-garde make-up designer Toshiro Takeda to create full prosthetic masks for our female models, who were bedecked in glamorous evening wear.

In mid-1998, Trade New Zealand decided that along with Wools of New Zealand it would sponsor four New Zealand brands to show at London Fashion Week: WORLD, NOM*d, Zambesi and Karen Walker. We were thrilled — to be chosen as a representative by the government's official trade promotion arm was a great honour. It soon appeared, however, that Karen Walker preferred to work on her own.

Karen didn't seem to show much collegial spirit. When we arrived in London, she set herself up in a hotel rather than work out of New Zealand House, where the rest of us were based. We were all happy to work together on things like model castings and meetings with hair and make-up stylists, but Karen did most things separately.

Karen had brought her own personal PR person, Michael Bragg, who had previously worked for Simon Lock, the creative force behind Mercedes Australian Fashion Week.

No opportunity for publicity was overlooked. TVNZ current affairs host Paul Holmes had requested an interview with Francis and me. F and I took the Underground to the studio, where we were ushered into a green room to await the satellite link to New Zealand. Suprisingly Karen was also there with Michael.

The shows were held at the Natural History Museum in Kensington, and WORLD was lucky enough to go first. Our show was called 2525. Brent had come to London with us, and our futuristic designs were set off beautifully by his fantastic little hairpieces, which could be whipped off the models' heads in a few seconds, ready for the next designer's show.

One evening before the shows I took my set square, pencil and scissors and went up to the magnificent penthouse that took up the whole top floor of New Zealand House, with a 360-degree view over London to make Origami shapes from holographic card. I later attached these with stick-on velcro to the black outfits to add colour. I just looked at the outfits and made shapes I felt complimented the collection. I was in the room alone and it was dark outside, with all of the lights of central London twinkling. There was a knock on the door and one of the people employed on the team came in with a friend, and asked if I minded if they hung out with me for a while. I said, 'Not at all, I would be happy to have company.' Then he took a package out of his pocket and proceeded to roll a joint.

I carried on with what I was doing, pretending I had not noticed, and the guy offered me one. I said no, as it wasn't my buzz, but I added that I thought it was odd that we were in New Zealand House, getting ready to represent the country, and a guy was smoking a frikkin' joint there! They laughed and asked if I minded. I said they could do what they wanted — if they got caught by security it had nothing to do with me — so they continued to get out of it, and I continued cutting out my shapes. I don't know what was in the joint but they got mighty high!

I love the atmosphere at a runway show — you spend hours getting ready, watching the models have their hair set and their make-up done, getting more and more nervous with each passing hour. I love going out onto the catwalk before a show, when all the bags are being placed on seats, and the guests' names are put onto the two front rows. It's all exceptionally quiet and serene, but you know that in a few hours the whole place will erupt into complete bedlam.

When all the sound and light checks are complete, the guests start trickling in, the photographers push and jostle for the best position at the end of the runway and, finally, the lights go down.

Francis stands backstage with his trusty stopwatch, ushering the models out into the glare of flashbulbs — and in a few moments, all the work of six months is over. A show can cost anything from $40,000 upwards, especially when you're into theatrical effects and flamboyant creations as we are.

The London show was a great success. The reviews were excellent, and our entire collection was immediately bought by Liberty and Selfridges, another venerable old department store. Both these fashion powerhouses understood us completely, and no New Zealand designer has managed the same feat either before or since. It was a great lift to our confidence, and it was especially interesting to monitor the reaction to that news on the New Zealand scene. Suddenly, we were taken a lot more seriously than ever before. I find this an infuriating drawback to life in the Antipodes — that it's only when someone achieves on an international stage that their accomplishments are appreciated.

26

'I don't do Row B'

Designers have always had a prickly relationship with the fashion press. London designer Alexander McQueen was famous for banning fashion historian Colin McDowell from his shows for a few seasons after some snarky reviews, which caused no end of fuss — the other members of the media rallied around McDowell and even many of McQueen's designer peers, who would no doubt have secretly loved to do the same, tutted disapprovingly. Personally, I believe McQueen had every right to do this. If I'm running a show, I can decide who gets in and who doesn't, regardless of how high and mighty they think they are.

It's a symbiotic relationship. Fashion writers and stylists need the designers, and although established labels might have the luxury of not worrying too much what individual journalists think, it's crucial for start-up labels and independent designers to be appreciated by the media if they are to make any kind of mark on the public consciousness.

In our two decades with WORLD, we've had generally excellent relations with the media, and have found many editors and stylists who truly understand our work and have been great supporters. There are a few women writers — and they are always women — who think for themselves and have little or no interest in what others think. They're the professionals I really like dealing with. In a small place like New Zealand, it's really important to avoid getting caught up in other people's fights. I tend to be very black-and-white: if you shit on me, I'll shit on you. I always make a point, however, of making my own decisions about people.

So while we've had some excellent dealings with the media, there have been some notable exceptions.

Journalists can be a designer's greatest advocate, or their most powerful critic — often in the same season. Anyone who operates a business in a creative industry is wide open to both situations. Writers, artists, musicians and designers are all in the same boat; we do what we do because we love it, but part of the deal is that we open our souls to the public and media and await their comments. Sometimes I find it almost laughable that people for whom I have little or no respect are in a position to openly criticise us — especially when they've no idea how we got to where we are, or what it's like to run a fashion business. It's very easy to sit behind a desk and say: 'I don't like that.'

I'm often disappointed by the lack of adventure in some New Zealand stylists and fashion editors. There are, sadly, a bunch of fashionistas in this country who have boxed WORLD as whack-jobs, and just won't make any effort to get what we're about. A good stylist sees all the designers and their ranges, and then works out what will work for them, but there have been some seasons at WORLD when certain stylists have simply failed to come and see the range. For them, it's all a bit too hard — they're so used to copying ideas from overseas mags that it's hard to cope when they see original ideas in front of their faces. Still they show us pictures from overseas shows and tell us how to 'recreate' the look for a fraction of the price, using pieces from 'New Zealand designers' who have copied the original ideas. It staggers me.

When Pebbles started expressing interest in working as a stylist, we instilled in her the need to be broad-minded. When she is styling a shoot, she will go to every shop and see what they have, as well as second-hand shops and everything in between. She then comes back and styles it all together.

Sometimes, Pebbles will refuse to use our garments. She doesn't want any appearance of nepotism, and I'm totally fine with this. I've never told her what I think she should do, and most of the time I'm blissfully unaware of what she's up to until it appears in print. She's grown up around fashion and fabrics, so I guess it's natural for her to want to be involved with the industry, but she's not interested in designing at present — perhaps because she's seen how unglamorous it really is at the coalface.

It's fascinating for me to watch how Pebbles works. Even at her young age, she knows it would be foolish to just stick to the old favourites — she might miss out on something really incredible.

It just baffles me that anyone would rule a certain designer's work out of contention. You wouldn't hear a restaurant reviewer saying: 'I'm not going to eat at that restaurant any more, because they used spinach in one of their dishes last season, and I loathe spinach.' Fashion's the same — consumers and the media need to be open-minded. There's always something on every menu to dislike, and that's because chefs cater for all types. Similarly, there is something in every range that a certain individual will not identify with. But if the stylists and editors don't keep coming back to try, how will they ever know?

Thank God, there is a new generation of stylists coming through the ranks that do not think like the old, boring guard. They are not afraid to see and experiment — they go in with both eyes open, as opposed to one. I'm excited to work with people like that — but as you'll discover, the old guard can still be pretty powerful.

When New Zealand Fashion Week began in 2000, again under the direction of Pieter Stewart, we were excited to be involved. We kept up our splash-making tendencies, staging shows with audiences of up to 1500, spectacular hair and make-up and — always — a huge buzz.

A full-on Fashion Week is a totally different affair to a small show — there are international buyers, media from around the world, and usually very few (if any) members of the public. It's an industry showcase, and there's a competitive energy that can be both thrilling and draining.

Dealing with the media, however, began to wear me down. Over the years there were many hissy fits and near-disasters involving members of the media, but the final straw came in 2004 when the then fashion editor of the *Sunday Star-Times*, Stacy Gregg, objected to being seated in Row B at our show.

We'd spent months preparing our show and were hugely excited about our off-site venue, the old Masonic Lodge on Mount Street, in the centre of Auckland city. I'd noticed the hall while driving past one evening, and had leapt out of the car, stuck my head through the door and asked if we could use it for a show. No woman had ever set foot in the main area of the lodge before, but the kindly gents inside were quick to agree. When I asked how much they would charge for the use of the building, the Masons nominated a sum, but said they would donate the entire fee to a breast cancer research charity.

On the night of the show, we couldn't wait to show our latest work in such an exciting space. We worked out a detailed seating plan, with four rows of seats on each side of the catwalk. The front rows were filled with our personal sponsors and international media who had been flown over by NZFW for the event. We decided that rather than split up the New Zealand media, we would seat them all together in the second row. One of the international delegates was a New Zealand-born model, Angela Dunn, who has done extraordinarily well overseas, and we decided we'd give her the best seat in the house, at the end of the runway. Sadly, we'd had to knock back her request to bring along her parents, who run a pharmacy in Auckland. I would have loved to have accommodated them, but we had a jam-packed house as it was. In the end Angela never showed up.

As the crowd filled the room, I could see the media were all in place. Then, just a few minutes before showtime, I noticed Stacy

Gregg walking out. 'I'm leaving,' she said when I rushed over to see what was wrong. 'I don't do Row B.'

I was astonished. I tried to explain that I'd had to give front-row seats to the international delegates and sponsors, and that all New Zealand media were sitting in Row B, but Stacy just didn't want to hear. She continued to gather her belongings and make for the door, while I grew increasingly frantic. It all seemed too horrible to be true — an influential journalist was walking out of my show because she didn't like her chair? I'd never heard of such behaviour.

I rushed over to Francis and told him what was happening.

'Fuck her, let her go,' F said. I was dreadfully upset — none of the time, effort or love we'd invested in the show seemed to matter to Stacy. In retrospect, I should have told her to fuck herself, and thrown her out on the street. Instead, I asked her to sit down.

'It'll be very embarrassing for me if you leave,' I said.

With a face like thunder, Stacy eventually sat down and watched the show with the other fashion mag editors, all of whom seemed to be perfectly content in Row B. After the show, Stacy was first out the door, and as she passed me I asked what she thought.

'It was great,' she said, rushing towards the exit.

I was fuming. A crew from the TVNZ programme *Sunday* was filming the show for a documentary on WORLD, and I walked up to the camera and let fly with a rant about what had happened. I didn't name Stacy, which in retrospect I also regret. To be frank, I would have enjoyed telling her to get fucked. That's what I should have done.

I wrote a letter to Stacy's editor complaining about her conduct, and pointing out that she was not Anna Wintour, and we were not in New York. A few weeks later, I rang Stacy to ask for a meeting, which she flatly refused.

'I will never forgive you for what you've done,' she said.

I believe that in revenge for my letter to her editor, Stacy published what I consider to be a vindictive story in *Sunday*, the newspaper's glossy magazine section.

The title of the article was 'Boars and Bitches'. The first part was a reference to another designer, who had sent her models out wearing boars' heads. I took the word 'bitch' to refer to me. The story didn't mention anything about our clothes — it was just a rambling narrative about my behaviour, complete with denials that our dispute had anything to do with the seating placement.

After the *Sunday* magazine story was published, the phone rang all day with editors from rival mags telling me how disgusted they were with Stacy's efforts. A former newspaper editor rang to say she would never have allowed her staff to write such rubbish. 'It shows a real weakness in leadership,' she said. Only two designers called me — Trelise Cooper and Cris Roberts (née Elrick) from the label Pearl. 'Today's news is tomorrow's fish and chip paper,' they both said, and I took great comfort from their support. I thought it showed great camaraderie.

I didn't really care what Stacy said about me, as my opinion of her couldn't have gone any lower, but I was irritated that she completely ignored the topic she was supposedly there to write about: the clothes. It also grated on me that she had used so much space to attack me — space that could have been used so much more usefully to write about some of the young designers who had shown at Fashion Week.

Another New Zealand journalist who seems to have misunderstood WORLD is Cathrin Schaer, who has written for various publications over the years, including the influential *New Zealand Herald*. In the late 1990s, Cathrin reported that our show in Sydney had feature models with 'clown faces'. I was staggered — in fact, Brent had made up the models with white faces, featuring cut-out felt shapes, including eyes and ears. It was a tribute to Picasso's paintings, and all the international journalists at the show got the reference immediately, describing the spectacular look in favourable terms in their stories.

I approached Cathrin at the Fashion Week venue and explained that they weren't clown faces. 'I don't know anything about art,' she snapped. Well, she got that right.

A recent article in the *New Zealand Listener* quoted Cathrin describing the clown-face incident. She said I had approached her in a Sydney restaurant and lambasted her in front of all her friends, which was completely untrue. I approached her at the Fashion Week venue, and I was polite and considerate. I'm not nasty or stupid enough to abuse someone in public. The whole episode was another example of how personal dislikes spill into the fashion media in New Zealand.

In 2008, I discovered another unpleasant side of the media's power. All of a sudden, gossip columns began printing suggestive items hinting heavily that I was having an affair with a younger man. I'd love to know who I'm supposedly cheating with — the truth is that I've been married for nearly 20 years, and I've never even looked at another man, let alone had an affair. The idea is just too preposterous for words. Francis trusts me completely, but to my enormous irritation I found myself having to reassure him that I was not having an affair.

'Of course I know you're not,' he said. 'I trust you.'

If I were having an affair, I would have no problem putting my hand up and admitting it. I'm upfront in everything I do, and this would be no exception — I don't tell lies. One journalist confided that I should feel very flattered to have people thinking I could attract a younger man, but I did not quite see it that way. I asked another journalist who commented on this farce to please let me know when she had located this young lothario, as I would love to meet him!

We're now highly experienced at staging international events, and have held runway shows in London, Hong Kong, Singapore, Sydney, New Zealand and Paris. The exposure has been brilliant — our label has been stocked across Australia, Europe, the United Kingdom, the United States, Russia and Asia.

We're happy working on the brilliant relationship we enjoy with our established stockists and loyal customers. They are bold and individual enough to understand where we're coming from; season after season, they continue to support us, and that is the most important recognition we could ever hope for.

27

The flipside of fame

As our business became more and more successful, Francis and I found ourselves the subject of a great deal of personal attention. For the most part, we loved meeting the public and revelled in the knowledge that our designs were appreciated. There was, however, a serious downside.

Like many well-known people, I had the misfortune to attract a stalker; a situation that seriously shook my confidence.

'You're a very hard lady to get hold of,' said a male voice one day in 2001 when I picked up the phone at work. It was the beginning of an ordeal during which this man, who told me his name was Steve, harassed me with innumerable phone calls, personal visits and demands for my attention. Somehow, he had become obsessed with me after seeing my photograph in the media, and had decided he had to get to know me. I'm still not sure exactly what he wanted from me — he made up all sorts of stories about having ideas for new garments and wanting to discuss the business of fashion — but when I declined to meet with him or take his calls, he became increasingly aggressive and abusive. He began making dozens of calls every day, visiting my workplace and ringing my friends and relatives, demanding to speak to me. It was clear he was never going to give up.

The police were unable to do anything to help. After I made a formal complaint that I was being harassed, they told me they had traced the calls and warned Steve to stay away from me — but because of the Privacy Act, they said they couldn't give me any of his details, not even his name or address.

The warning didn't have any effect; Steve just kept calling, over and over again. I decided to hire a private investigator, and within a day the PI had furnished me with Steve's name, address, occupation and a series of photographs of him; an unattractive, balding man in his fifties, who had a pot belly and a cigarette permanently attached to his bottom lip. The PI also told me Steve had been in prison on armed robbery charges. Fucking brilliant; this man had a gun and was after me!

Still, the police insisted they could do nothing unless he threatened to harm or kill me. By now, Steve had taken to coming into the stores and demanding to see me — and my aunt and uncle told of being woken in the middle of the night by a strange man who sat outside their house in his car, with the engine running. Finally, the police charged Steve with misuse of a telephone, and started driving by my house each night to make sure he was not staking me out. I was terribly afraid something might happen, and we began ensuring Pebbles was never alone, dropping her at school each day and picking her up in the afternoons.

The Steve situation did little to help my emotional wellbeing. I felt vulnerable, exposed and bruised by the whole drama, and even more inclined to withdraw into my shell. I was having immense trouble sleeping. With the help and support of my family and Dr Cooper, I was still pursuing medical and psychological avenues of treatment, but the mental strain of dealing with such a problematic situation left me with little energy.

While we were awaiting the court hearing, I decided to take matters into my own hands, ringing Steve's employers to let them know what their staffer was up to on the work phone. Next thing I knew, the Privacy Commission contacted me to say Steve had lodged a complaint about my being aware of his previous convictions. The Commission wanted to know exactly how I had obtained this information — which made me furious. I was the victim of harassment, and now I was being treated as the culprit.

Steve pleaded guilty to the charge of misusing a telephone, and was bound over for twelve months and ordered not to approach me. The matter had now been dragging on for a year, and just when I thought it was over, I received a letter from Steve's lawyer demanding a written apology to Steve, money to cover his legal costs, and $50,000 compensation for the humiliation and indignity he had suffered in defending the charges.

I explained the situation to a prominent criminal barrister who worked in our building, and he kindly offered to write a letter telling Steve and his idiot solicitor to go to hell. Again, I thought everything was over — but in early 2003, I was sitting at the computer in my workroom when all of a sudden Steve appeared in front of my desk. The court order had lapsed, and he was seizing the opportunity to finally come face-to-face with me. I was terrified. I stood up and ordered him out of the building, but he refused to leave, shouting abuse at me.

'I'm going to get you,' he screamed. Francis and two staff members came rushing to investigate the commotion, the police were called, and Steve was arrested and charged again. This time, the court ordered him to stay away from me permanently or face jail.

After years of no contact, he appeared again in 2008, out of the blue. He drew up outside my store in High Street, leapt out of his car, holding up the traffic, spat all over my shop window and got back into the car. When my store assistant ran out and demanded, 'What the hell are you doing?' Steve said, 'That was for the bitch Denise.' Again the police came, and went to visit Steve. I knew immediately it was him from the description, and I just wish he would bog off and get a life. I had no idea who he was before he started harassing me. It is just one of those things, the police told me, when you have a high profile.

In 2004, we had a nice reminder of the good side of fame. WORLD as a brand has always been very proactive with regard to working with charities. For three years we had a float in the HERO parade, which used to be held on Ponsonby Road in the nineties, and was such a great buzz to be involved in. We had worked with the AIDS Foundation and other organisations for years, and always helped out if we could.

In 2004 I was approached by a group of schoolgirls from a Christian school in Mt Albert, asking if I would help out with clothes for a fashion show they were having to raise money for an orphanage in Tanzania. I asked them what sort of publicity they were getting, as no publicity means no one knows, which means no money comes in! They said the media were not interested, so I said I would try to help them out.

The girls and boys from the school were about fifteen and very sweet. I made it very clear from day one that I'm agnostic, and not to try and convince me otherwise, as I could not work with people trying to convert me.

The students were travelling to Tanzania to see the orphanage they were trying to raise money for, and I agreed to go with them, to try and help get some publicity. A man called Al, who also belonged to the church, was a cameraman and he was going to go along and film, so he and I approached the gorgeous Carol Hirschfeld at *Campbell Live*, and she and John Campbell agreed they would use the footage, which was tremendous.

One of the students' parents owned a travel company, and they covered the airfares, but we had to pay for everything else, including accommodation and food, which was fine. I went along and had my medical jabs, which was appalling. Show me a needle and I faint — I hate them — I could never be a drug addict, it's too scary!

Some of the parents were coming along too, and a fashion writer called Sophie, who worked for a New Zealand magazine. She also brought along her guitar-playing boyfriend, William. I could not fathom why he was coming, as he was not going to be covering anything or helping the students, but all would become apparent.

We flew to Nairobi and had a day to spend there, so Sophie and I decided to go walkabout. She and William had had one of many arguments, and were not speaking, so she and I ventured off for a walk. Within minutes a young man came up to us and asked, 'Are you from New Zealand?' He had been walking behind us and had heard our accents. We were shocked, and said 'Yes'. He then told us he was going to study at Otago University, and would we please have a coffee with him as he wanted to learn more about New Zealand, although from what he was saying, he already seemed to know a fair bit. We went to a McDonalds, and as we were chatting it quickly dawned on me that he wanted nothing more than money.

Although the town was swarming with people, they seemed to disappear as quickly as they appeared. Sophie and I ordered coffee, and the young man said he did not want anything, which set my alarm bells ringing. After a while he started to talk about his family, and how they needed money. I was very stern, and explained that we were on our way to Tanzania to help the poor children in the orphanage, and would not be giving him anything. He talked about the All Blacks, the North and South Islands etc., and was very well-informed. When he realised we were not going to hand over any money he became quite forceful, so I got up and whispered to Sophie not to give him any money, and we went to pay the bill. I returned to the table and said we were leaving, and we walked out.

I suddenly realised how easy it is for tourists to be sucked in. I have always thought I was pretty streetwise, as I usually know when I am being conned, but not this time. We left the McDonalds and walked down towards a market, but suddenly found ourselves in what I can only describe as Bob Marley country. Shanty towns with lots of people with no money, and here were two little white women, all alone. It was not a good look — we could have disappeared in a second and nobody would have had any idea where we were. I did not fancy being garroted and ending up in a ditch, so I suggested we make our way back to the hotel and meet up with Al and William.

When we left Nairobi we had to sit on a bus and drive for hours to our final destination in Arusha. On the way we had to cross the border, at which there were gift shops and a Customs hall that was basically a big shed that had just been plonked in the middle of nothing. The roads were dirt tracks, and the ride was bumpy and laborious. At the border we were told we could use the toilet, and I thought this would be a good idea, as we still had a five-hour journey ahead of us. The girls and I queued up, and when I opened the door to the outside toilet I was not only thrown back by the smell, but the fact that it was a hole in the ground. I had seen this as a teenager when I visited Tunisia on holiday, and also in Hong Kong. When Pebbles was little we went to Hong Kong, and one time when we were in a department store we decided to use the toilets. We again queued, then I told Pebbles to go into the cubicle that had just become vacant, which she did. No sooner had she gone in than she came running out, saying in a very loud voice, 'Mummy, somebody's stolen the toilet!' I peered in and saw she had gone into the cubicle with the hole in the ground, so we came out and waited for a more conventional one to become free, but it made me laugh out loud. The little dot thought somebody had run off with the toilet!

I decided to let one of the girls go in before me while I decided whether I really needed to go that badly or if I could hold it in, but the more I thought about it, the more urgent the need became. There was also no toilet paper, but I had tissues with me. The door to this hole in the ground did not close, so I asked one of the students to keep it closed while I used the toilet. While they were waiting the girls had been talking about how you have to squat to avoid peeing in your pants, and I was trying to take heed of this information. When my turn came I went in, undid my trousers and pulled them and my knickers down. I let out the longest wee imaginable, and as I stood up I realised I had not peed in the hole in the ground but all over my knickers and trousers. All over everywhere. I was sodden in piss. I just stood there like a rabbit in the headlights, not knowing what to do. In the end I just came out of the cubicle and announced to the girls what I had done. I don't think any of them could stand up for laughing. They thought it was hysterical to be with a fashion designer who had wet herself. I could see no reason now to be coy, so I told Al that my bag would have to be unstrapped from the top of the bus and got down for me so I could change.

Sod's law ensured that my bag was not on the top but buried underneath the other 30 people's luggage, so a local climbed on the top of the roof of the bus and began throwing bags down onto the dry, cracked earth. The whole bus now knew my predicament, but all I could think of was that there was no way I could travel for five hours in wet pants. I would get nappy rash!

Finally my bag was unearthed, and I grabbed it and went to try and find somewhere to change, while the other bags were hauled back onto the roof of the bus. I went up to a female Customs official and tried to explain what I had done. She just looked at me, so I mimed it. Laughing, she showed me into the empty Customs hall, which was a completely bare wooden room, with not a stick of furniture. I always travel with Wet Wipes, so I cleaned myself up, put my wet garments into a plastic bag and went and sat back on the bus, to the sound of sniggers.

Before we were able to get on the bus we were accosted by what felt like hundreds of locals all plying their trade — they were selling beads, necklaces, wooden carved animals, you name it. They would not let up, they would swarm all over you, and you had to be very careful about your money, belongings and passport.

Sophie had taken her camera so she would have photos to accompany the article she was going to write and she constantly had this poking out of the bus window. We drove for hundreds of miles through barren land, on and on, and now and again we would see a Masai warrior, walking in the middle of nowhere, with his red and blue cloak and wooden walking stick. We learnt very early on not to try and photograph them. We had been told two conflicting stories about why we should not do this — one was that each time the Masai are photographed they feel a piece of their soul is taken away, and the other was that they did not like people using their images for personal gain. If they saw a camera they would wave wildly and cover their faces, becoming very upset.

We spent that night in a hotel on the way — I think it was NZ$30 a night, which was all good. A clean bed and a shower to boot!

We also slept on the bus as we drove along, and the students said I snored, which I did not want to believe but unfortunately know to be true. It is very embarrassing as you are not aware you are doing it so therefore cannot stop it! Apparently I snore very loudly, which is no more than I would expect, as everything else I do is loud. So now that is out in the public arena, and Pebbles can no longer blackmail me with threats to tell people I snore like a hog in mud!

We eventually arrived in Arusha, and saw that we were staying in an enormous white stucco colonial-style house in the middle of nowhere, which an American couple had gifted to the church in Tanzania. I had not been expecting anything quite so nice. We were shown upstairs to a room with two beds and a shower. Sophie and I shared a room the first night, but after that she announced she could not sleep with me, as my snoring kept her awake. So she camped on the floor in a sleeping bag with the girls next door, and I had my own room.

When we arrived the pastor, Glorious Shu, said there were two rules — no smoking and no alcohol. Bummer, I had brought a bottle of wine with me. I figured some rules are made to be broken, so after I had unpacked I asked Sophie and William to join me for a drink. But guess what, they didn't drink, so I sat alone on the balcony and drank it myself. I didn't want to ask the students as they were underage, and I didn't think that would make a good example. But after all that travelling, I decided getting caught drinking wine was the least of my problems.

So we settled in, and our real journey began. On the second day, William dumped Sophie, so she was in floods of tears. Quite frankly, I did not want to see him. I thought he could have picked a better time and place to dump his girlfriend of over a year than at the start of a trip in a strange country; if he felt that way about her he should not have come, but people are funny creatures.

Meals were held in a large dining room — the food was laid out on the balcony at the front of the house and we would all help ourselves. I was quite prepared for starvation and had taken lots of bars of healthy-looking stuff to munch on, which is not me at all. But the food was amazing and there was always plenty of it, even for growing teenage boys, who manage to consume so much it's remarkable.

If we needed to go into town Glorious would arrange for a driver to take us on a small bus, and he would take us to certain shops. If we purchased something we soon learnt the driver received a kickback from the store owner. I was a bit taken aback by this at first, but the place was so poverty stricken you could hardly blame them for trying tricks like this.

The day came to set off for the orphanage, and we drove up on the bus. All the children, aged from five to thirteen, were lined up outside the school in their uniforms with enormous smiles, and were singing the most wonderful songs. The younger ones had little paper hats on which they had made, and they were so excited to see us. I walked along and said hello to all of them.

We then sat down outside, and Pastor Shu held an assembly. He introduced us to the children, and the smiles never left their faces. I had bought things for the children which were light to carry, and which they would enjoy — balloons and a pump, and paper, crayons and colouring pencils. We blew up the balloons, and the boys kicked around footballs. The girls were all so happy to teach us their songs and how they danced, which seemed to come so naturally to them all. It is so much a part of their culture — when they sing they automatically dance without thinking about it.

I toured their classrooms, and where they slept and showered etc. On the shower-room floor was a wooden box with circles cut out of it, and each hole was filled with a very well-used toothbrush. My first thought was that I should have taken them new ones.

One little boy, aged about five, took me to show me his bed. It was in a dormitory, and was very simple, with a sheet and a blanket, but where the pillow should have been there was a very old, brown and battered leather suitcase. I asked one of the teachers why he kept it there. She said he used it as his pillow as it contained all his worldly possessions, and he felt safe if he had his head resting on it when he was asleep. This really started to tug at the old heartstrings. Some of the children had lost their parents to AIDS, some had been abandoned on the doorstep as babies, and nobody knew who or where their parents were. Each child treated the others like brothers and sisters, and that is what they were.

All each of them had in common was each other. There was no one else they had in the world. A few were lucky enough to know their parents, and visited them twice a year, but the families were too poor to keep them and had given them over to the orphanage. The heartache on both sides was palpable; the parents must have been as distraught as the children to be in this predicament, but unfortunately, it is a very sad fact of life in that part of the world.

After we had seen the children's rooms we went to another building which housed the newborns. We had to wear gowns, and the room was filled with little cribs with the tiniest babies. They had been dumped — it was almost a daily occurrence. Some of the babies' mothers were also there, and they were abashed by our presence. They were very young girls, about sixteen years of age, and had been sent away to have their babies as their families could not afford to keep them, or the stigma attached to an unwed young mother was too much for them to bear. I cuddled the cute little bundles who, when they were older, would be sent over to the school with the other children.

All of the older children spoke their native tongue as well as perfect English. One little boy pointed up at the sky, and asked me how we had got to their school. I explained that we had got on an aeroplane in New Zealand and flown over.

He then asked, 'But how do you get on it?'

I said, 'What do you mean?' and he replied, 'It's always up in the sky. How can you get on it? And how can you fit in it?'

He thought from seeing planes in the sky that they were small, and wondered how we managed to fit in them and how we got on them as they were always in the sky. The thought process was fascinating to me. I sat him down and told him there are places all over the world, in every country, called airports. And just like buses stop to pick up passengers, so do planes. They land at the airport, and we pay money to get on them, and when they land they are really quite enormous. I said we each had a seat, and there were toilets and food on the plane. When the plane landed, it was cleaned and refuelled, and after we were all seated and strapped in, the plane took off and we went very high and flew across the sky, then we landed at another airport in another country. He was mesmerised by my story — he had never realised how it worked.

One of the girls, who was aged about eleven, came up to me and slowly slid her hand into mine. I looked down at her, and she just smiled at me, and I smiled back, not a word was spoken. She clung to me, and it was all too obvious how desperately these children needed love. They are no different from any other being on the planet. Love is the one thing we all crave, and no amount of money will buy it. If you find it, even fleetingly, you are very lucky. Not that they did not receive love, but with so many children it would be very difficult to give any real special time to them individually. There would be no sitting on the bed at night reading a bedtime story, as I did with Pebbles, until she fell into slumber; no kiss and cuddle. There were too many of them, and they all had to be fed and watered daily, and kept clean and educated, which was an enormous task. This young girl did not have a tremendous grasp of English for some reason, but her eyes spoke volumes.

The next day we returned to the orphanage. We had been warned that we would have to help with the children who had wounds that needed cleaning, which did not sound bad, as they all looked very healthy. I was expecting grazed knees and cuts, but how wrong I was. We positioned ourselves on a patio of the school, and the children had to queue up to see us. Each time I thought we had reached the end of the line, another one appeared, each worse than the last. The children had enormous, festering, pussy scabs on their heads.

The headmaster of the Mt Albert school had brought his wife Sue, who was a nurse (it was she who had given me my jabs before we left). Sue said the scabs were probably from insect bites that had become infected. We had to take off each scab, clean the wound, put anti-bacterial cream on it, then apply a sterilised dressing. We all put on our disposable gloves, and had swabs and creams laid out on the tables in front of us. After each child was treated I gave them a lollipop, which I had also taken with me.

All the children's afro hair was kept very short, but the scabs on some of them were so large and deep I was gagging at times. The worst was the eleven-year-old girl who spoke little English. Her head was just covered in these sores. Each bite had become infected and had festered. Sue asked why these had not been treated and was told by the staff that when the doctor saw them, he sent them to the hospital, which was very expensive. Sue realised that all the children needed was to be administered antibiotics, and that expensive hospital visits were not necessary. Prevention is better than cure, and this was never truer than in this situation.

The eleven-year-old sat in front of me, and Sue and some of the students were all lined up, seeing about four children at a time. As I began to peel off the scabs, the little girl screamed — loud, impassioned, heart-rending screams. She could not understand what we were doing and why we were hurting her so. She began struggling, trying to escape. When one large scab came off, pus just flowed out, yellow, dirty pus. The wound was very deep and bloody, and we had to clean it out completely before dressing it. The girl began screaming and crying, like a wounded animal, and her eyes were begging me to stop. She kept looking into my eyes, and I could read every word, although none was spoken — it was the universal language of someone in intense pain, which we can all recognise.

By now I was in tears and losing it. I was completely out of my comfort zone, and there was only one thing I could do. I screamed to Sue to help me dress her wounds. Sue came over and I jumped down off the patio, at which she was seated, and I knelt on the ground and just hugged and stroked her and told her it was all going to be OK, while Sue worked on her head. It took ages, and the poor girl was so distraught, but it needed to be done; her head was by far the worst I had seen. I just held her close to me, and she hugged me back, and I kissed her and told her it was all going to be fine, we were going to make her better, and that we would never hurt her, it just had to be done. I thought about my darling Pebbles at home, and my heart just bled for this poor girl.

Then she pulled away from me, stopped crying, and looked at me with a startled expression. She lifted her hand and wiped away my tears, and kissed me, and tried to comfort me. I was a blubbering wreck, I had never come into contact with anything like this. Her compassion toward me was remarkable — what a girl. Her head was covered in dressings, but after that, whenever she saw me she made a bee-line for me. She would push the other children out of the way, grab my hand and smile, and follow me everywhere. I just wanted to bring her home.

The next day we had to return to finish what we had started. Sue and I also had to go into town, as we had run out of supplies — we had not anticipated what a large job we had to deal with. We bought up all the cream and dressings in the chemist and headed back to the orphanage for another day. Within days, so many of the children's heads and sores had improved. Sue ensured the teachers now knew what to do when the children got these bites, and how simple it was to stop any infection if they were kept clean, and given the right drugs.

Meanwhile Sophie and William continued their arguing, though they did this in private, and each day we did not know if the relationship was on or off. On the journey back Sophie,

William, Al and I decided to have dinner in a restaurant in Nairobi before flying out that night. Al had visited there many times and knew the good places to go. We bundled out of the taxi and into a restaurant called The Thorn Tree, which was famous as it had a large thorn tree growing in the middle of the outside deck, and travellers pinned messages to the trunk. We sat down and enjoyed a very pleasant meal, and felt we were on the way home.

Then when we came to leave Al realised he had left his bag in the taxi! After much calling around we managed to locate the company, then we had to grab another taxi and dash to the office, where the driver had left the bag, before we got our flight. Al was very lucky to have got it back.

Once home, I eagerly awaited the article about our trip in the magazine. Each week nothing appeared, and I kept calling Sophie and leaving messages. I also called Al and William, who both said they had not seen or heard from Sophie and had no idea what was going on. I spoke with the editor of the magazine, and she had not heard anything either, and had not been able to get hold of Sophie, which I found astonishing.

No article was ever delivered, and she did not return to the magazine. I was very cross, as Sophie and William had had their fares paid by one of the parents, and neither had done anything towards increasing the public awareness of the children's plight and the journey to Tanzania. I felt the money could have been put to much better use. I told the editor that had I known this was going to happen I would have written the article myself! By now weeks had passed, and although the editor had been keeping space spare in the hope the article would appear, nothing had happened and it was now too late.

My piece appeared on *Campbell Live*, along with an '0900' number that people could call to leave an automatic $20 donation towards the orphanage. We were trying to raise money to buy a large plot of land with a stream, which would be used to build a school to house the children once they reached the age of thirteen.

Beyond this age there was no room at the orphanage to house them for longer, and nowhere for them to go. So many of the children had no family, and those who did have family could not really return to their old lives in the villages as they now spoke fluent English and had an education. It would all have been for nothing if they were herding cattle and they could not use the education they had received for their and their families' betterment. They would be in limbo.

A few days after the *Campbell Live* programme I received a call at my office from a WORLD customer. She told me she had watched the piece and wanted to donate some money. I told her that she could call the 0900 number and donate $20, and she said, 'I would like to donate a little more than that.' I said, 'Oh, how much?' and her response nearly had me falling off my chair. '$100,000,' she replied. I said, 'How much?' She repeated it — one hundred thousand dollars — which was the total amount needed to buy the land and build the school.

I took her details and immediately rang Al and John, another member of the church who had come with us on the trip. They were as overwhelmed as I was. The woman said she was only doing this as I was involved, and she trusted me. I wanted to ensure everything went smoothly, so Al, John and I flew down to meet her. I promised her complete anonymity, and therefore cannot say where we went, but John took down all the plans, and the details of how the money was going to be set up etc. I too was concerned, as we were dealing with a very large amount of money and I wanted to ensure it went exactly where it should and did not get lost in any system. The woman was told that she would be welcome to visit the orphanage, and she said she would very much like to do this and she would like me to go with her.

Soon after this I had William and Al over for dinner and we talked about the trip and the children, and I said how much I was looking forward to seeing them again. A while after this I opened the newspaper to read that another fashion designer was going to visit the orphanage that I had raised all the money for, without my knowledge. I could not believe what I was reading. I rang Al, who said William had arranged everything and that he (Al) was also going, and that William had told him he had informed me. I made it very clear that I had not been informed, and was not happy at all. I did not care that this particular person was going, but I had gone there and got the coverage, and because of this we had received over $119,000 — and now I was not returning, but someone else!

Al felt so bad about what had happened that he decided to boycott this trip, and William kept totally clear of me, although he arranged the next fashion show to help raise funds for the children at the orphanage. The benefactor was coming to Auckland to attend the show, and she asked me to go with her. I told her the situation and said I could not possibly go, as I would probably put my hands around William's scrawny neck and throttle him. I also spoke with John who was very nonchalant about the whole thing. I was speechless. I felt they had got their money, I had done my bit, and I could now fuck off — and these were Christians! People who prayed every day to God to do the right thing, and they had, in my view, got it so wrong. I felt thoroughly used and abused.

Al, John and I met the woman at the Hilton Hotel in Auckland, where she was staying, and I told John exactly how I felt. He really could not have cared less — it seemed to me he had the goose that had laid the golden egg and that was all he cared about. I was furious. The woman again said that she would like to travel with me, and Al and John said they were travelling to Tanzania in November 2007 and we could go along then.

Since that rather unpleasant episode Francis and I have been very careful about which charities we align ourselves with. We are approached regularly to help this charity and that charity, and one half of me wants to help, but I had been badly burnt and was not going to deal with anyone who was not 100 per cent kosher. While I don't feel there was anything untoward financially, I felt it was handled badly. The lines of communication were severed and it all turned very akward. To this day, I have no idea if the school was built and what happened, and I would love to see how the children had progressed, as at the end of the day that was all that mattered to me.

For many years we had worked under the radar with Andrew Young, the CEO of the Starship Foundation, and I decided children's health and well-being was still the area I was most passionate about. The Starship encompassed so much for me, not only with children who had met with terrible accidents or had life-threatening illnesses but also those who have been subjected to the horrors of child abuse, which appals me. The work these people do is phenomenal.

I feel a lot of celebrities will align themselves with any charity that asks so that they can receive the publicity, and the same for functions. That is so the wrong reason to be involved with anything — you have to have some passion for the charity. Some celebs will go to the opening of a toilet lid, but I could not be bothered.

Andrew and I bumped into each other here and there, and we often talked about how WORLD could help the Starship Foundation further. One day I approached Andrew and said I would like to design a range of T-shirts for children aged from 0 to 14, with proceeds going to the hospital. I cold-called The Warehouse in 2006, as I had done my homework and wanted a retailer that fitted the criteria I had — it had to have stores throughout New Zealand, be large enough to handle the production and distribution of such a large project, able to run TV ads and magazine media, be happy to give the profits to a worthy cause, and have a philanthropic view on life. There was only one name that kept coming up. So I rang and rocked up for a meeting, and I was greeted so warmly and with such enthusiasm that I knew I had done the right thing. I was told on the spot that they would be delighted to be part of the project. F and I designed a range of T-shirts, and within six weeks of their hitting the stores we had raised $225,000 for the hospital. We repeated this exercise in 2008, upping the age to sixteen, as the feedback had been so great. Again $5 from the sale of every T-shirt goes towards the children, who are the future of New Zealand.

28

Making it work

As you might have gathered, Francis and I have grown our business through trial and error. By making plenty of mistakes — and learning from our catastrophes — we've honed an efficient, reliable system that makes it possible to run such a complex business as ours. In any fashion company, creativity must somehow thrive alongside efficiency and accountability, and that can be a delicate balance. Too much rampant creative energy and the practical stuff suffers — and conversely, an excessive focus on spreadsheets and formulae will stifle the energy and dynamism. We've worked very hard to make sure everything hums along smoothly in a practical sense — and that helps to ensure we have the mental space to find inspiration.

I have the added complication of working with my husband. The common wisdom is that romantic partners should be very cautious about working together, but I can genuinely say we've never found it difficult. F is my best friend and I am his. I'm very lucky to have him in both spheres of life; he is a truly great man. I would never have married anybody who wasn't — but my appreciation of all his qualities has grown over the years. F has the wonderful ability to be able to communicate with anyone. He loves people, and is a great natural retailer. He lives and breathes fashion — it is his first passion.

Sometimes, when he and Brent Lawler get together and start raving about fashion, I have to leave the room. In fact, F is so enthusiastic that he tends to be a workaholic. Once I get home and shut the front door, I just want to switch off, play with the dogs and talk to Pebbs. Francis can't relax at all, and will continue sketching ideas all the time, even while we watch TV. If we disagree on either a personal or a work matter, we deal with it instantaneously. We don't hold grudges; after we've resolved a dispute, life goes on as normal. F is very easygoing, thank God, because I am not. When I erupt, it's more spectacular than any volcano. But in our entire 20-year relationship, we've never sworn at each another or had a major row.

Over the years, I've devoted a lot of thought to exactly how to manage a business that absorbs so much of our energy, and the best way to ensure equal weight is given to the practicalities and the flights of fancy. We're still learning every day, but here are some of our philosophies, distilled over 20 years of experimentation.

Communicate with everyone, all the time. This is an absolute must with any business, and the one area where the vast majority of struggling businesses go wrong. Just like a healthy relationship, a good business needs well-maintained lines of communication. We are constantly in touch with all our staff, suppliers, wholesalers and crucial contacts like the bank, so everyone knows what is expected of them, and what they can expect from us. Lack of communication can only lead to problems.

Never turn up late for an appointment. It's tardy and shows no respect. If you are running late, call the person you are seeing to inform them. If you can't attend a meeting on time, what else do you not care about? I have no time for slackers.

Have an incredible work ethic. This seems to be harder and harder to find in people. It does not matter how talented or amazing you might be; unless you can put in the hard graft, you ain't gonna make it. Clock-watching is completely at odds with running a successful business, in my view. If you're a boss, you need to be available to the business all the time. Often, that means missing out on relaxation time or having to cancel social occasions; that's just the reality of life in business. If a business problem arises, we fix it without delay, because ignoring an impending disaster never makes it go away. I always see WORLD as being like a child. It has to be fed, watered and nurtured if we are to get the best out of it.

Deal with people respectfully and — if possible — calmly. This is crucial in every business, and especially in retail. Every day, you meet so many people with diverse cultures and personalities, and it's vital to get along with all of them. Staff, customers, suppliers, contacts — even when they make me want to throw a brick at their heads, it's imperative to try and get along with everyone. As I've learnt from Francis, remaining calm is a big part of the secret. If there's conflict, I try to let everyone have a fair say, then express my own view and try to work out a way we can all meet somewhere in the middle. It's also crucial to be fair. In one of my first fashion jobs in New Zealand, I worked with a girl who was the boss's muse, and she got all sorts of preferential treatment. I vowed then that if I were ever a boss, I would treat all my staff equally.

Don't give in. Whatever the drama or dilemma, we always figure out a solution eventually. Being dogged and determined means we've always stuck in there, and it's taken us a long way. Francis and I are always amazed at what we have achieved, as neither of us has ever done any sort of business qualification or had a mentor. We've learnt the hard way; by making mistakes and learning from them. Sometimes it feels we take one step forward and two back, but we have to keep going. Just when things seem impossible, a new opportunity arises, and we thank heavens we didn't give up.

Keep all the balls in the air. The early years of WORLD were a real juggling act, as we had baby Pebbs and a new business. Both needed me full-time. Pebbles has always come first, and she got used to always being taken here, there and everywhere with us. Neither Francis nor I had any family network in New Zealand, and I've never used a nanny. Little Pebbs would be quite happy playing in the workroom while we toiled. She would take fabric swatches and make collages with glue for hours, and sometimes I felt terrible, but as long as she was with us, she was happy.

Be organised. I am very methodical. My mother is a Virgo and is a tidy freak, and I've picked up her traits. F can never find anything, even a phone number, and he asks me a million times a day for contacts and dates and numbers. He refuses to write anything down, no matter how many times I suggest it. I've found that in business, it makes my life much easier if I have all my contacts, appointments, reminders and records at my fingertips. I never know when I might need some obscure piece of information, and a good filing system has made everything accessible.

Flexibility. Preserving a flexible attitude can make everything so much less stressful. I might have every intention of spending the day doing a specific task — but if something unexpected happens, I have to drop everything and fix the problem. Every day, prioritise what's most important and urgent, and don't worry too much about a mucked-up schedule. The best-laid plans won't help a bit if pressing concerns are allowed to get worse and worse.

Be honest. If we say we'll do something, we always do it. Letting people down can so easily wreck a reputation and create more work and stress for the future. We're punctilious about meeting deadlines. If we say we will despatch an order on a certain day, we'll make sure it's ready even if it means working through the night. Protecting our relationships, and our reputation for reliability, makes the fatigue worthwhile.

The show must go on. Our business is like a perpetual-motion machine — nothing ever stops. We have to get everything ready for the next collection so far in advance that we're constantly projecting our minds into the next two or three seasons; thinking about cold weather in the middle of summer, and imagining winter while spring is just blossoming. There's no point in procrastinating — regardless of how busy we are, time will not wait. Each deadline must be met, otherwise the machine will grind to a halt. There's also very little room for excuses. Feel sick? Bad luck — we can't just miss a season because we're feeling off-colour.

Laugh. You have to be able to laugh at yourself, and all the crazy things that happen, or you will go nuts. We have had some of our best times when we are at our most stressed. Before a show, we'll be racing around madly getting everything together and someone will cut the tension with a funny remark. Everyone cracks up, and we're reminded that without the laughter, there's no point.

29

Opening up

I never wanted the world to know I suffered from depression. Although I was hugely relieved to be diagnosed and have the opportunity to get treatment, I didn't discuss the issue with friends or colleagues. Apart from my family and some very close friends, nobody knew.

One day in 2006, I got a call from an acquaintance, Janet Wilson, a respected television producer and journalist, and the wife of the then head of TVNZ news and current affairs, Bill Ralston. 'How would you feel about joining a TV ad campaign to raise awareness of depression?' Janet asked. I was startled at first, but she went on to explain that a prominent advertising executive named Kevin Denholm had come up with the idea for an ad campaign to lessen the stigma associated with mental illness. The ads were for the National Depression Initiative, which was a project of the Ministry of Health.

'It's not going to be about feeling sorry for the poor depressed people,' Janet said. The idea was to encourage people who suffer depression to seek help, and realise they are not alone. One in four New Zealanders suffers depression at some time in their lives, and this ad campaign was designed to encourage young people who were suffering to share their problems with family and friends. There would be a series of ads featuring well-known New Zealanders from various fields of endeavour, and the theme was that depression can strike anyone, no matter what you do or who you are.

I told Janet I'd have to think it over. I wasn't sure if I was ready to announce my affliction to the world. I put down the phone and continued working — and about ten minutes later there was a knock at my office door and a bespectacled young man entered. 'Hi, I'm Kevin,' he said. 'I think Janet Wilson has contacted you.'

'Bloody hell,' I replied, 'you don't waste much time. Were you standing outside my door waiting?'

Kevin just laughed — but I still think he really was standing there waiting to get the OK from Janet before knocking.

We chatted about the idea, and Kevin was so enthusiastic, and so keen for me to come on board, that I decided to go ahead and do it. I was still shy about revealing my condition, but I thought if I could help one young person avoid suicide, or seek treatment, it was worth washing my dirty laundry in public.

There was only one hesitation — I had recently been asked to feature in a TV ad campaign for a big company.

Out of courtesy, I decided to inform their ad agency about the ads for the National Depression Initiative. I couldn't see why they'd have a problem — it was not a promotion for any product or service. There was no conflict of interest.

They didn't raise any objection at first, but then the account director asked me to come in for a meeting, and seemed terribly embarrassed. Eventually, he blurted it out: 'You've been dropped from the campaign.' The problem, he explained with much sighing and shaking of his head, was that the client wasn't happy about me appearing in a mental health ad.

I couldn't believe what I was hearing. I told him I wasn't going to be lying on the floor in the foetal position crying 'Woe is me'; I was merely trying to alleviate the stigma surrounding mental health.

What followed next had me so astounded and upset that I

wrote it down, word for word.

'It's not the sort of thing they want to be associated with,' he said.

'Am I hearing you right?' I said. 'Do you mean they don't want to be associated with people with mental health problems?'

He nodded. 'Yes,' he said, adding that the decision had nothing to do with him.

For the first time, I was beginning to see the stigma attached to mental health problems. If I had not admitted my depression, they would have continued thinking I was a great representative for their brand. As soon as they knew I might have a mental illness, they couldn't back away fast enough. Because I had kept quiet about my depression for so long, I had never been confronted with discrimination. Now it was staring me in the face.

I went back to the office and burst into tears. I was livid. I rang the head of the agency, and told him what had happened.

'Will you say this in public?' I asked him. 'This is totally discriminatory — are they brave enough to actually be honest about the fact they don't want to be associated with me because of my mental health issues?'

He denied there was any link between the depression campaign and their decision to rescind their offer to me. He said the account director should not have said what he did, and that he was mistaken.

I didn't believe a word of it. The account director had let the cat out of the bag — and quite rightly so. He was just passing on what a bunch of hypocritical arseholes his bosses were at that time. The head of the agency was backtracking furiously; he certainly didn't want any of this to come out.

Funnily enough, all my shyness about admitting depression dissolved. I was no longer shy — the experience had filled me with righteous anger. I wanted everyone to know what had happened to me. I talked to many friends and acquaintances about how upset I was, and how badly I felt I had been treated. I felt I was being punished for having a mental illness. It was hardly as if I was saying I had a sexually transmitted disease — and if I had said that, so what?

I'm still angry and hurt about the issue when I look back at it, and can only hope the former executives are embarrassed about their actions. It's an indication of how far we have come as a society — today, no company would dare be so discriminatory. Our awareness of mental health problems is so much greater, in part due to awareness campaigns like the one I participated in.

The National Depression Initiative campaign, 'Like Minds, Like Mine', was a big deal, and the process of shooting the ads was intensive. Singer Mahinarangi Tocker and former All Black John Kirwan were among the other celebrities taking place, and when Mahinarangi and I met at the post-shooting wrap party, we clicked immediately.

'I was shy about meeting you,' Mahinarangi confided. 'You're so famous and I'm not really fashionable enough.'

I was amazed that such a beautiful, talented woman would be intimidated by me, although I know it happens often. The fashion industry can seem intimidating from the outside, but of course the reality is that fashion people are just as consumed by insecurities and complexities as everyone else.

Mahinarangi and I laughed together all evening, and we continued meeting up over the years. Anyone watching us would have been surprised to learn we were two depressives — or, as I prefer to say, nuts. We shared the same warped sense of humour, and I was very upset when in April 2008 I heard the news that Mahinarangi had died of complications following an asthma attack. What a beautiful, honest woman she was.

The campaign exceeded everyone's wildest expectations. I'm sure the corporates were kicking themselves — the campaign would only have given their own ads featuring me greater impact. I decided that if they ever approached me again I would refuse to work with them, no matter how much money they offered. A million dollars? I would tell them where to stick it.

Suddenly, I was catapulted into a new realm of life I'd never even imagined. The ads touched so many people; every day, I would meet someone who wanted to tell me about their reactions.

There was a lawyer who worked near us in High Street at the time, and he and I had been nodding acquaintances for years. I would always think how lucky he was: he drove a flash car, had lots of money, ran his own practice and had the privilege of working in a profession where everything he needed was in his head. All a lawyer needs is his books, a laptop and a small office, whereas a fashion designer needs rolls of fabrics, scissors, set squares, rulers, notches, patterns, racks, and somewhere to cut out. I've often thought wistfully of how nice it must be to be unencumbered by all that stuff.

After the campaign began screening, this fellow came up to me and said: 'I like the ad; we have something in common. I've suffered depression for years.'

I was gobsmacked. To me he looked like the man who had everything, but when you scratch the surface just a little, it's obvious our assumptions about other people are rarely correct.

The most emotional encounter I had was in the supermarket. Ever since childhood, I've maintained my ability to attract strangers who tell me their personal stories, and many of my encounters seem to be in supermarkets. I was standing by the bread counter, feeling rather baffled by the range of products on offer (Francis hates white bread, I'm not keen on brown, and Pebbles always wants something different, so I spend a lot of time gazing at the shelves), when a teenage boy, about sixteen or seventeen years old, approached me.

He was dressed as a goth, with black clothes and pale make-up. 'Excuse me,' he said, in a quiet, educated voice; 'I just want to thank you for doing those ads. I've had depression for so long, and I could never talk about it. Since the ads have been on I don't feel so alone, and I want to thank you for what you have done for me.'

I just wanted to drop my shopping and hug him. My eyes filled with tears. He said he had tried to commit suicide in the past, but was feeling better now that depression was being talked about in the open. I was so humbled; I had never really thought that my actions could have such an intense effect on someone's life. I was so glad I'd agreed to do the campaign; knowing I had helped just one person get back on track gave me a wonderful sense of achievement. It made all the difficulties worthwhile.

After we had chatted for a bit, I wished him all the best for the future and we went our separate ways. To this day, countless people come up to me and talk about the campaign, but he is the one I remember most. He seemed a very confident teenager, self-assured and articulate, but there was so much pain underneath.

Francis sometimes calls depression 'the Gift'. One day when we had been talking to someone who also suffered from depression, F said: 'Oh, you have the Gift!' We all laughed, and it brought a lighter note to the conversation. Although it's an odd way to refer to such a painful affliction, it can help us to see a positive side to the condition that plays such a big part in our lives. Working on the ad campaign made me see another way in which depression can be regarded as a gift — it has given me the opportunity to help others, and it's nothing to be embarrassed about, it's just what it is.

30

Her Majesty's finest

It had to be a joke. In 2002, an envelope arrived from the Prime Minister's office, containing a formal letter advising me that the Prime Minister wished to recommend that Queen Elizabeth II bestow an honour on me for my services to the New Zealand fashion industry. If I accepted, I would become a Member of the New Zealand Order of Merit (MNZM), the New Zealand equivalent of an English MBE.

The letter asked me to call the Prime Minister's office to inform them of my acceptance. I rang the number, convinced it was all a big hoax organised by one of my friends.

'Is this a wind-up?' I asked the terribly proper sounding man who answered the phone.

'No madam,' he said; 'Queen Elizabeth II is not in the habit of playing jokes.'

I put the phone down very sheepishly and pulled Francis aside to tell him the news; I was to be the first female New Zealand fashion designer to receive such an honour. I had made history! It had to be our little secret until it was formally approved by Her Maj and publicly announced, but to my continuing amazement, it all proceeded as planned. A few months later, Pebbs, F and I flew to Wellington to receive my medal from the Governor-General, Dame Silvia Cartwright.

What on earth was I to wear? F had bought me a black Philip Treacy hat years earlier, and I made an ivory silk coat to go with it. As usual, I worked on the garment up to the last minute, stitching buttons on in the car on the way to Auckland Airport.

As she handed me the medal, Dame Silvia commented: 'You're the best-dressed woman in the room.' I didn't mention the frantic last-minute buttons.

As we stood around nibbling tiny sandwiches and admiring the Government House art collection — all of which Francis wanted — it occurred to me that I was the least likely person I could think of to be in this position. In our family, I was the black sheep whom nobody expected to amount to much — I don't think any of my relatives thought fashion would be a real career for me. My English friends were all thrilled — New Zealanders tend to be rather blasé about gongs and honours, but they still have enormous cachet in the UK.

It was undoubtedly the best thing to have happened in my career. The whole experience was humbling; I was surrounded by famous New Zealanders who had achieved great things — but I wished F had been receiving a medal too. Ours has always been a 50/50 partnership, and he was the instigator of WORLD. Generous as always, he was thrilled for me. Pebbs, however, was a little harder to impress — at the same ceremony was one of her schoolmates, whose father was receiving an Order of New Zealand medal, the equivalent of a knighthood. As far as Pebbs was concerned, I still had a way to go.

In 2005, I decided we needed to buy our own head office. Over the years we had spent hundreds of thousands of dollars in rent for our workroom, an expense we could do without. I spent ages hunting for the right site.

'Don't show me anything unless you really like it,' said Francis, who loathes any thought of real estate matters. 'I'm not traipsing around looking at offices!'

Soon, I'd found the perfect spot, a 150-year-old former Wesleyan chapel in the CBD; the oldest surviving brick church in New Zealand. It needed a new kitchen, bathroom, wiring and heating, but apart from that it met all my criteria. It was a single-level stand-alone building with carparking, and I loved it.

I put in a tender without mentioning it to Francis, which is probably the naughtiest thing I have ever done. I loved it so much that I didn't want to run the risk of him saying it was too expensive. One evening when we were driving home after seeing a movie, the agent rang to say my tender was successful.

'What have you bought now?' asked Francis jokingly when I had finished the call.

'A church!' I said. He nearly crashed the car, and when I told him the price, he was beside himself.

'Any chance of seeing the most expensive purchase of my life?' he asked.

Of course, when he saw the site he loved it as much as I did, and we've been very happy there with our staff of 28, including machinists, pattern-cutters, administrative staff, production manager and assistant, and designers. The church, which is haunted, is a great place to be. I had always wanted to find a site with some character — and we got more than we bargained for. One morning, we had a work-experience girl in the workroom. She looked up at the ceiling and screamed: 'There's a woman floating up there!'

The rest of us laughed it off, thinking she was simply over-imaginative — but now, I believe she might have been telling the truth. We've since discovered that the church, which was built in 1859, was for many years the home of Auckland's first spiritualist group, the Auckland Society for Spiritual Progress (later the Auckland branch of the Spiritualist Church of New Zealand). The organisation was led by Elizabeth Harris, an outspoken campaigner for political reform and advocate of the role of women as guardians of morality. Spiritualist connections with the chapel endured unti the late 1920s, and it was also the meeting hall of the

Star of Auckland Lodge of the Independent Order of Oddfellows, which I've always thought appropriate. We're pretty odd fellows too, in our own way.

We always seem to be in haunted spaces. In 1999, when we opened our large Deluxe store at 57 High Street, the space had been derelict and boarded up for 30 years. It took ten months to paint off all the graffiti and fix all the holes in the floor. We'd vaguely known of its existence for years; it is hidden just off High Street, up a few little stairs. Francis was intrigued by it, and in the late nineties when we were looking for a larger space, he persuaded me we should take it over.

The Deluxe store had been built in the early twentieth century as a private concert chamber and theatre by Lewis Eady, who owned a music store on adjacent Queen Street. It was lucky to escape the wrecking ball and could easily have been demolished or substantially altered by some eager developer in the 1980s or 1990s, when Auckland was changing so rapidly. We restored it to all its former glory, using cream and gold heritage paints, and in 1999 we invited Prime Minister Jenny Shipley to open the store. I asked the son of Lewis Eady — who still owned a shop in Newmarket — to come along to the opening, and he came with some trepidation, knowing it would make him sad to revisit the memory-soaked old spot, which he had sold with great reluctance. He brought along a sepia-toned photograph of a couple who had got married in the space in 1929. It was a gorgeous photo; all the wedding guests were wearing hats, and looked so smart. When I turned the picture over, I was astounded to see that the date of the wedding was the very same as our opening, exactly 70 years later. Since its renovation, the store now has a heritage grade listing.

As we settled into the store, the alarm was always going off in the middle of the night. When we arrived to investigate, we'd find a bag thrown across the floor, or something moved out of place. We were puzzled — there seemed no way these items could have moved on their own. After a couple of months this stopped, but one day a customer was standing in the store, talking to a staff member, when she glanced towards the mezzanine level and screamed. 'There's a man standing up there!' she shouted. Nobody else could see anyone, but again she insisted someone was standing on the upper level. Thoroughly spooked, she hurried out of the shop, never to be seen again.

In late 2006, Francis saw premises in Melbourne that really took his fancy. 'Let's open a Melbourne store,' he said excitedly. At the same time, a lovely little site had become available in Vulcan Lane in Auckland, just around the corner from High Street, which we knew would be the perfect spot to launch our beauty store concept, stocking exotic and unusual perfumes and cosmetics.

We sat down and did the figures, and they were not stacking up. 'It's one or the other,' I said. F opted for Melbourne, but I was still concerned. I felt Auckland would be easier, as we were based here and could keep a close eye on exactly what was happening with a new venture. With much grumbling and moaning, F eventually succumbed, and we agreed Melbourne would be next on our agenda.

I think it was the right decision. In 2007 we opened two new stores (the beauty shops in Wellington and Ponsonby) and moved our Ponsonby clothing store to a larger site, all at the same time. We were in debt up to our eyeballs. It was horrific. We were redoing three new stores from top to bottom — painting; installing lighting, air-conditioning, flooring and fittings; commissioning clothing-racks; buying stock; coordinating architects and builders, and paying rent, even before we started trading.

It just about crucified us, and although I'm usually pretty calm, I did have the odd sleepless night. 'How on earth will we ever get out of this?' I'd wonder in the wee hours. Money was flowing out like we'd opened an artery, and nothing was coming in to cover it. As Francis now acknowledges, opening a Melbourne store at the same time would have brought us to our knees. We've been through so much to bring the business to this stage that I'm just not willing to let it die. Sometimes, sacrifices need to be made to keep the venture alive.

F is very good, and will always admit when he is wrong. I feel bad when I have to be the bad cop, as I know his determination and foresight are phenomenal. The truth is that money and creative people don't mix terribly well. F loathes learning how little we have in the account, so it has become my responsibility to be the financial conscience of our partnership — and that's all right. I've learnt over the years that being strict on ourselves is crucial: the higher you climb, the harder you fall.

31

Father figures

In 2002, I had a brush with my own mortality — and the afterlife.

I would never normally have described myself as a spiritual person, even though as a child my mother always went to the Balham Spiritualist Society, and the mediums would do house calls and readings for you. Sometimes my mum would gather a few friends, as well as my crazed grandmother and the Gin Queen, and a spiritualist would come round. I was always very excited, as I immediately thought they were going to whip up some ghosts and we could have a bit of fun, but that never happened.

One day, one of these people, a very tall gentleman, was there when my sister and I came into the room. He told my sister she would marry a short, dark-haired man, and said I would marry a tall, fair-haired man. Forever after I would eye up every fair-haired boy that walked past me as a potential suitor. It all turned to nothing, when my sister married a very tall, fair-haired man and I married an average height dark-haired man.

I was never sure if I really believed in the afterlife, but in my twenties I would often visit the spiritualist society in Belgrave Square, London. For a few pounds, you could sit in the room with a clairvoyant and they would pick people from the audience to pass on messages. Scott Crolla had a sister called Romayne, and she truly believed she was a medium. She told me to get picked out from an audience all you had to do was wear a red top, as mediums were attracted to bright colours. I tried this many times, but alas, it always failed.

When we first arrived in London we lived in a house in Trinity Road in Tooting, and I vividly remember once waking up and going downstairs to the kitchen in the middle of the night. There was a being in the room, and it ordered me to sit down, pointing at a chair, which I did. I was terrified, and have never forgotten the experience, or what the 'being' looked like — it scared the life out of me. It looked like a cross between the devil and what we imagine aliens to look like, way before Steven Spielberg and *Close Encounters of the Third Kind*. It was very aggressive and I just did as it told me. It then let me return to my room. I am sure it was not a dream, as it has stayed with me ever since, and I never spoke about it to anyone as I was rigid with fear. I was about three years old at the time.

The next time I had any true confirmation of the afterlife was in 2002. I had my period as normal, but after two weeks it failed to stop. I was bleeding non-stop, and as the weeks turned to months it got worse and worse. The doctor could not work out what it was, but after four months I was severely weakened and was having to take a complete change of clothes to work. I could not go out, as the bleeding was beyond bad — nothing could control it. I was soon wearing enormous maternity pads, and even these were not working. I would go straight from home to work, a journey of about five minutes, and would have to change my underwear when I arrived.

One day I was about to board a flight to Sydney with a friend, when I said I would just pop to the bathroom at the airport to change my clothes. As I took my pants down, I started haemorrhaging all over the floor. I didn't know what to do, as there was no way to stem the blood. It was pouring out faster than I could clean it up — it was like a really bad horror movie. But work always came first. I cleaned myself up as best I could, changed my clothes, and went outside. When the flight was called I was in a terrible state and did not know if I should even get on the plane. My friend says she remembers me saying that 'tennis balls' were coming out of me, and I am sure I did say that, as the blood was in enormous fist-sized clumps. I boarded the plane but spent most of the journey in the toilet. When we got to Sydney I had to time everything I did, to ensure I was never too far away from a toilet, and believe me, that is not a great way to spend your life!

When I got home I sought a specialist gynaecologist. They didn't know the cause either, and ran a battery of tests, but nothing showed up. It wasn't cancer, which many people had thought, but it had now been happening for six months non-stop. Being a vegetarian, I also suffered terrible anaemia, and the blood loss was not helping. I was now losing blood faster than my body could renew it, and I was pale, drawn and very lethargic. I found it almost impossible to get out of bed, I was so tired all the time. It took me forever to make a decision, as I could not think straight. I just wanted it to stop.

At night I had to sleep on a pile of towels, and was up most of the time. One particular night I awoke, and felt a really weird sensation. I went to the bathroom and sat on the toilet, and felt something was not right. I held toilet paper under me and waited, and suddenly something came out. I peered at it, and it was what can only be described as a large piece of grey flesh. I gagged, put it in a container, and took it to the doctor for analysis the next day. The results came back, and it was found that my uterus was disintegrating. There was now only one thing to be done — I had to have my womb removed. I was beside myself with worry, but was told there was no alternative. The procedure had to be done immediately. I was very lucky to have health insurance, and was put into a private hospital straight away.

Prior to this, I had always been very healthy, and had only ever been in hospital after my overdose at the age of fourteen, and when giving birth to Pebbs. I was very scared about being put under anaesthetic, as I thought I would never wake up. I checked into the hospital and was shown to my room, which overlooked Ellerslie racecourse. The nurse came in and told me to have a shower and brush my teeth. I explained that I was not having anything done to my mouth, but she said: 'Oh no, it's because some people have really bad breath, and it almost anaesthetises the anaesthetist as they have to be very close to the mouth!'

So I brushed my teeth. I kissed Francis and Pebbles and told them how much I loved them, and was then wheeled into surgery. The doctors were lovely. They explained that they thought I was too young for a full hysterectomy and they would remove only my uterus, and not my ovaries. And it would be done by laser — I was not even going to be cut!

They gave me a sedative, and when the anaesthetist administered the drugs, I was told to count to ten. I think I reached three before I drifted off into a very deep sleep. I have never taken drugs, and have to have a severe headache even to take a painkiller, so any strong drugs send me completely off in no time at all. I do believe that when you are under, you are halfway between life and death — you are on a beautiful plateau in between. I cannot explain why I think that, but for people to be still alive, yet able to have open-heart surgery and brain surgery and eye surgery, and not feel a thing, must surely mean you are halfway to the other side.

Before all this happened, Francis had been telling me he had arranged a surprise for me. I had no idea what it was. He and Pebbs were both in on it, but they were keeping it very quiet. I imagined the surprise was a holiday, or maybe a new bag. While I was in a state of unconsciousness, my father appeared and spoke to me. He held my hand, and he said: 'Francis has arranged for you to go on the last flight of Concorde.'

When I awoke after the surgery, Francis and Pebbs were in the room with me. I looked at Francis and said, through my haze, 'My father has just told me the surprise.'

Francis looked at me, then at Pebbles, and said: 'What is it then?' So I told him.

The colour drained from his face and he looked at Pebbles, and I went back to sleep.

He had in fact booked me on the last-ever Concorde flight, as I am a speed freak — I love anything with force and power. Francis could not believe my father had told me this, but he knew it was true, as there was no way I could ever have guessed something so unusual. I decided I would not take the flight, as I felt maybe my father had told me because he did not want me to take it. I feared Concorde was going to crash. After many attempts, I convinced Francis to cancel the flight.

Of course, Concorde did not crash, and I have no idea why my father would have wanted to tell me the secret. It was all too weird, but it happened. I have never figured out why he would have wanted to scupper my surprise, but there was no other way for me to find out what it was, as F and I had never even discussed such a thing.

While I was in hospital recovering, although suffering from no pain whatsoever, which I just found incredible, I was still too scared to go to the toilet. After the surgery I had had a catheter put in for the day, as I was so drowsy, and after that I could go for a wee, but I was too frightened to attempt anything else, much as I wanted to. The first night after the surgery, Pebbles, being a kid, wanted to see what I had for dinner, and ended up eating all my food. I was told that if you wanted you could order dinner for your family also, and have it together in your room, so the next night I decided I would do that.

So I ordered dinner for the three of us, and told Francis and Pebbs to be at the hospital by seven. We ate dinner and chatted, then I said I thought I should attempt to go to the toilet, as I had not been for a couple of days. Pebbs immediately jumped into my bed, put the covers over herself, and watched the TV attached to the wall. She thought this was the height of luxury, especially as it also had SKY. Then she started to play with the buttons that put the bed into all sorts of different positions. Francis asked if I needed any help in the bathroom, which was off the bedroom, but

I said I would be fine.

I slowly walked to the bathroom, pulled my knickers down and sat on the toilet, then waited for nature to take its course. All the time I was on edge, and I kept expecting an enormous surge of pain, but it never came.

Suddenly a nurse burst into the room, and I heard her ask Pebbles, 'Are you the patient?' I heard Pebbles say, 'No, she's in the toilet,' then the nurse burst in. I just sat on the toilet, desperately trying to pull my knickers up, but I was too slow. I am extremely weird about stuff like that, and am not used to strangers being there.

The nurse said, 'Are you all right?' I looked at her quizzically and said, 'Yes, why?'

She said, 'Well, you pressed the emergency button!'

I told her I had not, all the time just wanting her to go, as I thought the smell might kill her. When I came out of the bathroom Francis and Pebbles were both falling about laughing. While she was playing with the buttons on the bed, Pebbs had accidentally pressed the emergency button which had summoned the nurse. They both thought it was hysterically funny, particularly as they knew of my toilet hang-ups. I shouted that I could not even have a shit in peace.

I laugh about it now, but at the time I didn't know whether to laugh or cry with embarrassment.

The next time I had a brush with the 'other side' was on Wednesday the 9th of January 2008. I was alone in the house, watching *Coronation Street*, when I saw out of the corner of my eye something move in the hallway. I had the door of the lounge open, and there, outside my bedroom door, to my left, was a large dark figure. The light was on in the hall and it was very clear. I just stared at it, unable to move. It was a dark shape in the outline of a man. It then slowly dissipated. I just sat still on the couch. The whole room seemed to have gone silent, and both the dogs were asleep on the floor. I thought about the day and the date, and realised it was 33 years to the day since my father had died.

I had no idea if it was him, but I felt he had a message for me, although I did not know what it was. Francis was in Paris, and on the following Friday, the 11th of January, I spoke to him and told him what had happened. Friday the 11th was also the day Sir Edmund Hillary died, and Francis said, 'Oh, it must have been Sir Ed!'

I was gobsmacked, and asked, 'Why would Sir Edmund Hillary appear to me?'

Francis replied, 'Maybe he knew he was leaving this mortal coil and came to see you — especially as you say it was a large figure.'

'Sir Ed and I were hardly close mates,' I said, 'and he didn't die until Friday and this happened on the Wednesday. And I am sure if Sir Ed knew he was on the way out he was not thinking, "Oh, I must pop in and see Denise in Freemans Bay before I leave this mortal coil"!'

Sometimes my husband's thought processes truly amaze me. It caused much amusement among my friends that he could even think such a farcical thing, at such a dark time in New Zealand's history, but death and shock have funny ways of turning our humour very black.

On the Saturday I met my great friend Angie T for lunch, and we had a huge catch-up and talked about everything. She said she was having a barbecue that night and she wanted me to come. I said no, but she absolutely insisted. She said that her friend Kelvin Cruikshank was going to be there, the man who appears on the TV programme *Sensing Murder*. She had once asked me if I wanted a reading with him, as he had a cancellation, but I was not able to go, and since then his appointment book had been full. She told me he has a five-year waiting list. He was currently on holiday, and Angie said he managed to block out messages coming through so he could relax.

After much coaxing I agreed to go to the barbecue. I arrived last, and found it was just Angie and her husband Wayne, Kelvin, another friend and me. We sat down and drank and ate, and had a great time. Kelvin told me he did not have a five-year waiting list, as Angie had said, but a ten-year waiting list!

I started telling them about the 'apparition' in my hallway, laughing as I said how Francis had thought it was Sir Edmund Hillary, but I thought it was my father. Kelvin looked up at me and said, 'No, it was not your father, it was your partner's father. I know that because your father is here, and he has told me it was not him, but that it was your partner's father.'

We all looked at him absolutely gobsmacked. I explained that Francis does not know who his actual father is, which has always been a bone of contention between him and his mother. She will not tell him, and he has always wanted to know, even just a name, so he could have some closure on that part of his life. I can understand that, although not having been in that position, I cannot fully grasp it.

Kelvin was now telling me that Francis's father was a spirit. I asked why on earth Francis's father would appear to me, as I had been alone in the house that night, and Francis was not even there. Kelvin said he obviously wanted me to pass the message on. Francis has never been very spiritual, and while he is not a disbeliever, he is one of those people who would have to see it for himself before he could believe it. I feel spirits know the people who are open to seeing them, and consequently appear to them. I could be wrong, but that's my perception.

We carried on talking, and as Angie asked Kelvin something we noticed he had sort of disassociated his attention from us. Then he told Angie that he could not talk to her, as he had 'three people talking to him'.

He then looked at me and said he had my father with him, and that he would not leave. He had been talking to Kelvin ever since I arrived, and he could no longer block him out — he was too strong, and would not go. Kelvin told me to be quiet and just listen, then he just talked and talked.

He told me a woman called Margaret was with my father, which threw me completely as my dear Aunt Margaret had passed over in August, and she and my father had been very close. In fact, my father had been going out with her best friend for many years.

Huge problems connected to her will had also just surfaced, and he explained what had happened, which made perfect sense. Kelvin described my father to a T — how he looked, what he was wearing, and his character. My father also told Kelvin to get his hair cut, which I found quite funny! He also said he had someone there whose name began with a B — a Bill or William. I couldn't immediately get this, but Kelvin was drawing a large B on the table with his finger, and kept saying B, B, B. Then it clicked — my mother's late husband was William, and we all called him Billy.

The whole experience was surreal. Angie was sitting there with tears streaming down her face. She had often asked Kelvin to speak to her father, but he had explained that the spirits had to contact him, he cannot contact them. He said that my father was very insistent that the message he had must go through to me.

When Kelvin left the room, their friend turned to me and said the moment I walked in Kelvin had tensed up. It was an altogether wonderful and exhilarating experience, and I was very glad that I had been persuaded to go along. I felt so humbled to have been able to have a one-to-one reading with such a prominent psychic.

Bottoms, sadly, are a theme in my medical history.

Francis was away overseas again, and a friend suggested I pop over for a glass of wine and he would get some takeaways in. I am always far more social when I am alone, and tend to go out all the time, which is not always a good thing.

On this night we had a very nice meal of veggie stuff and couscous, too much wine, and I got home after a very nice evening and lots of chat. Midway through the night I awoke feeling not too well, and I visited the bathroom quite a few times.

The next day that awful feeling had not subsided, and the feeling of dehydration began to set in, along with chronic stomach cramping. After about a week of feeling wretched, but thinking it would pass, I visited my local GP and told him I had campylobacter.

I usually make a self-diagnosis — I have no medical background whatsoever, and I am sure this infuriates my GP no end, but he never tells me off. He usually just listens, then tells me how wrong I am.

I have already diagnosed myself as needing a hip and knee replacement after two catastrophic falls, but he disagrees with this. This time he told me that I probably did not have campylobacter, but some other long-fangled ailment that I will not even attempt to pronounce. He gave me some antibiotics and sent me on my merry way, after saying 'Ahhh' when I said I had eaten takeaway couscous — apparently you should not eat any reheated rice or pasta as it tends to make a lovely living environment for bacteria. I crawled to the chemist to get my prescription filled, at the same time passing this invaluable knowledge on to everyone I met, none of whom had any idea that reheating wheat was bad.

As the days progressed I felt better, then after the week, when I had finished the tablets, the pain came back, threefold. In fact, I was doubled over with pain. Fearing I was close to death, I called out an emergency doctor in the middle of the night. When I later read the form he had filled in I saw that he had written, 'The patient opened the front door'. Well, there's a surprise — since I was the only person in the house it was pretty obvious I had no choice if he wanted to come in, as I have yet to teach the dogs the trick of opening the door.

The doctor pressed and prodded and told me to drink lots of water and Gastrolyte, then said if I was no better by Monday I should visit my GP again, but he felt I would be as right as rain. Wrong! On Monday I was back at the doctor's, and he said I had to give a sample! This is the most disgusting thing to do, and I cannot imagine the poor human being who has to look at it and analyse it — what a job! So I did what I could, and the results came back a few days later to say the 'sample' was not sufficient and I had to do more!

I could not keep anything in, so the chances of getting a bigger sample were looking decidedly grim, but I tried. I was by now totally bedridden; in fact, I could hardly move. I just slept and had terrible nightmares, but the doctor was reluctant to give me any more medication until he found out what the problem was. My self-diagnosis by now was cancer, but he said he doubted that, and that I should wait for the results.

A few days later the doctor rang and asked me to go in to see him. When I went into his consulting room he asked, 'Have you been gardening?'

'Are you serious,' I replied. 'I can hardly get out of bed!'

'No, before you became sick, were you gardening?'

Sick or not sick, I have not got a clue about anything in the garden. The last time I cut down all the 'weeds' Francis came home and asked, looking rather startled, 'Where's the cherry tree?'

'What cherry tree?' I replied.

It turned out that what I thought was a weed was a cherry tree, and since then I have been banished to the house. I now leave the gardening to Mike from Green Acres, because at least he knows what he's doing.

The doctor told me that the results showed that my sickness was from bacteria in soil!

I rummaged as hard as I could through my now-addled brain, and all I could come up with was the fact that I played ball with the dog every night. The Jack Russell has an obsessive compulsive disorder, and I have to throw the ball into the garden (come rain or shine) and he retrieves it. We do this over and over again until he is exhausted. Maybe that was how a tiny bit of soil had got onto my hands and into my mouth.

The doc agreed that this was the most likely scenario, and said he would give me the 'Rolls Royce' of antibiotics. If these did not do the trick, we would have to resort to the 'other option', which he did not want to discuss with me unless I needed it.

I then told him point blank that I would not move until I knew what the other option was. He said he was not going to tell me, and I repeated that I was not going to move until he did.

When he did tell me I thought I was hallucinating. Was I

hearing right? I repeated what he had said to confirm that I was not sicker than I had thought, but no, he said that was the next option. I left his room with my sphincter tightly closed and raced outside to call Francis, who was by now home again.

'He said WHAT?' Francis asked, so I repeated myself, then I listened to his hysterical laughter and knew he would put the phone down and tell everybody at work.

The 'other option' was faecal bacteriotherapy: having somebody else's faeces injected into your bowel — not your anus, but right up into your bowel — which put the other person's bacteria into your body, and started your own bacteria growing again.

I was flabbergasted, and asked the doctor if it was anybody's in particular, or just a random person picked off the street. He confirmed that there are people who do this for a living (not full-time, I presume) and that they come in and poo in a container and it is put in a plastic syringe and poop is whooped up your botty!

I told him I was a vegetarian, and could not have any old poop put in me, as that person may have had sausages for tea, and my body would not react well!

He said the people were screened, and I was anxious to know who they were, as I have yet to meet anybody who says they poo for a living! What a conversation stopper at a dinner party: 'What do you do for a living?' 'Oh, I shit in containers and it is then put into strangers' bottoms!'

I felt sick and better, all at the same time. Of course, this story has been recounted many, many times to friends and acquaintances at parties, and the look of complete and utter horror always tells me nobody else had heard of it either.

Even my most gay friends, who tell me all the sordid things they get up to, confess to never having heard anything quite so disgusting; even one of my dearest friends, who shall remain nameless for obvious reasons, who has frequented every gay haunt there is, was shocked. He was once asked to be the 'door bitch' at Stonewall, the infamous gay bar in Sydney. So there he was in full drag at the door telling people who could and could not gain entry that night. He said a man came up to him at the door, and told him he was completely straight, was married with two children, and had never been with another woman before, but was compelled towards my friend. My friend said, 'He thought I was a woman!' How a man of over six feet, built like a brick shithouse and dressed in a wig, dress and size-14 shoes, could be mistaken for a 'woman' I have no idea. But my friend left his door job, went to the attic of the club and did whatever it was they do with this 'very straight man', then returned to his position on the door.

The manager then approached my friend and said he was firing him for the night. My friend took great umbrage at this and said, 'I was only away from the door for an hour, for goodness' sake — you can't fire me for that.' The manager looked at him and said, 'It's not because you were away from the door for an hour, but because you have shit all up the back of your dress!'

This story at least made me feel slightly better about my close brush with the horrors of faeces donation.

32

If the hat fits

When I read in a Wellington newspaper that the renowned London-based hat designer Philip Treacy was to come to New Zealand to open his exhibition 'When Philip Met Isabella' at The New Dowse art museum, I was thrilled.

It was an even bigger thrill when I called the Dowse and found that Philip was also coming to Auckland, for an evening at the Auckland War Memorial Museum.

The organisers asked if I would like to introduce Philip at the evening, and say a few words, to which I agreed.

Six months before Philip's October 2007 visit, and long before I was aware he was being brought out to New Zealand, Francis had viewed his collection of hats in Paris. He had ordered a selection, as they were too fantastic not to, and these were due to arrive in September, just before Philip.

Philip arrived in Auckland on the 9th of October, and the British Council and The New Dowse arranged a very small cocktail evening for him on Wednesday the 10th (which also happened to be Pebbles' eighteenth birthday). It was to be a small, select group of those who would be involved in interviewing Philip the next evening. I was asked if I would like to attend the gathering, which was to be held at 6pm at the Metropolis Hotel bar in the

Chancery, in Auckland city, where Philip was staying. The other people who would be attending were Claire Regnault from the New Dowse, Anne (whose surname I never found out) from the British Council, my super-friend Stacy Gregg, writer Douglas Lloyd Jenkins (Stacy and Douglas were going to interview Philip), Philip and his friend Ursula. Philip was originally to arrive a week earlier, with Detmar Blow (the late Isabella's husband), but when Philip's schedule was put back a week Detmar was unable to come. So Philip brought the quite fabulous Ursula, who he had met in college as a teenager and who was now an interior designer in Ireland.

Just as I was about to leave the house to head down to Metropolis, my mobile rang. It was Claire to say that there could be a problem. When I asked what it was, she said she had not realised that Stacy and I did not get along. I was quite flabbergasted, and asked if Stacy had told her that. I was assured she had not. I told Claire that I was quite grown up enough to be in a room with a person who disliked me as much as I did them without causing a fuss; I can even be quite civil (you learn this with age). This seemed to reassure her.

Then she said that the hotel bar was quite dull, and that we were now going to be heading to a different location. She asked if I could suggest anywhere, and I said maybe SPQR in Ponsonby. Claire then said she would call me back when they had decided where to go.

The rain had begun to pour down outside in absolute buckets, and as we were not going to be having a 'cocktail party', but merely drinks at a bar, I took off my Philip Treacy hat and changed into less formal wear. About 20 minutes later Claire called to say we would now be meeting at a new restaurant that had opened in Ponsonby Road, called Magnum. I had been there before and knew it had a large bar in the middle of the area. I thought this could be a problem for seven people who did not really know each other, as we would all be seated in a line, as opposed to opposite each other. Coupled with this was the fact that Magnum, being new, was likely to be packed tighter than meat in a sausage.

When I arrived Douglas Lloyd Jenkins was perched on a stool at the small, rather high bar table, right by the entrance. While I have nothing against bar stools per se, I just wish they were a little shorter, as I always have a great problem trying to climb on them. I either have to be pulled up by a friend, or the stool tips and I fall over — either way, I prefer to stand. Claire was there, standing with Anne, and Philip and Ursula had just arrived. Stacy was apparently in the toilet. I said hello to everyone, then Ursula suddenly realised she had left her bag in the taxi, so she and Philip went outside and started calling the taxi company to try and locate it.

I was getting jostled from all sides as it was very busy, and the table was very small for us all to stand around. Stacy returned from the toilet, and avoided making eye contact with me. I said, 'Hello Stacy,' in a friendly voice, as I thought it would be dickhead stupid not to; she replied, 'Hello Denise,' and that was that.

I had met Magnum's maître d' at another dinner a few weeks earlier, as she was a friend of friends of mine. So now I asked her if there was any chance of getting a table for seven, as we were unable to hold any type of conversation standing in the entranceway around a teeny, tiny, tall table. She asked if we would be eating, and when I said 'No', she said, 'Eee, probably not then,' which I fully understood.

So we all made small talk. Stacy kept her face away from me and talked to Douglas, and Claire, Anne and I chatted while Philip and Ursula were still outside. Then a taxi drew up, Ursula's bag was returned, and she and Philip came inside. By now Magnum was so full, and we were being banged and knocked so much, that it was very hard to have a conversation of any sort. There was also a slight awkwardness, similar to that of a first date, when you are looking forward to seeing a person, but when you do, you don't really know what to say!

While Philip and Ursula were outside I had noticed that they both smoked, so now I asked them if they would like to go outside and have a cigarette. They both jumped at the chance. There was one small table with two chairs right at the end of the outside seating area, which faced the street. It was enclosed by clear plastic roll-down shutters, as the rain was now torrential. We pulled up a third chair and started talking, and the three of us got on like a house on fire. Philip ordered glasses of Taittinger champagne, and we quite lost ourselves talking about fashion. Philip told me he had visited a great shop in Vulcan Lane that day, called WORLDBeauty, and purchased some items — he was quite shocked to learn it was my store.

I asked if they had eaten, and he said no, and suggested the three of us go on somewhere after to eat. We had got so engrossed in conversation that we had quite forgotten the reason we were actually there was to discuss the format for the talk at the museum the next day, which of course included the others and not just the three of us.

After a long while the others came out and joined us, and Claire said we really needed to discuss the format for the following day. So we pulled up a few chairs and Philip spoke to Douglas and Stacy about what the museum evening would involve. Philip then asked me if I would mind if they joined us for dinner, and I said 'Absolutely not.' So he told the others we were going to eat after, but they all declined the invitation, and we carried on.

As the evening progressed, I excused myself to go to the loo, which was located at the back of the restaurant. When I opened the door the two cubicles were occupied, so I stood and waited. Just then the main door opened, and a short, slim and not unattractive woman walked in. She took one look at me and said, quite aggressively, 'What's your name?' I was so shocked and taken aback I spluttered, 'Denise.' She said, 'I thought it was you. I have been wanting to meet you for so long. I'm bipolar too.'

Before I had a chance to tell her I was not in fact bipolar, but suffer from depression, she launched into the story of her life — how at eighteen she had had a car accident, and after this she had suffered from bipolar, then she started to lift her clothes to show me the scars. I was like a rabbit caught in the headlights, and my mouth just kept opening and closing like a fish, with nothing coming out. She said she had been into my store, and she wanted to be a fashion designer. She wanted to meet me for coffee, as she felt I could help her with her mental problems. I was completely overwhelmed.

Just then the lock on one of the doors slid across, and I flew into the toilet. I also flew out again, and joined Philip and Ursula back at the table outside, not mentioning what had just happened in the bathroom.

Suddenly, the woman appeared at our table. She looked at the three of us and said, 'Hi, I'm bipolar, just like Denise. People think I'm mad, but I'm not really!'

I could actually see the blood drain from Philip's face. There was no escape for us, we were backed into the corner. The woman launched into her tale of wanting to be a fashion designer etc., while having no clue at all that she was talking to Philip Treacy! She rabbited on and on and on, and none of us could get a word in edgeways. She explained that she wanted to go back to fashion school to learn how to use CAD (computer-aided design, which enables you to sketch, on computer — go figure). At this point Philip interrupted and said in his very Irish accent, 'Woy would'ya bother? Woy don't you just sit down and sketch — that's what real designers do. You don't have to learn CAD to be a designer.'

The woman continued to talk rapidly about herself and things that had nothing to do with any of us, and we were very polite, but it was getting embarrassing now. Ursula had just bought a round of drinks, and had put a $20 note and a $10 note on the table. A gust of wind blew up, and the $10 note twittered onto the floor, right by her feet. Suddenly, this woman swooped down, picked up the $10 note and waved it about, saying, 'Ooh, look, I've just found $10!'

I said, 'It actually belongs to this lady,' pointing to Ursula. The woman held it up, almost waving it, then said 'Oh' in a rather downbeat way. Ursula, being the lovely lady she is, said, 'No problem, you keep it if you want,' at which point the woman promptly stuffed it into the back pocket of her jeans and walked off. I was absolutely mortified, and I apologised, but they were both very calm about it.

Philip then said, 'Are you bipolar?'

I said I was not, but that I had taken part in a TV campaign for depression. We had a chat about this, as his best friend and mentor, the fashion icon Isabella Blow, had suffered from depression for many years. She had in fact committed suicide just a few months earlier, which Philip was obviously still trying very hard to deal with.

He told me how brave he thought I was to do the ad, and I also explained that even before the mental health campaign, I had always been a magnet for strange people. I can be the only person sitting in a cinema, and one other person will walk in, and out of the whole empty space they will seat themselves next to me. Friends are amused and confused when we are out, by the number of people who come up and start a conversation with me. When they leave my friends will say, 'Who were they?' and I'll say, 'I have no frikkin' idea.' Unfortunately, it's just the way it has always been — I attract the weird and wonderful.

Suddenly, the woman reappeared. She brought a chair over and placed it next to mine. I was watching her out of the corner of my eye, as I did not want to encourage conversation. She then went and got another chair, and placed this behind Ursula. She then sat on one chair and put her feet across onto the other one, like a bridge, which meant we could not get out from where we were seated unless we spoke to her. Philip was facing her, but he was too polite to say anything. We just carried on talking, as she craned her neck, trying to listen in to what we were saying. Without saying so, I think we all thought it was better to just stay where we were for a while, which we did.

After about 20 minutes the woman got up and left, and soon after we followed. The others had left long ago, and I suggested we make our way down to SPQR for a pizza. On the walk down, Philip bought some flowers from the late-night dairy, saying how much he liked to have flowers in his room. He asked if I would like him to buy me some, but I declined.

While we were chatting Philip had mentioned that he was being awarded a CBE from the Queen. I said that in 2002 I had received an MNZM, which was previously an MBE, and we got chatting about the Queen. Philip said he had met her before, and then out of the blue received a letter from Buckingham Palace asking if he would design a star to sit atop the Christmas tree in the Palace.

It was such an odd request, he thought, but nevertheless an incredible honour. He said he had designed a fabulous star that could be worn as a hat as well as a Christmas tree ornament. When it was finished he delivered it personally to Buckingham Palace, at a specified time. He said he thought he was just going to drop it in, but when he arrived he was shown into a room, where there were not only choirboys singing hymns, but the Queen! His office assistant had failed to tell him that he was expected to stay for this.

I thought this was incredibly amusing, but I would most definitely not have thought so if it had been me.

We sat outside SPQR and ate pizza hungrily, as it was very late by then. Later I dropped them back at their hotel, and we said we would catch up the next night at the museum.

The following evening I arrived wearing my Philip Treacy hat. An assortment of people had come to hear Philip speak, some with beautiful bought hats, some with no hats, and some with hats they had obviously made, that really should not have been allowed to see the light of day. Stacy arrived in a matching dress and leggings with rather loud prints, which resembled pyjamas, and platform shoes, which she was obviously having trouble walking in.

I introduced Philip to the assembled audience, and of course mispronounced the name of the town he was from, and he corrected me from his chair. I had been practising Ahascragh all day, but had not mastered it at all. I also mentioned that he had designed a star for the Queen's Christmas tree, and shot him a quick look, as he had told me nobody really knew about this, but he smiled back at me, so I know he was fine with it.

After that he was interviewed by Douglas and Stacy. Philip told how he had originally wanted to be a fashion designer, and that he had always made hats to finish his outfits and complete a look. One day, when he was still in college, he asked his tutor whether he should continue with clothing or move into hats. She said 'Hats', and thus a comet shot into our stratosphere.

Philip then showed a couple of DVDs of his latest couture shows. They were absolutely breathtaking — both the hats and the clothes were exquisite. It was hard to believe it was possible for hats to be so beautiful. The shows were held in a tiny salon, with only a few rows of seats, and while I was watching I couldn't help wondering whether he had experienced any of the nonsense that I had with people thinking they should be seated according to their so-called rank. When I asked him later he said he had, and that he had only two words to say to people like that: 'Fock off!' I laughed and told him I could not have agreed with him more!

We also discussed the media, and I asked him whether he gave out freebies. So many New Zealand and worldwide designers do this, to ensure they get good treatment from journalists; it's always very easy to see who does it, by the number of pictures and words they receive in the media. It's almost an unspoken rule that this needs to be done. It's rare for a fashion writer or journalist to purchase an outfit from a designer, and if they do, you can bet it's because they have already received some of the collection for free.

Philip told me he had never done this, and never would. He said the reason was that one hat could take one of his staff eight hours to hand-sew, and he felt it was insulting to that person if it was then given away free to someone who would probably not appreciate it.

My philosophy is that if they really like it and want it, they'll buy it. I know of some media people who save all their freebies and give them away as Christmas presents! It was so refreshing to meet someone who, although so famous in his field, still held the belief that his work was worth something, and did not use it as a tool to garner media space.

I also mentioned that the hats we had ordered were late, and I wanted to know where they were. He turned to me and said, 'Noy, I could give ya bullshit and make up lots of excuses, but I won't. The reason your hats are late is Ralph Lauren's fault!' Apparently Ralph Lauren had asked him to design a hat range, and this had put everything else on the back burner. I told him jokingly that I was going to write to Ralph Lauren and complain!

The museum show ended with a question and answer session, then Anne announced that everybody was welcome to join Philip downstairs for a glass of champagne. She added that Philip would be happy to sign copies of his book, which was available from the museum bookstore in the foyer.

Philip then came up and thanked me for my introductory talk, and asked if I wanted to go for a cigarette with him and Ursula before he had to go downstairs. I said I would, so the three of us climbed the stairs of the auditorium to his dressing room. You entered a little area, and to the right was a small room with two two-seater couches, a table and chair, a mirror and a small cupboard. Next door to this was a teeny, tiny toilet with a small sink. Neither of the rooms had windows.

Philip suddenly noticed there were sprinklers in the room. I said you were not allowed to smoke in the museum, because of the fire danger. Philip was quite frantic and said, 'I have to have a cigarette before I go downstairs — what am I going to do? I certainly don't want to burn down the Auckland Museum, especially after the fabulous refurbishment!'

Just then Anne walked in with a bottle of Deutz, so that Philip could have a drink. She had brought only two glasses, but that was fine, and she left soon after. Philip suggested we cover the sprinklers, but then was mortified at the thought that the alarm would go off and we would be caught. He dashed into the toilet and yelled, 'In here, there are no sprinklers.' So the three of us crammed into the toilet and locked the door.

Philip climbed onto the lid of the toilet, lit his cigarette and held it up high so the smoke would go directly out through the extractor fan. He inhaled deeply, obviously relieved to be smoking, while the three of us chatted.

Just then we heard the outer door open, and a small voice saying, 'Hello, hello, where are you?'

I just froze. Not because Philip might be caught smoking, but because the three of us were in a locked toilet together, which was not a good look. We all looked at each other. My immediate reaction was to flush the toilet, which I did.

Philip looked at me and said, 'What did you do that for?' I said, 'We are in the toilet!' and he said, 'She will think we are all having a crap together!'

By now I was laughing, crying, and just freaking out. Ursula whispered, 'She will not, she will think we are all snorting coke!'

My legs just turned to jelly now, as we realised that Anne was not going anywhere until we came out. Philip was waving his arms around frantically trying to get rid of the smoke. Finally we composed ourselves, Philip stepped down from the toilet, I washed my hands in the sink, we unbolted the door, and the three of us very sheepishly walked out into the other room. We just stood there, like three kids caught smoking behind the bike shed — none of us said a word.

Anne looked at us and said, 'I have brought you another glass.'

Ursula thanked her, then added in her Irish lilt, 'I don't suppose you would have any of that lovely, smelly spray stuff that gets rid of bad smells, would you?'

Anne glanced at me, and said icily, 'No, I do not have any of that "lovely, smelly spray stuff that gets rid of bad smells".'

That was it, I was buggered. She obviously thought we had had a gigantic shit-fest together in the toilet.

Anne then looked at Philip and said, 'Could you please come downstairs, as your guests are waiting.' He said, 'Absolutely, I'm coming now, right now.'

Anne left, closing the door, and we all collapsed into fits of giggles. I told them it was all right for them — they would be on a plane out of here in a few days, but I lived here!

I could just imagine Anne getting back to Wellington, and with a very neat hand crossing my name off any future invitation lists, and noting: 'Denise L'Estrange-Corbet is not to be invited to any future gatherings we hold, as I have severe reservations about her moral conduct. She is either a coke dealer, or has a perversion which has not yet been reported in the media.'

Philip went downstairs to queues of fans waiting to have their books signed, and this took him a couple of hours. When I left he gave me a big hug and thanked me for everything. We had got on tremendously well, and he was such a sweetie. At Christmas he sent Francis and me a beautiful handwritten card with a picture of him and Isabella Blow on the front.

I felt very honoured to have been able to spend so much time with such a creative genius. I was also relieved that the gossip columnists milling around had missed the best scoop of the evening!

33

Characters

We've met some fairly unusual people along the way, and I've learnt plenty of difficult lessons about trust, faith and human nature.

Two years after we opened our first store, I took on a workroom in High Street. It was in a building awaiting refurbishment, and I managed to rent the whole floor for just $50 per week. There was a very large central area, two offices, a kitchen and two toilets, so we were quite self-contained.

One day I got a call from the store staff, asking me to come down. When I arrived the shop assistant whispered, 'A woman went into the changing room to try a garment on, and another woman went in there with her. They've been in there for ages.'

I looked towards the changing room, from which came muffled laughter. The assistant said she had asked several times if the women needed any help, or if they wanted to try alternative sizes, but they had just kept saying they were fine.

I went up to the curtain. 'Is there anything I can help you with?' I asked.

'No,' came the insouciant response.

I waited a while. 'What do you think they're doing?' I asked the shop assistant.

'I don't think I want to know,' she replied.

This was getting ridiculous. I decided I had to do something I've never dreamt of before or since. I strode up to the changing room, and with one mighty tug I pulled the curtain back.

There they were. One of the women was standing, and the other was on her knees. I don't need to go into graphic detail, but the shock set my temper off. Enraged and embarrassed, I screamed: 'How dare you do that in my store?! Get your clothes on and GET OUT NOW!'

One of the 'ladies' hurriedly put her clothes on and ran out of the shop, utterly humiliated. The other, casually dressed, sauntered up to the counter, looked me straight in the eye and purchased a garment. As the sale went through, I stood there spluttering in disbelief. Just a few moments earlier, this person had been caught doing the wild thing in my changing room, but she apparently didn't have the slightest notion of shame.

Today, I would probably burst out laughing, but I had never had to deal with anything like that before. When I related the experience to F, he was astounded. 'Thank God I wasn't there,' he said. 'I probably would have fainted.'

I only ever seemed to be summoned to the workroom when something mortifying was going on. One Monday morning, the High Street store manager rang me sounding distressed. A customer had bought a pair of cream vinyl crocodile-print trousers the previous Friday, and had now returned to the store screaming and swearing that the trousers were wet.

'I told her there's no way we would have sold the trousers wet, and that they must have got wet after she left,' the manager told me. I knew she was right — when we sell any garment it is wrapped in tissue then put into a paper carrier-bag. Any dampness, no matter how slight, would have been noticed.

I went down to find the sodden carrier-bag, the dripping trousers, and the irate customer. The manager stood there looking awkward. One look told me all I needed to know — the trousers were soaked in urine.

'How dare you accuse me of urinating in these pants?!' the customer roared when I told her what I thought. To my mind, there was no doubt — the pants stank of urine, and the lining of the vinyl was clearly stained yellow.

'There's nothing I can do about it,' I told her. 'If you urinate in your pants, it's not my problem.' Even as I said the words, I was conscious of how odd they sounded.

The customer went ballistic, threatening to take us to every tribunal under the sun and sue us for everything we were worth. 'My father's a lawyer!' she shouted — the classic line, used by nine out of ten disgruntled shoppers. She swept out of the store, only to return the next day to continue the tirade.

Again, I came down to the store. 'Look,' I told her. 'Our staff work very hard, but they all manage to go to the toilet when they need to. None of us are in the habit of urinating in our clothes.'

Eventually I calmed her down and asked her to explain events after she had left the store.

'I bought the pants and put them in the back of my car on the Friday,' she said. 'On the Monday I went to get them out and found them soaking wet. It's not my fault.' She told me that if we did not give her a replacement, she would 'sue the arse off' us.

I asked her if there was any way anyone else could have worn the trousers, and she shook her head. 'The only person who borrowed my car at the weekend was my brother,' she said.

I asked her to call him on the store phone and ask if he had worn the trousers. She was reluctant to do this, but in the end agreed. As the manager and I stood there, she made the call — and suddenly, her face changed.

She hung up, turned to face us, and said: 'I'm so sorry.'

Not only had her brother borrowed the car, but he confessed he had taken the trousers out of the bag on Saturday night, worn them out to a nightclub, got really drunk, and pissed himself in the pants. He then got home, wrapped them back in the tissue and replaced them in the bag on the seat of her car.

The customer left the store in a hurry, apologising again and again as she left. I've no idea what happened to her brother, but I'd have hated to be in his shoes when she got hold of him.

Soon after I took on the workroom, fashion schools started contacting me to ask if they could send students to us for work experience. This was all new to me, but I agreed. One of the first students was a lovely single mother from down the line who came to work for us for three days. She was very sweet. Our assistant Nicky and I were the only two people in the workroom — F was always in the store — and we left the student alone if we had to pop out. She had been given things to get on with and all was good.

She asked me a ton of questions about how we had started, and told me how she had always been 'different from other people at school'. I told her I had learnt to accept people for who they were, as I was one of those misfits too.

When she finished her work experience I gave her a bag of scrap fabric, as she'd been saying how hard and expensive it was to buy fabrics in the town she was from.

A couple of weeks later, a package arrived for me. I opened it, and inside were several metres of fabric and a handbag. There was also a letter from this student, saying she had stolen these things from the workroom (this was before we had proper systems in place). She said she had been absolutely wracked with guilt as I had been so nice to her, and had decided to send them back.

My emotions were all over the place. I was grateful she had sent them back, and furious she had abused my trust in the way she had. Then I received a letter from the school, asking me to fill out a report on the student's work experience and how I had found her. I anguished over this for a week. Did I dob her in or not? I decided I had to report it — it was theft, pure and simple. I did not work my butt off, and then give someone the chance to work in the industry, only to have them steal from me.

The school was horrified, and failed her that year. I hope she learnt a hard, bitter lesson. I also felt I had to tell the school, otherwise she could do the same thing to someone else, and she might not feel so enthusiastic about admitting it. And, of course, had she not owned up, the blame could have fallen on Nicky when we eventually discovered the missing items, and I trusted Nicky absolutely.

We still had students for several years after that, but no longer. The staff are too busy and they are interrupted too often when there are students — they are always asking questions, and reports have to be filled out. It takes too much time for a full-time staff member to do this and it is just not worth it, as while they are doing this they are not concentrating on their own jobs. Hard as it may seem, that's the way it is. It is a tough and unforgiving industry, and if you want to learn the profession, you start at the bottom, making the tea and taking out the trash, which is where all my best staff have started if they did not have a qualification.

In the early years we had a girl who came to work for us one day a week. Francis had judged some competition she had entered and won, and she was so grateful that she made me a bag and asked F if she could work one day a week for free to learn the ropes.

She absolutely drove F to distraction. She would make the tea, and forget to put teabags in the pot. Then she would put teabags in the pot and forget to boil the kettle. She would forget to pass on messages, and forget to do the stuff she was asked, but she was very kind and sweet. I had a soft spot for her, but F would come home threatening to commit hara-kiri on her.

When he took her aside and mentioned things to her she would dissolve in tears and he did not know what to do; he cannot cope with crying females. There was no denying she was creative, and she would sit surrounded by fabrics in her own little world. I convinced F that even though she had faults she did have some great attributes. She was a good timekeeper, honest, creative, willing and hardworking, and you could not hope for more than that. So he said she could stay, but she had to pull her socks up.

She then went on to working three days a week, while she was still studying design, and she was now paid. Francis decided to let her do some designing, but all her sketches had to go before him. Again, it drove him insane. He would give her back the sketches asking, 'How is that going to work? What does the back of the garment look like?' She would sit at her desk in tears, and work with tears dripping onto the table, but she was persistent.

One day I pulled her aside and told her that criticism was something she had to take on board if she wanted to succeed. We had all been there — it was constructive criticism, and she had better get used to it as that is what it is like. F had given her a break, and she had to rise or fall on her own. I could not help her — if she wanted to be a designer, then that's what she had to go through.

When she came back the next day, she had changed. She had obviously thought things over and made a decision. She told F how grateful she was that he had given her a break, as her friends were working for mass-market clothing manufacturers who taught them nothing, and they were very envious that she worked for us. She said WORLD was the only brand she could identify with, and she would do everything in her power to learn from him.

I explained that she would learn things from Francis that no school would ever teach her. And if she could hack it with him, she had made it, as he is a hard taskmaster where design is concerned.

There are no short corners to be taken — a story has to be told, a thread has to run through the whole collection, and it has to be concise and sellable. If it's not sellable, there's no point.

She went in for many competitions, and won them all, including the Deutz Fashion Awards. She won a placement with Vivienne Westwood in London, and went off to work with her for a while. She came back to WORLD and was put in the position of womenswear designer, always under F's wing. After a couple of years she went back to London to work in the industry there. Francis, Benny Castles (our menswear designer) and I would always catch up with her in London, and she said she missed us terribly. After two years, she called to say she was coming back, and she slotted back into her old job like a duck to water. She stayed another two years, then left mid-2008 to return to London, as she had fallen in love, and her boyfriend was working in London.

Her name was Lou Davies. She worked for us for eight years, and I watched this teenager grow up into a confident, talented, beautiful star, but her dizziness still remains. In 2007 we booked out the five-star Partingtons restaurant at the Langham Hotel in Auckland one Sunday evening to have our Christmas party. They did not normally open on Sundays, but the Executive Chef decided he would do this for us; he even agreed to work that night himself.

All the staff were sent a memo telling them where and when the party was, and on the Friday they were all reminded again. We arrived at Partingtons for an hour of cocktails before dinner, and near the end of the hour I asked Benny if he had heard from Lou. He said no, and that he would call her. When he phoned he found she was working with her father on their vegetable garden in the Waitakeres, and had thought the dinner was the following week!

So we started eating, and Lou's dad dropped her in to town. We were all dressed up, and Lou arrived in her gardening clothes, with her hair all over the place. F said, 'God, Lou, you will never change!' and we all laughed.

She worked as our womenswear designer for five years, and was a delight to work with. We all adore her, and she was always distraught when she had to leave, as WORLD was her second family. We had been through so much with her in the years she spent with us. She once wrote F and me a letter telling us how grateful she was for all we had done for her, and for giving her a break. She also thanked F for being so harsh on her, as without this she would never have found the strength to survive in this industry. We know now she can walk into any top designer in London and get a job, no problem, as she had made the grade.

No matter how much you learn, you will never know everything. F and I are still learning; every day challenges are put before us, be it with staff, customers, the range, suppliers, landlords, etc., and we have to rise to those challenges and deal with them to the best of our ability, or we too will fail.

No one is irreplaceable or infallible — do not think you are for a minute, because you are not. It is like being the star of the show — if you are not there an understudy is always waiting in the wings to replace you, and you must always remember that.

When Lou eventually comes back, she will work for us again. She has always said she could never ever work for another New Zealand designer, as she is in love with what we do, and we are her second family. That is what is great about the industry — sometimes, stars come before you, and understand you and everything you do. They are always in your life, even when they are overseas; they always keep in contact, and great, lasting friendships are born.

34

Today

It's quite hard to put my finger on a specific time when I realised the business was running profitably and solidly. When we first began, people told us if we lasted seven years, everything would fall into place. It wasn't quite true — after seven years, we were still pretty nervous. There have been times when we've been surrounded by empty shops as the economy tanked, and there was a time when we feared our home-base store on High Street would have to move if we were to survive.

We've always chosen to ride out the storm, however. All these years, the remark Rupert made on our first day of trading has remained in my head: 'Is this it?' That put-down, and his belief that all our optimism was simply folly, have resonated through all our successes.

Why have we managed to make it? I think it's because we've kept our feet on the ground.

I am not into the wanky fashion parties, and I only go to the events I really want to attend — I usually accept about a quarter of the invitations I receive. Some designers and so-called celebs are so up themselves it makes me cringe; they talk about nothing but themselves, their greatness, their talents, their charitable works and their million-dollar orders. I take it all with a pinch of salt, and tend to keep away from events that all designers are invited to, as I often find them dreadfully dull. One designer in particular is so boring she sends me to sleep. Whenever she strikes up conversation at a party, I have to make an excuse to get away before I lapse into a coma.

It's the falseness I don't like. There are plenty of people in fashion who are incapable of telling the truth about their businesses: everything is always wonderful, business is booming, the range is being stocked here, there and everywhere. Interestingly, when I drop into the international department stores to see whose clothes are being stocked, I often can't find the ranges of the designers who boast the loudest. It's all bollocks, and I've never been good at putting up with bollocks.

I have no problem being honest. If it's quiet in retail, I'll say so. The truth is nothing to be ashamed of. There is no one in the industry I feel the need to impress; I do what I do and I do it well, and if you don't like it, that's fine.

After nineteen years of trading, it's still really tough. The bills come in just as they did before, except that now they are astronomical. The wages have to be paid each week, and they astound me. Everything is the same as when we had just one tiny jewel of a store, but now it's all on a much bigger scale. In our weekly board meetings, Sue the General Manager tells us how much we have in the bank, what we can spend and what has to be paid. Then we decide what we'd like to do — and what we can afford to do (a distinction F absolutely hates; he's a true creative).

We can't run off on tangents now as once we could. Today, our responsibilities are too great for pure adventurism. Our people have families to feed and mortgages to pay, and the choices we make could be disastrous for them. We hold votes at our board meetings to decide on contentious issues, and F can get quite riled when he's overruled. Even though we are married, I'm willing to speak up against his view if I feel a decision is wrong for our business. To his credit, F is wonderful at accepting that it's not personal. He knows I'd never be so petty or stupid as to let our emotional and business lives overlap.

We're still determined to maintain a sense of humour about fashion. Before the 2005 election we did a range of political T-shirts, giving popularity rankings to the top politicians. We extended the joke to New Zealand artists like Dick Frizzell and Ralph Hotere, and we were delighted when Dick came into the store and told us he was happy to have a higher score than some of his peers.

Our 2008 range included slogans like 'Fashion Week Promotional T-shirt (this t-shirt is not connected to any Fashion Week in particular, but Fashion Week in general)' and 'Post-modernism saved Fashion Week'. They were a big hit in our Sydney store during that city's Fashion Week in May 2008, and were snapped up by Christina Neault, the head of New York agency IMG, which runs most of the world's fashion weeks.

Another little taste of celebrity endorsement came in March 2008, when Francis and Pebbles were visiting Hong Kong together for the opening of the new Louis Vuitton store. They had a few hours to kill before the opening, and decided to hit the shops. They were mooching around Fendi when a man approached Francis to ask where he got the shirt he was wearing. It was a white shirt with gold military buttons, from one of our recent collections.

'It's one of mine,' F said.

The man looked perplexed, so F explained: 'I'm a designer from New Zealand. Our brand is called WORLD, and this is a shirt from our collection.' The man said he'd be very grateful if F could help him get hold of one of the shirts, and then asked if he could take F's photo.

By now, everyone in the shop was staring at this little scene. F laughed. 'Shouldn't I be the one asking for your picture?' he asked — for the man was Kanye West, the American R&B artist. He was in town to perform at the very same Louis Vuitton opening. That night, Kanye's entourage gave Pebbs front-row tickets, and while performing, Kanye came over to Pebbles, grabbing her hand as he sang.

Later in the evening, one of his bouncers came over and told Pebbles that Kanye had requested her phone number. She wasn't forthcoming with it, as she has a boyfriend and doesn't see herself as a groupie by any stretch of the imagination.

That's just one of the odd little episodes that seem to take place every so often, to interrupt the daily realities of business.

My temper can still surface. In my defence, I must say that once I've voiced my opinion, I let the anger go and completely drop the issue. I never rehash arguments or bring the past up again. I've learnt to accept my temper — that's just the way I am.

Our wonderful customers are still with us. One of our original regulars was a woman who would trundle into the shop with her sweet baby boy in his pram. Today, the baby is a teenager and he still shops with us. 'Mum has all her WORLD clothes,' he said recently, which caused us both to shudder — who knows what might be lurking in her cupboards from those early years?

The future of the fashion business fascinates me. Design is all about evolution, so it's impossible to predict its likely course, but one certain area of development is fabric technology. Before long, designers will be using fabrics technologically advanced enough to keep the wearer cool in summer and warm in winter — and I'm not talking natural fibres. Laboratory-made fabrics will define the clothing of the near future. Can you imagine wearing a dress in the height of summer that has intrinsic cooling properties? Bliss, I say.

Fashion has been done to death. There's nothing we can create that has not been done throughout the history of design, but each time a fad recreates itself, there's a slight twist that makes it interesting. Another change we in the industry have to face is the changing shape of women's bodies. The 22-inch waist has disappeared; the body shape of the western female has utterly changed because of our diets — and the evidence is in every vintage store in any first-world city. None of the clothes fit today's young women — even the shoes, hats and gloves are too small.

We noticed about twelve years ago that we had to lengthen our trouser legs, as today's girls had amazonian pins — not necessarily as slim as once they were, but certainly longer.

Our plans are to keep expanding our business, opening more retail stores and continually improving our existing shops. WORLD will become a truly global brand — we have only just begun.

Francis and I have always made sure we are not only figureheads, but on the ground at all times. We no longer travel together overseas, so one of us can remain at home to keep the business ticking over. Eight stores is a lot for an independent company. They are not franchises; we own every garment, fixture and fitting in each and every store. That has been really tough, but we've always been happy to grow our business slowly. We're the tortoise, not the hare.

Our partnership is as strong as it has ever been. Francis and I are highly respectful of each other, and we adore running our business together. I'm so glad I took him up on his suggestion of starting a company together, all those years ago in the bus stop on Queen Street.

In 2008, for the first time in my life, I decided to have a birthday party for myself. I've never had one before because I've always thought nobody would turn up, and if it was a disaster, I'd be too embarrassed to face the world.

But at 48, I'm too old to worry about that kind of thing any more. Birthdays only come around once every four years, so I figure I might as well make the most of them. I arranged for my very good friends Michele and Wendy to cater, and invited 30 of my closest and dearest mates to celebrate with me at our house.

The day started with a constant stream of phone calls, txts and emails from friends all over the world, and flowers just kept arriving, until I ran out of vases and had to use our big cooking pots. I ordered an enormous croquembouche; a glorious tower of 75 profiteroles, which were covered in blue, pink, yellow and green chocolate. Lou Davies made me an amazing gingerbread house with icing and chocolate pebbles all over it, like something Hansel and Gretel might like to eat, with a lotus-flower candle in the middle.

The evening was warm and delightful, and at about 11pm we lit the candles on the croquembouche and the gingerbread house. When alight, the lotus-blossom candle not only started to open up, but played a tinny version of 'Happy Birthday', which couldn't be stopped. Cris Elrick took the candle out of the room so we could hear ourselves think, then returned to make a lovely speech, after which she asked Pebbles if she'd like to say a few words. Pebbs nodded, cleared her throat and said literally a few words: 'Happy Birthday Mum.' Everyone laughed, and I stepped forward to say a few words of my own.

Suddenly, our friend Josh popped his head around the kitchen door with an announcement.

'The bathroom is on fire,' he said, 'but it's under control.'

We had all by now had far too much to drink, and as everyone erupted in laughter, I assumed it was a joke. Cris ran off to investigate, and I stayed there, continuing my speech.

While the cakes were being cut, I went to the bathroom to see what the joke was all about.

I nearly had a heart attack. When the lotus-blossom candle could not be silenced, Cris had brought it into the bathroom and put it on the white vanity, shutting the door to give us some peace and quiet. The candle had then exploded, and as well as sending hot wax flying all over the bathroom cabinet, bathroom door, electric toothbrush and mirror, it had set the white wooden vanity on fire.

In the attempt to put it out, Maddy, Josh's girlfriend, had grabbed my brand new white Egyptian cotton towel, wrapped it around the candle and put it in the bath. Luckily, the bath is cast iron and not plastic, otherwise it would have melted from the heat.

I just stood there looking at the blackened bathroom. I was

speechless. Cris burst into tears of mortification, but made me feel slightly better by saying: 'If we had left it on the gingerbread house, it would have exploded in your face.'

I decided on the spot it was not going to spoil my birthday. The celebrations carried on until the early hours of the morning, but every day when I enter the bathroom, I'm confronted with brown, bubbly burn marks on my white vanity and I laugh.

It was another memorable day, just like the ice-skating bloodbath and all the other dramas that have followed me through a life of leap-year birthdays. I've no idea what awaits on the next February 29, in 2012, but I'm sure of one thing: it won't be boring.

As I've been writing this book, I have spent a lot of time wondering how to finish it — but it has been decided for me by fate.

After ten years, I have had to go back into therapy. I began seeing a psychotherapist again in 2008, as I was having a difficult time. I was caught in a downward spiral, and knew the pills were not going to get me out of it. I was suicidal; constantly in tears and thinking of how I could end my life painlessly (I'm a dreadful coward, and no matter how depressed I am, I'm terrified of suffering a slow, painful death). I confided in a friend who also has 'the Gift', and she persuaded me to seek therapy.

I never wanted to return to counselling. This time, I was determined not to keep going over and over the same ground. 'I don't want to focus on the past,' I told the psychotherapist. 'I've been there, done that — and I don't like it. I just want to focus on my current situation.' To my huge relief, the counsellor agreed, and we have begun working together.

Although I didn't want to return to therapy, I do not feel it is a step backwards. It's just another rung on the ladder of life. We all fall down sometimes, and need to be helped up. There's nothing wrong with that.

Life is a fraught journey, and if you can recognise when you need help, you are on the way to getting better. I know I will recover, and I also know I will fall down again. That's just the way life goes.

If I've learnt anything in my crazy journey through the world, it's this: you can never judge from the outside what is really going on. All that glitters is not gold.

Acknowledgements

This book would never have been written without Debbie Tawse, the founder of Celebrity Speakers, who dragged me into Michael Moynahan's office at Random House all those years ago and said, 'You need her to write a book; she has a great story.'

Debs, I'm sorry I never got my A into G to start this before you left us, but it was the catalyst that finally got me started.

I thank you for your unfailing support and belief in me.

Debbie passed away on 26 December 2006.

To my friend Mahinarangi Tocker, who died on 15 April 2008 — keep singing, little songbird.

To my dear Aunt Margaret who passed away on 25 September 2007. You were just my biggest fan, and never faltered in your love and support of me. I never did get the ring, but the memories I have can never be taken away. I love and miss you dreadfully.

To Michael Moynahan and Jenny Hellen from Random House for listening to my ramblings, and for giving me so much freedom.
To Claire Harvey, who had to edit those ramblings.
I could not have done it without you all.

And finally, to all my very dear friends, scattered over the globe. I love you and thank you all for putting up with me these years.